NATHANIEL TOLLE

PUMPKIN CINEMA

The Best Movies For Halloween

Schiffer Publishing Ltd®

4880 Lower Valley Road • Atglen, PA 19310

ACKNOWLEDGMENTS

I'd like to raise my glass of cider to the following people:

My parents, Michael and Julia Tolle, for their love and support, and for being cool enough to let me watch scary movies at an early age.

Summer Violett, for being the greatest friend anyone could ask for, and for having pumpkin televisions at her wedding.

Helena Rudolph, for patiently watching countless hours of Halloween television episodes with me in the summer, spring, and winter months, and for many fantastic movie recommendations.

Christine LaPorte, for setting the bar when it comes to Halloween enthusiasm, and for making sure my Octobers are fun-filled.

Tina Libby, my wonderful editor and fellow pop culture aficionado, who I hope will never stop recommending awesome films, books, and TV shows to me.

My brother, Nick, for introducing me to several of these films and for teaching me what a cannibalistic humanoid underground dweller is.

The bloody good staff at The Lovecraft Bar, for keeping horror alive and well in the Land of Ports.

Mike Clark, whose awe-inspiring video store, Movie Madness, had every single obscure movie I was seeking.

Pamela Apkarian-Russell, the Halloween Queen, for taking the time to answer all of my questions.

The Wenzel Family, for their incredible Halloween Fantasy Trail in Oregon City.

The Great Pumpkin, for always finding me in the most sincere of pumpkin patches.

I can't say thank you enough to Pete Schiffer, Jesse Marth, Matt Goodman, Alex Potter, and everybody else at Schiffer Publishing.

Lastly, thank you to whoever is reading this right now—you know who you are.

Copyright © 2014 by Nathaniel Tolle

Library of Congress Control Number: 2014942355

Stock Images Used:
Halloween Striped Candy Corn
Halloween Striped Candy Corn against a background by bhofack22
Stock Photo 37412503

Halloween Pumpkin Candy
Colorful group of halloween candy in shape of pumpkins on white background by MoonBloom
Stock Photo 49772423

Halloween
Halloween decorations by LoriMartin
Stock Photo 180838

Sweet Halloween Candy Corn in a White Bowl by HHLtDave5
Stock Photo 49954622

Cover & Interior designed by Matt Goodman
Type set in Trade Gothic

ISBN: 978-0-7643-4723-8
Printed in China

Published by Schiffer Publishing, Ltd.
4880 Lower Valley Road
Atglen, PA 19310
Phone: (610) 593-1777; Fax: (610) 593-2002
E-mail: Info@schifferbooks.com

For our complete selection of fine books on this and related subjects, please visit our website at www.schifferbooks.com. You may also write for a free catalog.

This book may be purchased from the publisher. Please try your bookstore first.

We are always looking for people to write books on new and related subjects. If you have an idea for a book, please contact us at proposals@schifferbooks.com.

Schiffer Publishing's titles are available at special discounts for bulk purchases for sales promotions or premiums. Special editions, including personalized covers, corporate imprints, and excerpts can be created in large quantities for special needs. For more information, contact the publisher.

CONTENTS

INTRODUCTION:
THIS IS HALLOWEEN

Throughout the neighborhood, the noises of scampering trick-or-treaters, haunted house sound effects blasting from porches and through open windows, and barking hounds are slowly becoming more sporadic and distant. The fierce October wind is carrying dead leaves along empty streets that were filled with children only an hour ago. One by one, the porch lights turn off, ending the open invitation to the remainder of the ghouls and goblins lurking through the neighborhood. The flickering glow of the orange-fleshed faces is subsiding, but their smoky fragrance still looms in the air, blending with the familiar scents of fall foliage, home-baked goods, and latex from store-bought costumes.

A ten-year-old boy donned in a morbidly amusing Zombie Pinocchio costume enters his house along with two of his friends, one dressed as a Vampire Tourist and the other as a psychotic bunny rabbit. Over their shoulders, they are each lugging a bulging pillowcase full of the night's delicious rewards given to them from people who they hadn't seen since last All Hollows' Eve and probably won't see again until the next one. These three boys have seen each other almost every day since the school year began, but never quite like this. A short time ago they were ordinary kids on the school bus but since then have undergone a bizarre metamorphosis and united in a ritual that has brought them much closer together. With their costumes on, they waited by the front door until they were greeted by a dusk that seemed to promise one of the most thrilling nights of their lives, where anything was possible. Then it was finally time to run into the final hours of October, masquerading as strange creatures of the night, and even for the Psycho Bunny, who could only breathe through tiny holes in his mask, the air had never tasted so sweet. The odyssey began with empty pillowcases, but thanks to the kindness of strangers and the spirits of a 3,000 year-old-holiday, they now have enough candy to last until Christmastime.

The Vampire Tourist is especially exhausted, since his map prevented him from using both hands to carry his pillowcase. The three boys collapse on a set of couches as Psycho Bunny removes his mask and feels overwhelmed with the aesthetics in the room—for in the past few hours, he had only been permitted to see through holes that sometimes did not line up correctly. After removing their shoes to comfort their aching feet, they raid the refrigerator for some much-deserved sodas.

Then they return to the living room and pour out the goodies from their pillowcases, making three enormous mountains of sugar to run their fingers through as if they were pieces of gold in a pirate's treasure chest. After tearing open the miniature disguised bags (holding multiple treats) that a few houses offered, the trading officially begins, and they suddenly turn into articulate negotiators in order to rid themselves of the disgraced unnamable candies in orange paper wrappers. Once the three boys are all satisfied and have a copious amount of sugar and caffeine in their systems, they turn off all the lights and spend the next couple of hours happily staring at the television screen.

The elderly couple that lives next door is once again feeling that peculiar liberation from being assured that Chuck and Charlotte's House of Horrors—heavily armed with fog machines, strobe lights, bubbling cauldrons, rattling chains, animatronic ghouls, surround sound speakers, and scarecrows that excitedly spring to life when you stand too close—was the highlight of the trick-or-treaters' night. It took three weeks of hard work, and every time they were outside adding onto their labor of love, they received words of gratitude from neighbors that were all excited to see what they would come up with this year. One afternoon they were even greeted by a couple of neighborhood kids who volunteered to assist with draping the bushes and trees with cobwebs, for which they were rewarded with hot apple cider afterwards.

As the sun started to fall a few hours earlier, they had felt pangs of nervousness that reminded them of first dates, the first day of school, and having to walk out on stage during plays and recitals—memories that seemed like several lifetimes ago. What if the trick-or-treaters didn't show up this time? What if the constantly-changing world was no longer interested in the Halloween traditions they've held dear since childhood? Their annual pre-Halloween paranoia was soon pacified when Harry Potter, a butterfly-fairy, a mummy, Medusa, and Spongebob Squarepants (illuminated by several shaky flashlight beams from the grownups trying their best to keep up) literally sprinted towards their house. From that point the giggles and shrieks from children seemed to play in a continuous loop for three hours, making Chuck and Charlotte feel not only young and energetic, but also fortunate that they decided to buy all that extra candy just in case. But now it has been over fifteen minutes since the last "trick-or-treat," so they decide it's time to officially close the House of Horrors by turning off the porch light and going inside, all while sharing their lists of the top five costumes of the night. Once again their lists are identical, reminding them just how in sync they are when it comes to their favorite holiday. Now, for the 38th Halloween in a row, they begin a horror movie marathon that will last until the sun comes up.

The house directly across the street is hosting a large group of college students who have spent the last couple of hours socializing, flirting, and rapidly filling up their cups of witchy ginger punch. They show off their costumes and live vicariously through their characters, enjoying such a refreshing diversion from the mundane worlds of schoolwork and customer service. Spooky music is blasting through the speakers. Decorations, some cute, some grotesque, cover every nook and cranny, so the tallest guy has to duck every time he enters a different room. Strobe lights fill the living room and send a few people into a dizzying stupor.

A student dressed as a Candy Corn Cockroach is feeling confident, interesting, and accepted for the first time in exactly a year. He's been in good spirits all day long thanks to an enjoyable day of carving jack-o'-lanterns, reading scary stories in a graveyard, and walking around his neighborhood to admire the many great decorations while listening to some of his favorite Halloween music. Now he finds himself in a haunted manor where every room he enters is filled with creative and beautiful-looking people who immediately greet him with approving smiles and compliments. He realizes that he'll be invisible to most of them again the next day, but on the bright side, at least he'll be able to grab a snack without knocking things down with four additional roach arms. A couple of hours go by and the party dwindles down to ten sole survivors, feeling somewhat tired but by no means ready for Halloween to be over. So they gather in front of the TV, and after making predictions on who will scream the loudest, are transported to a different world with a fresh set of characters. It doesn't take long for the Candy Corn Cockroach and the others to remember just how much fun watching a scary movie can be.

These three houses have catered to different agendas all night, but now a passerby will notice the same shadowy gleam bouncing against their windows, serving as the only source of light. Everybody inside is hoping for one last thrill, but for some of them, the movie might make or break their Halloween, so hopefully they were wise with their selections.

Most people watch a movie on Halloween, and in many cases, it is the night's final activity. Since this magical holiday only comes once a year, it is extremely important to find a movie that contributes to the ambience and keeps the energy flowing; you can't afford to let this night end on a sour note. The giddiness caused by the night's prior adventures could dissipate if you spend precious Halloween time watching something that fails to excite, amuse, frighten, and fascinate. This book will serve as a companion for when you visit a video store and browse through Netflix not only on Halloween, but for the entire month of October, where nights fall early and brim with the kind of menace that beckons you to stay indoors. Scary movies and gloomy autumn nights feed off each other magnificently well, and the titles I have selected should both kick-start your Halloween season and let it end on a high note.

From 1993–2004, I kept a list where I wrote down every single movie I watched and gave it a rating from 0–5 stars—there was no good reason at the time other than simply being a dork. But it sure came in handy when I started writing this book. The first thing I did was make a separate list of horror movies I had given at least three stars to, and that I could envision watching on Halloween. Then I read horror movie guides like John Stanley's *Creature Features* and James O'Neill's *Terror on Tape* to find films that seemed interesting and that could possibly fit all my criteria. Internet forums, such as the ones on Bloody-Disgusting.com and Halloween.com, proved to be equally helpful in learning about films that had eluded me, and websites such as RareHalloweenVideos.Blogspot.com (which I highly recommend checking out) and *Wikipedia* led me to films that actually took place around Halloweentime. This resulted in a list of several hundreds of movies, and for three years, I would get to them all while doing my best to pretend it was Halloween to see which ones gave out the appropriate holiday vibes. The employees at the Portland video store Movie Madness surely thought I was a deeply disturbed individual for wanting to watch *Pooh's Heffalump Halloween Movie* on Super Bowl Sunday, *Hack-O-Lantern* on Easter weekend, *Halloween 6: The Curse of Michael Myers* when most people were putting up their Christmas decorations, and that piece of garbage *Teen Wolf Too* when it was actually autumn.

For choosing the greatest movies to watch in October, I concentrated on a simple set of guidelines.

It has to be fun to watch. You obviously want to be in the best possible mood, so the film needs to evoke smiles and laughter, not melancholy. This is especially important for when you have friends over because it is up to you to keep the mood energetic and uplifting—be miserable on your own time. This category disqualifies many respected titles like *The Texas Chainsaw Massacre*, *The Vanishing*, *28 Days Later*, *The Descent*, *The Mist*, *Open Water*, *The Hills Have Eyes*, *Jacob's Ladder*, *The Fly*, and *Pet Sematary*.

It cannot repeatedly present seasons, locations, and weather that contrast with autumn. Even though *Jaws* is a masterpiece in every possible way, summertime and swimming do not mesh well with dead leaves and trick-or-treating. This would also exempt *The Shining*, *The Thing*, *Misery*, and *Black Christmas*.

It cannot have a running time of over two hours. Every second is valuable, so sitting in front of the television for too long is not productive whatsoever, even when it involves Sigourney Weaver and aliens.

It cannot be mean-spirited and cruel. It is hard to feel joyous and celebratory when you are witnessing the exploitation of pain and suffering found in films like *The Last House on the Left*, *Audition*, *Martyrs*, and *Wolf Creek*.

If it is not scary, then it has to be directly associated with Halloween. This qualifies non-horror titles like *Hocus Pocus* and *The Halloween Tree*. I had to break this rule once—because when it comes to *Troll 2*, there are no rules.

If it is a sequel, it has to make sense to those who have never seen the original.

It must have a fairly quick pace. You don't want anyone falling asleep during the movie, so in addition to keeping heaps of treats and caffeine nearby, your movie shouldn't take long to deliver the goods. This sadly excludes *The Uninvited*, *Nosferatu*, and *Dracula*.

If it takes place on Halloween, I'm much more likely to look past its shortcomings because for some reason, there haven't been a whole lot of films directly associated with Halloween. So I chose to include deeply flawed films like *Double, Double, Toil, and Trouble* and *Ernest Scared Stupid* because at least the Halloween spirits lie within them.

One of the hardest decisions to make was whether or not to include Frank DaLaggia's 1988 supernatural horror-fantasy *Lady in White*. On one hand, the first half-hour is filled with some of the most enchanting Halloween imagery captured on film: cemeteries and sidewalks buried underneath multiple layers of fall foliage, bowls of candy corn at the local candy shop, beams of sunshine peeking through trees of flaming colors, a boy in a Dracula cape and mask riding a bike with a jack-o'-lantern in its basket, and by far the most festive looking elementary school classroom ever (so it's no wonder why each student brought a costume and a pumpkin to school). Adding in a very likable main character, charming small town, and interesting story, after the first 30 minutes it becomes hard to imagine a more appropriate movie for Halloween. But on the other hand, this movie is a real downer thanks to a significant chunk of time being dedicated to the civil rights struggle and a subplot where an African-American janitor is wrongfully accused of the murders of 11 children. A serial killer who preys on children is already pretty heavy material, but the sight of a racist white woman assassinating an innocent black man is way too troubling for me to give *Lady in White* a full recommendation for the most fun holiday of the year.

The almost two-hour running time doesn't help either. So, I think you should just watch the first half-hour on Halloween and then save the rest for a dreary, freezing cold night in November when you're suffering from seasonal depression disorder or post-Halloween depression.

From the moment your pumpkin season begins to when you drift off (extremely late!) on Halloween night, I hope this book will be useful. Everyone will commence their Pumpkin Cinema season at different times—some will be unable to resist the ghostly manors that seem to mysteriously sprout overnight inside department stores in the dead of August, while others prefer to let their hearts decide when the time is right to once again welcome Halloween. One of my friends has the hardest time admitting that summer has ended and year after year, succumbs to a crushing funk when 5 p.m. now means headlights in the mocking darkness, instead of sleeveless gardening to wafts of charcoal briquettes and freshly cut grass and the tune of birds and distant child laughter. But just as inevitable as her post-summer depression is the moment of jubilation once she smells the autumn spirits in the air for the first time, immediately breaking her spell and triggering a continuous flow of things to look forward to, and you better believe that *It's the Great Pumpkin, Charlie Brown* is high on that list.

Some of the films in this book will be brand new to you, some you've already bestowed as perennial Halloween favorites, and some you've even enjoyed for years and never really understood its stormy October night potential. Some will fill you with enchanting, innocent whimsy reminiscent of *Pinocchio* and *The Wizard of Oz*, while others will obliterate your psyche until you're too frozen from fear to reach for the popcorn bowl. Some are almost a century old from other countries and some flooded mainstream American theaters in 2013. Some will reunite you with old Halloween favorites like witches, scarecrows, vampires, werewolves, black cats, skeletons, zombies, and ghosts, and others will introduce you to a new batch of majestic monstrosities, like vegetarian goblins, parasitic slugs from outer space, pumpkin enforcers in pajamas, fluffy crate monsters, enigmatic carnival barkers, humanoid fish, homicidal landlords, manic mannequins, demonic trees, and Halloween hounds. Whatever your age or preferences, this book has you covered and will protect you from *Trick 'R Treat*'s Sam, who always watches you to make sure you're not only following all the rules of his sacred holiday, but also watching the most appropriate films possible.

Happy haunting, and may the Great Pumpkin always find you.

FEATURE-LENGTH FLICKS-A-FRIGHT THAT GO BUMP IN THE NIGHT

ABBOTT AND COSTELLO MEET FRANKENSTEIN (1948)

🎬 **Director:** Charles Barton
⭐ **Cast:** Bud Abbott, Lou Costello, Bela Lugosi, Lon Chaney Jr., Glenn Strange
🎞️ **Length:** 83 minutes
👤 **Rating:** PG

🎞️ **Synopsis:** A pair of bumbling railway baggers visits McDougal's House of Horrors to deliver two special crates that may or may not contain the remnants of certain famous monsters.

Although nowhere near as funny as Abbott and Costello's *Hold That Ghost* and nowhere near as scary as the classic Universal monster movies, this horror-comedy hybrid works like a charm for a dark and stormy October night companion. In fact, you're hit with a wave of Halloween nostalgia immediately, since accompanying the opening credits is playful, simple animation featuring skeletons, Frankenstein, The Wolfman, and other Halloween mascots. The whole movie conjures images of our earliest Halloweens, when our wide-eyed innocence first clashed with the macabre.

It's a pretty goofy swan song to the once-terrifying Universal monsters, but at least Frankenstein, Dracula, and The Wolfman all received ample screen time to remind audiences of their power and attraction. Unfortunately, Boris Karloff chose not to bring his classic monster back to life (Glenn Strange once again took over, as he did with *House of Frankenstein* and *House of Dracula*), believing that its reputation would be destroyed by surrendering to comedy; however, always the affable professional, he helped out with the film's publicity and even appeared in future meetings with Abbott and Costello.

Reprising their classic roles, Bela Lugosi and Lon Chaney Jr. have surprisingly good chemistry with Abbott and Costello, and it's a real treat to see these four stars together in one movie. Like in previous pictures, Bud plays the bossy leader, while Lou is the ultimate goofball who always seems to get into trouble despite good intentions. One of the best scenes finds them wandering inside McDougal's House of Horrors in the midst of a thunderstorm, where Lou has the misfortune of seeing the monsters rise from their coffin crates only to have them inconveniently disappear once Bud responds to his cries. A similar misunderstanding takes place in Dracula's castle when a trap door hilariously separates the characters numerous times. Equally delightful are the transformation scenes of a clumsy and slow bat morphing into the Count, and the dissolves of clean-shaven Chaney becoming the hideous wolf, which reminds us how CGI often takes the fun out of everything.

The film starts strong but ends even stronger, as Dracula attempts a simple brain transplant so the Monster will be forever obedient. A cat and mouse chase ensues that resembles some *Three Stooges* shorts, and waiting at the finish line is yet another Universal monster making a special appearance.

Lobby card for *Abbott and Costello Meet Frankenstein* (1948). Universal International Pictures.

THE ABOMINABLE DR. PHIBES (1971)

Director: Robert Fuest
Cast: Vincent Price, Joseph Cotten, Virginia North, Peter Jeffrey, Hugh Griffith
Length: 94 minutes
Rating: Not Rated

Synopsis: Dr. Phibes, who is believed to be deceased from a car accident long ago, seeks revenge on the doctors he blames for the death of his wife. One by one he murders them using the 10 biblical plagues of Egypt as peculiar artistic inspiration.

Billed as Vincent Price's 100th feature film, the truly one-of-a-kind *The Abominable Dr. Phibes* is distinguished for its elegant art-deco sets, breathtakingly bizarre dance routines, extravagant early 20th-century costumes, hammy performances, lovely renditions of songs like "Somewhere Over the Rainbow" and "One for My Baby and One More for the Road," and death scenes so absurd and creative they make Jigsaw's methods seem lazy in comparison. But while the carnage in the *Saw* films is ugly and brutal, here it is played mostly for laughs, because even though the film goes all over the place, not for a second does it lose its zany tone.

In what can only be described as the most mesmerizing of opening scenes, the iconic, velvet-voiced St. Louis native Vincent Price plays the most Halloweenish of all musical instruments, the organ, and then lets his spooky mechanical band, Dr. Phibes' Clockwork Wizards, take over so he may dance with his assistant, the beautiful and equally mysterious Vulnavia. Spellbound and engaged, you are now ready to dive into Dr. Phibes' depravity as a man is shredded to death by bats while he lay in his bed—the first in a series of elaborate murders based on the ten curses visited upon the Pharaohs for keeping the Israelites in bondage. Next up: boils, frogs, blood, hail, rats, beasts, locusts, death of the first born, and darkness. Your mind will explore a most fascinating territory as you try to envision the possibilities, but chances are you won't predict correctly. Scotland Yard is justifiably baffled by the bizarre series of murders, leading Superintendent Waverly to respond, "A brass unicorn has been catapulted across a London street and impaled an eminent surgeon. Words fail me, gentlemen."

In a scene that showcases the film's ability to be morbidly funny without sacrificing class, Dr. Phibes and Vulnavia are all dressed up and dining inside their home, drenched in mood lighting and facing backdrops of silhouetted figures beside Le Casino de Monte Carlo, giving the impression that they are out in the world. While looking into Vulnavia's eyes, Dr. Phibes takes a glass of wine and pours it through the hole in the side of his neck. Since you can't actually see the hole at any point, you are giggling instead of squirming. And when a character at a crowded masquerade party is stumbling through the crowd in a mad, dizzying panic when his animal costume is tightening at an alarming rate thanks to a hidden contraption, director Robert Fuest again shows he is expertly disciplined about what to show and what not to show to give us the greatest possible reaction.

Lastly, there is even a scene that makes you aware of just how easy we have it when it comes to porn, for the poor suckers in the 1920s must have required enormous coordination to use one hand to constantly crank the film projector.

ALL HALLOWS' EVE (2013)

Director: Damien Leone
Cast: Katie Maguire, Mike Giannelli, Catherine Callahan, Kayla Lian
Length: 83 minutes
Rating: Not Rated

Synopsis: On Halloween night, a boy returns home from trick-or-treating and is surprised to find a VHS tape in his sack. He and his sister persuade their babysitter to let them watch the mysterious tape, which consists of three short and scary films.

Giving credence to Lon Chaney Sr.'s statement that nothing on earth is more frightening than a clown after midnight is the presence of Art the Clown (played by Mike Giannelli), who makes frequent appearances throughout *All Hallows' Eve*, a direct-to-video horror anthology that deserves to achieve cult status in the upcoming years. Damien Leone wrote, directed, and edited this film and he does an outstanding job in each department; he also performed the makeup effects and it's obvious he learned a lot from Tom Savini, who Leone called his personal hero in a Dread Central interview. Two existing short films—2008's *The 9th Circle* and 2011's *Terrifier*—were spliced together with a new short film about an alien invasion as well as a wraparound story to add onto the recent resurgence of the important horror anthology subgenre.

All Hallows' Eve gets off to a terrific start as two children and their babysitter named Sarah, played by Katie Maguire in an especially strong performance, return home from trick-or-treating. With *Night of the Living Dead* playing on TV, the kids pour out their hard-earned treasures onto the floor, and the boy finds within his mountain of un-trademarked candy an unmarked VHS tape, which he has no recollection of receiving. The kids persuade Sarah to let them watch the tape and that sets up "The 9th Circle," about a young woman who is trying to read a book as she waits at a train station late at night with a creepy-as-hell clown sitting right next to her. She is eventually drugged and awakens to find herself chained in a dungeon, along with two other girls. This segment features Lucifer himself in an inspired scene that is perfect for Halloween viewing, with its misty atmosphere, hideous demons, and meticulous sound effects of distant moans and bubbling cauldrons.

Sarah refuses to give into the kids' protests as she turns off the tape and sends them upstairs to bed. But her curiosity gets the best of her and she watches the rest of the tape while sipping red wine. There is a radical shift in tone for the next story, about a woman playing cat and mouse with an alien who has crashed nearby and is looking for a late-night human snack. While the alien isn't frightening whatsoever, it has the ability to turn off all the lights and disable electronic devices to lend a decent amount of suspense.

Next up is easily the scariest entry, which begins with a gorgeous woman pulling into Last Chance Gas with an empty tank, and minutes later, speeding away in hysterics after witnessing Art the Clown eviscerating the gas station employee. The powerful Grindhouse effect makes perfect sense for this tale, which significantly ups the gore factor and somehow makes Art even more terrifying than he was before as he relentlessly chases the poor woman while laughing and taunting. I only wish Leone had used some restraint here because the ending goes way too far, inflicting brutal and distasteful acts of misogyny into what had been a fun and spooky Halloween movie. So I'd highly recommend watching something a little more wholesome immediately after so you won't have to fall asleep with disturbing and hateful images clouding your mind. But no matter how much you watch afterwards, you will still go to bed feeling just as spooked as the two children in *All Hallows' Eve*, because the method in which their babysitter and Art the Clown eventually meet is a twisted and masterful act of storytelling.

AMERICAN NIGHTMARE (2002)

Director: Jon Keeyes
Cast: Debbie Rochon, Brandy Little, Johnny Sneed, Chris Ryan, Robert McCollum
Length: 93 minutes
Rating: R

Synopsis: On Halloween night, a group of friends confess their biggest fears on a radio show, which gives inventive ideas to the serial killer who is stalking them.

The characters in this direct-to-video cheapie are horror movie experts, but that doesn't make them any less vulnerable when they confront their worst nightmares. They casually recite lines from everything from *Andy Warhol's Frankenstein* to *From Dusk Till Dawn*, but aren't sharp enough to call the police when death visits their little town. Writer-director Jon Keeyes further corroborates his horror aficionado status by naming a character Caligari and offering chilling spoofs of *The Vanishing*, *Psycho*, and *When a Stranger Calls*.

Notwithstanding a piggy bank budget (which is evident immediately with the opening credits) and a somewhat inconsistent audio track, Keeyes and his surprisingly convincing group of young actors succeed in taking us on a wicked ride that runs smoothly; that is until they crash into a truncated final scene that resolves nothing. There is a chance that the ending could anger your friends, so if you decide to present this film on Halloween, have something fun planned for immediately afterwards (it would be a good time to use your spare blood packs for a gruesome gag).

The spookiest moments of *American Nightmare* are when a frenetic chase scene comes to a vicious conclusion, when an online instant message scares one character to tears, and when a girl must confront her phobia of being buried alive.

THE AMERICAN SCREAM (2012)

Director: Michael Paul Stephenson
Cast: Victor Bariteau, Manny Souza, Matthew Brodeur, Richard Brodeur, Tina Bariteau
Length: 91 minutes
Rating: Not Rated

Synopsis: This documentary follows three families in Massachusetts who transform their houses into elaborate Halloween haunts every October, a painstaking ritual that takes an emotional and physical toll on them, but that provides infinite joy when the big night approaches and the trick-or-treaters stop by.

Unless you live in the most hopeless and uninspiring of towns, you know the nearby house that goes all out for Halloween. You make a point of driving by there often during October just so you can witness the slow transformation from ordinary house to haunted wonderland. The sleepy town of Fairhaven, Massachusetts has three of these houses in close proximity, and their owners are the subject of this fantastic documentary by Michael Paul Stephenson,

his first since *Best Worst Movie* explored the monumental cult phenomenon of *Troll 2* (a lovably incompetent b-movie that he starred in when he was a little boy).

These affable but clearly stressed out blue-collar characters may remind you a little of Roseanne and Dan Conner because they masterfully fulfill their oddball obsession despite not having much money or space to hold massive collections of zombie mannequins, Styrofoam tombstones, and animated ghoulies for the 11 months when they aren't displayed on their front lawns. As a result, Victor Bariteau, who gets most of the screen time, has a house that sometimes resembles those in *Hoarders*, and his two daughters are forced to share a small bedroom. The older of the two has inherited her father's love for Halloween and is the rare girl who will wear black clothes and mutilate dolls while also being one of the most popular girls at school—after all,

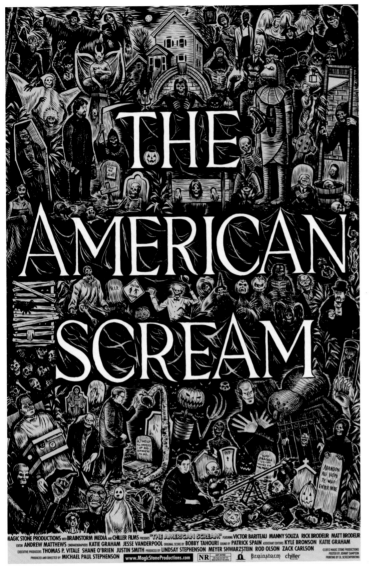

Poster for *The American Scream* (2012). Magic Stone Productions.

having so much fun playing make believe and trick-or-treating. Years of repression have turned him into a Halloween King of sorts, but his perfectionist nature makes you wonder if he's having any fun with his art. With less than a week to go before Halloween, he is exhausted and overwhelmed by how much still needs to be constructed, and because his family and friends like him so much, they put up with his mood swings and agree to be compliant team members.

Fellow home-haunters Matthew and Richard Brodeur, a father-son team who occasionally attend clown conventions, are also frustrated because with Halloween soon approaching, a storm has dismantled many of their unorthodox homemade props. Seemingly void of occupations, relationships, or companionship except each other, at least they have the time and necessary teamwork to save the big day.

The American Scream eloquently shows us a side to the Halloween lifestyle that we all observe, but rarely from behind the scenes, and the results are compelling and unexpectedly moving. Post-Halloween depression is not uncommon, but when you work as hard as people like Victor Bariteau, it's a practically agonizing to stow the witches back in the garage, reduce your still-freshly painted sets into pieces of lumber, and

her classmates all excitedly head over to her house on Halloween and find her successfully terrifying everyone, a rite of passage that the younger sister will soon attempt for the first time. Much like Wes Craven, Victor was raised in a household so religious that anything having to do with Halloween was strictly off-limits. A typical Halloween was spent alone in his bedroom, listening to the sounds of other kids

peel away the layers of ghoulishness to once again reveal a boring-looking house that nobody will bother to notice for another 11 months. When this film ends, you'll want to write a thank-you card to the owners of that one special house in your neighborhood because they sure do suffer for their art to make your Halloweens extra spooktacular.

AN AMERICAN WEREWOLF IN LONDON (1981)

⬚ **Director:** John Landis
★ **Cast:** David Naughton, Jenny Agutter, Griffin Dunne, John Woodvine, Brian Glover
◉ **Length:** 97 minutes
⬚ **Rating:** R

🗑 **Synopsis:** Two American college students are traveling through Northern England when they are attacked by a werewolf, sending one of them into a coffin and the other into a coma. The latter wakes up, but his road to recovery is harmed when his deceased friend pays him a visit and warns him that he will soon become a werewolf—and unless he commits suicide, many others will die.

Poster for *An American Werewolf in London* (1981). PolyGram Pictures.

It's not easy to name the greatest zombie film of all time, or best vampire film, but when talking about werewolves, there is one movie that is perched so far above the others. John Landis took an old formula, but added tongue-in-cheek humor, revolutionary special effects, stylish camerawork, award-winning make-up effects, and sophisticated dialogue to create the best lycanthrope film of all time.

Landis sets the mood perfectly, giving us two likeable young men named David and Jack wandering around the foggy English moors at night, gossiping about girls and telling lame knock-knock jokes. After walking around aimlessly in the cold weather, they hope to find temporary shelter in a pub called The Slaughtered Lamb. The creepy locals scare them away but warn them to beware the moon and stay close to the road. The two students find themselves back outside, and feeling even unluckier and colder as they're drenched from a storm. They drift unwisely off the road into a wide open field of darkness when they start hearing faint animal cries that seem to be getting closer and closer. At this point, Landis has us entirely in his palms, and he doesn't loosen his grip once in the entire film, always keeping us on edge by sprinkling doses of humor among some extremely frightening scenes, such as in the goofy dream sequence where David's relatives and his nurse get gunned down by a gang of mutant Nazis.

And obviously, *An American Werewolf in London* is known for having the most graphic, technically spectacular werewolf transformation scene ever, and still after all these years, despite various technological breakthroughs, nothing has even come close to matching the accomplishments of Rick Baker.

David Naughton's character reminds us all how similar werewolves are to vampires: they are able to function in society, socialize with friends, and even fall in love, but can't ignore their monstrous instincts no matter how hard they try. We honestly care for the characters in *An American Werewolf in London*, especially the two American students who were just in the wrong place at the wrong time. This gives the film a lot of emotion to go along with the gore and silliness, making its joyless, abrupt ending appropriate and satisfying enough.

A good portion of the comedy belongs to the scenes where the undead Jack keeps showing up to warn his friend, and to sincerely educate him on what he's been up to; at one point, Jack asks, "Have you ever talked to a corpse? It's boring!" He looks worse and worse each time we see him, and by the time he joins David at a porno theater, he has deteriorated to an articulate skeleton with hair. In the theater, he brings along David's latest victims, and reminds him that he has to sever the bloodline of the wolf, or they will all roam forever in limbo. David responds to this dire warning in one of the film's best lines:

"I will not be threatened by a walking meatloaf!" Be sure to hunt down the *An American Werewolf in London* Full Moon Edition DVD/Blu-Ray because it includes a stellar documentary called *Beware the Moon,* which gives the greatest werewolf movie of all time the credit it deserves.

AMITYVILLE II: THE POSSESSION (1982)

Director: Damiano Damiani
Cast: Jack Magner, James Olson, Burt Young, Rutanya Alda, Andrew Prine
Length: 104 minutes
Rating: R

Synopsis: After a family moves into a house built over an Indian burial ground, a demonic spirit possesses the oldest son and he goes on a killing spree. A local priest feels guilty for not doing more to help, so against his church's wishes, he decides to perform an exorcism on the boy.

Press kit photo for *Amityville II: The Possession* (1982). Orion Pictures.

The *Amityville Horror* series is mediocre at best so it's easy to overlook this second entry, a prequel to the original film. Loosely based on the murders committed by Ronald DeFeo Jr. of his entire family on November 13, 1974 at their home on 112 Ocean Avenue in Long Island, this is one of the most audacious and entertaining haunted house movies of the '80s.

As creepy-sounding children sing "la la la," reminiscent of the classic *Rosemary's Baby* score, we first see the Amityville house veiled behind skeleton trees and awaiting its new victims. The strongest element of this film is how it uses not a typical loving family, but a family so dysfunctional that even Jerry Springer and Maury would be lost for words. The father is physically abusive to his children and his wife, the mother is so religious that she asks a local priest to bless the entire house including the beds, and the two oldest siblings have an incestuous relationship. Thanks to films like *Poltergeist* and *Insidious*, we all know how an all-American ordinary family reacts to haunted houses, but a family constantly on the brink of war with each other gives an added dimension of hysteria.

The house does its usual tricks like bursting pipes, rotating beds, and guns shooting off automatically, but ups the ante considerably by speaking to the oldest son through his Walkman and having a spirit press violently against his stomach as bulbous growths invade his neck. Surely you can imagine the basement in the Amityville house being a tad on the unpleasant side, but nothing quite prepares you for the slimy, spewing secret room that almost seems like a place for all the evil to take a break and hang out for a bit. Peppered with unmistakable Italian horror touches (thanks to the director with the coolest name ever), the first hour of *Amityville II* is shocking, nauseating, and thrilling, but slows down considerably soon after the demonized boy hunts down his entire family on a stormy night. What follows is far less interesting, as the priest attempts to free the boy from the police station so that he can perform an exorcism. But even though the exciting Montelli family is gone, at least the blowing leaves, lightning, thunder, and impressive special effects stick around awhile longer. The screenplay was written by Tommy Lee Wallace, who would later write and direct *Halloween III: Season of the Witch, Fright Night Part 2*, and Stephen King's *It*.

ANDY WARHOL'S DRACULA/BLOOD FOR DRACULA (1974)

🎬 **Director:** Paul Morrissey
⭐ **Cast:** Udo Kier, Joe Dallesandro, Vittorio De Sica, Maxime McKendry, Arno Juerging
🎞️ **Length:** 103 minutes
👤 **Rating:** X

🎃 **Synopsis:** A sickly Count Dracula travels from Romania to Italy with his faithful servant in a desperate search for virgin blood. They arrive at a 17th century mansion owned by a deeply religious family with four beautiful daughters. Thanks to their promiscuous Communist gardener, the girls aren't so pure after all and their blood proves to be hazardous for the Count.

Poster for Andy Warhol's *Dracula* (1974). Bryanston Distributing.

Shot immediately after director Paul Morrissey wrapped up production for *Andy Warhol's Frankenstein/Flesh for Frankenstein*, this inherits the same X rating, principal cast members, and blend of silliness and seriousness. Although nowhere near as gory as its predecessor, it is far more humorous and technically adequate. The-one-and-only Udo Kier is very appealing as the Count who would look like an albino if it weren't for the daily application of rouge make-up to his face and black paint for his slicked-back hair, which is demonstrated in a mesmerizing opening title sequence. Once his morning ritual is complete, he resembles Mike Myers from his "Sprockets" skits on *Saturday Night Live*, but with a hypnotic stare and even thicker German accent. At one point, somebody describes him as "deadly pale, but then he is a vegetarian, and they all seem to look like that."

Three of the four Italian daughters that the Count has his eyes on are anything but virginal: they take turns fornicating with the family servant, engage in lesbianism, commit incest, and even take their clothes off while gardening just to rebel against their strict Catholic upbringings. It's no surprise that immediately after Dracula gulps from their necks, he violently vomits until he is too weak to even stand. These puking scenes are disgusting, but they are so prolonged and exaggerated that it's hard not to laugh. And be sure to look out for an unbilled Roman Polanski as he competes in a hilarious game of Copycat with Arno Juerging (who plays the bossiest and grumpiest Rendfield in any Dracula film). But seriously folks, this is Udo Kier playing Count Dracula, and a more delightful Halloween party guest I cannot imagine.

ARACHNOPHOBIA (1990)

Director: Frank Marshall
Cast: Jeff Daniels, Harley Jane Kozak, Julian Sands, John Goodman, Stuart Pankin, Henry Jones
Length: 103 minutes
Rating: PG-13

Synopsis: A dangerous spider is transferred from its home in a Venezuelan jungle to a small town in California when it hitches a ride in a coffin. It finds new sanctuary on the property of the town doctor, and when it mates, an army of eight legged killers is unleashed on the locals.

Lobby card for *Arachnophobia* (1990). Buena Vista Pictures.

Arachnophobia opens with a series of breathtaking shots as the camera pans through South American landscapes. But don't get too comfortable, because in only a matter of minutes, director Frank Marshall (who has produced many, many Steven Spielberg projects) grants us a skillfully constructed spider attack that assures us that this is a film capable of totally annihilating our nerves. The method in which the spider arrives in the American town of Canaima, a town so precarious it contains only one doctor, is clever and also quite horrific.

The always-compelling Jeff Daniels gives a commanding performance as a doctor whose arachnophobia is so intense—resulting from a traumatizing incident as a young child—that he cannot even muster the ability to remove a miniscule spider from his house. Also memorable are John Goodman as an exterminator with a rock 'n' roll attitude and Julian Sands as an arrogant scientist. With a repertoire that includes two *Warlock* films, *A Tale of a Vampire*, and *Gothic*, among others, the ravishing Sands should be considered one of horror's most capable leading men; after all, he was Anne Rice's personal choice to play Lestat in *Interview With the Vampire*.

Compared to other arachnid-horror flicks, the spiders in *Arachnophobia* are modestly-sized (with the exception of the Queen Spider), and Marshall allows them to move with fluid grace when they are not too busy transferring venom, making them all the more elusive. Their small size allows them to crawl inconspicuously into football helmets, cereal boxes, showers, and bowls of popcorn, which leads to several moments where the characters and the audiences shriek in unison.

If the idea of touching a tarantula doesn't make you squirm too uncomfortably, then 1977's *Kingdom of the Spiders* (starring William Shatner!) is also worth checking out, but not on Halloween night. There are several scenes in which thousands of real-life tarantulas crawl over helpless bodies, and that is too extreme for most people to handle, especially on a night that celebrates having fun.

ARMY OF DARKNESS (1992)

Director: Sam Raimi
Cast: Bruce Campbell, Embeth Davidtz, Marcus Gilbert, Richard Grove, Ted Raimi, Ian Abercrombie
Length: 80 minutes
Rating: R

Synopsis: Ash, the hero from the *Evil Dead* films, is transported to 1300 A.D. He journeys to find the "Book of the Dead," which will allow him to return home, but he makes a small but crucial mistake that releases the Army of the Dead.

Three Stooges slapstick and a storyline similar to *A Connecticut Yankee in King Arthur's Court* are partnered in this goofy monsterfest, part three of the *Evil Dead* series. Although far less scary and gory than the first two entries, Sam Raimi uses a much bigger budget to give us a slicker-looking film with more ingenious special effects and elaborate action scenes than you can count.

Watching this film is like riding a rollercoaster that only goes downhill. It has the kind of speedy pace where, if you leave the room for only a few seconds, you'll probably miss deaths, sight gags, and goofy one-liners (like "Yeah and maybe I am a Chinese jet pilot.") Despite having lots of practice, the hotshot muscleman Ash still has terrible luck with the virulent *Necronomicon*: he not only gets his fingers bitten by the cover, but he gets literally sucked inside the book, and when he returns, his head is drastically enlarged. Other amusing special effects include an army of bite-size Ashes who force his mouth open as one dives inside, as well as Ash growing a second body that he doesn't get along with.

At first, this doesn't have a distinct Halloween feel, but that changes when Ash enters a cemetery at night and participates in a slap-fight with a group of skeleton arms that emerge from the ground. It also contains some great-looking creature designs, most notably the winged Deadite that seizes Ash's love interest, and the pit demon that gobbles up those found guilty of crimes. Watching the skeleton warriors in action is also impressive—they are vicious fighters who can also play bones that sound like flutes.

Press kit photo for *Army of Darkness* (1992). Universal Pictures.

The inevitable war between the living and dead gets a little redundant for such a succinct running time, but its ending should put a big smile on your face.

Bridget Fonda, who starred with Bill Paxton and Billy Bob Thornton in Raimi's brilliant *A Simple Plan*, has a very brief cameo in the introduction. Although not quite on the same level as the first two entries, *Army of Darkness* is just as imaginative, ambitious, and bizarre, so it should please even the most demanding of fans.

ARSENIC AND OLD LACE (1944)

Director: Frank Capra
Cast: Cary Grant, Priscilla Lane, Raymond Massey, Josephine Hull, Jean Adair, Peter Lorre
Length: 118 minutes
Rating: Not Rated

Synopsis: A well-known theater critic gets married, but just before he's ready to enjoy his honeymoon, he discovers that his two sweet elderly aunts have a terrible habit of poisoning lonely old gentlemen and burying them in the basement.

Film still for *Arsenic and Old Lace* (1944). Warner Bros.

If you'd rather have a movie charm the pants off of you than scare you right out of your pants, then this Frank Capra classic is a fine choice, and it has enough Halloween aesthetics to look past that long running time. Based on a popular Broadway play starring Boris Karloff, *Arsenic and Old Lace* stars Cary Grant as Mortimer Brewster, a theater critic and well-known bachelor in Brooklyn; this role was originally offered

to Ronald Reagan but he turned it down. Mortimer has written such anti-marriage books as Marriage: A

Fraud and a Failure and Mind Over Matrimony, so a couple of journalists are shocked to see him at the city hall with his adoring girlfriend, in line to be wed. Before they begin their honeymoon to Niagara Falls, he returns to his childhood home to share the good news with his two maiden aunts and his brother, who believes that he is President Theodore Roosevelt. After Mortimer discovers a dead body in the window seat, his aunts nonchalantly confess that their generous spirits have enabled them to help out lonely old men by killing them and then having Teddy Roosevelt bury these "yellow fever victims" in the basement. A second sibling who has just escaped from an asylum also returns home, with scars holding his new face in place. Mortimer then begins to wonder if insanity runs in his family.

The plot sounds ghastly, but this isn't a horror movie whatsoever. The two aunts never once lose their wholesome and innocent demeanor even as the night gets crazier and crazier, and Cary Grant hams it up so much he resembles Curly from *The Three Stooges*. Add in a wickedly good Teddy Roosevelt impersonation, the most inept police officers you'll ever see, and Peter Lorre in one of his most adorable roles ever, and you have a movie that only intends to make you chuckle at its absurdity. And what makes it such an appropriate movie for October is that it's set on Halloween night (a great change to the Broadway version), making the insane events inside the Brewster house mirror the creepiness that's on the outside: a Brewster family graveyard filled with dead leaves and trick-or-treaters.

Reminding us how holiday traditions change over time is when a group of rowdy trick-or-treaters reach in through the back door, shouting unintelligible dialogue as the aunts hand out pies and jack-o'-lanterns. The custom of trick-or-treating has undergone various incarnations, beginning back in the Middle Ages when children and poor people would go "souling." By going door to door, they would receive cakes in return for praying for the homeowners' relatives who have passed away. In the city I trick-or-treated in, St. Louis, it was custom to tell a joke before getting a candy, and that tradition thankfully still stands.

BEETLEJUICE (1988)

Director: Tim Burton
Cast: Alec Baldwin, Geena Davis, Michael Keaton, Winona Ryder, Jeffrey Jones, Catherine O'Hara
Length: 92 minutes
Rating: PG

Synopsis: A married couple is killed in a car accident and find themselves trapped in their New England home as ghosts. Just as they are trying to understand their situation, a yuppie couple and their gothic daughter move into the house. After being unsuccessful in their attempts to scare the family enough to leave, they enlist the services of Betelguese, a mischief-making ghoul who specializes in exorcisms for the living.

Press kit photo for *Beetlejuice* (1988). Warner Bros.

Making a feature film debut as original and beloved as *Pee Wee's Big Adventure* can be a constant albatross for any director, but with his follow-up, auteur Tim Burton proved he had plenty more tricks up his sleeves. Known for internalizing a child's deepest, darkest nightmare and making it whimsical and enchanting, it's no surprise that he has multiple films that would be appropriate for the Halloween season.

Beetlejuice wastes no time in creeping us out, giving us a close-up of a tarantula immediately following one of Danny Elfman's (a long-time collaborator of Burton's) most bombastic scores. Alec Baldwin and Geena Davis are charming as the couple who just wanted to spend their vacation decorating their new house, but instead have to spend it as ghosts watching their house being taken over by a pretentious and persnickety couple, played by Jeffrey Jones and Catherine O'Hara. Winona Ryder is also excellent as the misunderstood teenager with the spidery, tangled hair and assortment of veils. If these five characters weren't engaging, then the film would crumble to pieces because "Betelguese," as dynamic and goofy as he is, couldn't hold it together by himself.

Michael Keaton plays the sardonic, horny, gravel-voiced ghost like an eccentric used car salesman who you know has a load of lemons in his lot. Fortunately, Burton uses him in small doses, because too much of Mr. Beetle Breakfast would probably give us all headaches. He does make us laugh,

though, especially when he pulls a ring off a severed finger and assures his bride-to-be that "she meant nothing to me." Another funny bit takes place at the business office for the recently deceased, full of lavish surroundings and rooms where lost souls are stored. It runs much like the DMV, so not even death can get you out of waiting in long lines. There he flirts with a pair of severed legs as her upper portion watches in disgust. And the way in which Robert Goulet's character is disposed of is a thing of Burton beauty—it's even more satisfying than his demise in *The Naked Gun 2 ½*.

BLACK SABBATH (1963)

🎬 **Director:** Mario Bava
⭐ **Cast:** Boris Karloff, Mark Damon, Michèle Mercier, Jacqueline Pierreux, Susy Andersen, Lidia Alfonsi
🎞 **Length:** 95 minutes
🎭 **Rating:** Not Rated

🎞 **Synopsis:** In this Italian horror anthology, a woman is being harassed by telephone calls from an escaped prisoner; the patriarch of a Russian family goes on a quest to kill his adversary, but returns home a vampire; and a nurse makes the deadly mistake of stealing a ring from the finger of a recently-deceased medium.

After a colorful introduction from Boris Karloff that resembles how Alfred Hitchcock began episodes of his television program, director Mario Bava presents three tantalizing tales, and just like in his previous masterpiece *Black Sunday*, he tosses ominous signs like breadcrumbs, giving his rich gothic atmosphere a real sense of dread.

The first tale, "The Telephone," is clearly the weakest of the three, but it does have its moments. The rather mundane plot is boosted by a claustrophobic setting and really nasty dialogue coming from the other end of the telephone line. It also paved the way for the most memorable scenes from *When a Stranger Calls* and *Scream*. A lesbian subplot was unforgivably cut for the American release and was replaced by more supernatural elements.

"The Wurdalak" fares much better, offering an eerie Russian countryside location drenched in fog, an assaulting soundtrack of spooky music and winds so forceful that they creep their way into every interior scene, grisly visuals like decapitated heads and skeletons, and one of Karloff's most intense performances. The complex destruction of the family

Poster for *Black Sabbath* (1963). American International Pictures.

justifies this tale commanding the bulk of the film's running time.

Bava doesn't allow you much time to catch your breath because "The Drop of Water" is the scariest of the three. It contains the kind of crippling tension that beckons you to look away from the television screen in order to salvage your few remaining nerves. If trick-or-treaters decide to ring your doorbell during the more hushed moments, then a chorus of screams could easily erupt from your party guests. While this film played theatrically in England, it attracted the attention of a certain rock band that was in the process of looking for a new name to go along with their much darker musical directions.

BLACK SUNDAY (1960)

Director: Mario Bava
Cast: Barbara Steele, John Richardson, Ivo Garrani, Andrea Checchi, Arturo Dominici, Enrico Olivieri
Length: 83 minutes
Rating: Not Rated

Synopsis: Two hundred years after being burned at the stake, an evil witch rises from the grave to stalk the descendents of her hunters and to possess her look-alike princess.

After working as a cinematographer for nearly 30 years, the reputable Mario Bava was ready for a mightier feat. His beautifully atmospheric *Black Sunday* paved the road for Italy's longstanding contribution to the horror genre and continues to be revered by new audiences. Shot in bleak but stunning black and white, it mirrors the uncanny camera angles from German expressionism and employs the kind of Gothic set pieces that propelled Universal's 1930s monster movies. It is especially generous to those wanting an appropriate viewing experience for a stormy October night. There are heavy uses of fog, rain, fire, howling, cobwebs, bats, skeleton bones, and unnerving music. Also contributing to the mood are bugs nestled on rotting corpses, shaking coffins, a vampire that rises from the grave during the separation between thunder and lightning, and a creepy castle that contains trap doors and dark pits.

In one of the most unforgettable opening scenes ever, the aforementioned witch is convicted by the Inquisition and has a spiked "mask of Satan" drilled into her face. With such a ghastly initial murder, the strangulations in the second half pale in comparison. Also unfortunately noticeable is the lousy dubbing that had become a common element in Italian imports.

Centering around Barbara Steele's dual roles as a maligning witch and innocent princess, *Black Sunday* unfolds like a fairy tale; it even contains love at first sight. The British beauty became a star as a result of the film's success, and would later work with movie messiahs like Federico Fellini before ultimately being typecast in horror pictures.

THE BLAIR WITCH PROJECT (1999)

Directors: Daniel Myrick, Eduardo Sánchez
Cast: Heather Donahue, Joshua Leonard, Michael C. Williams
Length: 86 minutes
Rating: R

Synopsis: "In October of 1994, three student filmmakers disappeared in the woods near Burkittsville, Maryland while shooting a documentary. A year later their footage was found." *(taken from the promotional poster)*

You have probably heard a thousand times from critics and movie buffs that often what you cannot see is scarier than what you can. Watch this film if you need proof that this statement is true. It doesn't happen often, but sometimes a horror film will come out of nowhere to take America by storm, to not only breathe new life into the genre but to give the public something they have never witnessed before. *The Blair Witch*

Project has a phenomenal history of how it became one of the most profitable films of all time. These filmmakers had a miniscule budget, but they were still able to make the most inventive and terrifying film in years. To watch this film is an experience that everybody should have, and on what better night than Halloween?

The Blair Witch Project became the icon it is today thanks to a smart and creative marketing campaign that convinced people that this was a true story, and that this really was the footage of three filmmakers who went into the woods and never came back. They produced fake documentaries on TV about these three students and stated in online movie databases that they were either deceased or still missing. Also sparking public interest were the movie trailers, which resembled a home movie of the most nightmarish vacation of all time, rather than a feature film. And because the film itself looks no more sophisticated than a home movie from your senile aunt, many people who watched *The Blair Witch Project* were amazed afterwards when they found out the truth. In fact, the film is completely improvised, with the actors having no idea what they were going to see or do, which is why the dialogue and reactions seem so natural and unrehearsed. And this was before the big, idiotic, boring, stupid, lame, brain-sucking reality show craze.

The three lead performances are convincing, so you can really feel their impending doom. After a few days of watching them walk around endlessly in the chilly October air, not being able to find a way out of the woods, not having any food, losing their tempers at each other, hearing intermittent cries from afar, and seemingly being stalked every night while they are asleep, you really feel like you're out there with them. This is the kind of film with an ending so powerful, you will sit completely still, staring at the ending credits, not saying a word, and trying to decipher what you have just seen (Chris Kentis's 2003 masterpiece *Open Water* had a very similar effect).

THE BLOB (1988)

Director: Chuck Russell
Cast: Kevin Dillon, Shawnee Smith, Donovan Leitch, Candy Clark, Michael Kenworthy, Jeffrey DeMunn
Length: 92 minutes
Rating: R

Synopsis: A secret government experiment goes terribly wrong, resulting in a mass of gooey gelatin that terrorizes a small town, consuming anyone in its path. With every meal, it grows bigger, and it's up to a pretty cheerleader and the local rebel to warn everybody before the blob takes over the whole town.

Made 30 years after the sci-fi drive-in pleaser that gave Steve McQueen his first starring role, this version of *The Blob* clearly lays out what it takes for a horror remake to succeed. It honors the original source material and keeps its tone in tact while updating the societal themes to fit with the times, taking advantage of technological upgrades to show us things that the original wasn't capable of showing, and restructuring the characters and their relationships so we don't get ahead of a story we've heard before. Also catching us off guard is how it repeatedly dispatches the kind of characters that 99% of horror films would keep around until the very end—women and children aren't off limits to this gelatin nightmare!

Among the carnage is a man getting sucked down into a tiny drain, a bum getting completely chewed in half, a child getting blobified in a sewer and returning as a bloody skeleton, and plenty more, but it's all in good, drive-in quality fun.

Affection for the 1980s isn't a prerequisite to enjoy a movie like this but man does it ever help, as everything from Shawnee Smith's wardrobe to the pumping hair metal soundtrack works like a time warp. The blatancy of how Kevin Dillon is portrayed as a "youth gone wild" will surely inspire early chuckles: when we first see him, he's a greasy, long-haired teen with a leather jacket, smoking a cigarette, guzzling the last of his beer before tossing the can aside, and performing dangerous motorcycle tricks without wearing a helmet. And we haven't even seen his cool swagger yet!

The Blob is an obvious winner for Halloween night no matter what kind of company you're in: from start to finish it's full of great horror action, likeable characters, stunning special effects, and well-executed comic relief. Its final scene in a sweaty, uncomfortable church service conducted by a reverend resembling Freddy Krueger seems to be promising a sequel that never came.

Press photo for *The Blob* (1988). TriStar Pictures.

BONES (2001)

Director: Ernest R. Dickerson
Cast: Snoop Dogg, Pam Grier, Michael T. Weiss, Clifton Powell, Bianca Lawson
Length: 96 minutes
Rating: R

Synopsis: Four youths renovate a condemned ghetto brownstone and turn it into a posh nightclub. What they don't know is the basement serves as a tomb for the corpse of Jimmy Bones, a benevolent inner city godfather who was murdered in the '70s by a crooked cop and backstabbing associates. With the help of a mysterious dog that chows on human flesh, the spirit of Jimmy Bones resurfaces to avenge his death.

Unfairly ripped to shreds by critics, *Bones* is a delightful romp with a slick look, an entertaining cast, in-your-face special effects, and by far the greatest shot you will ever see of a dog projectile vomiting thousands of squirmy maggots. Director Ernest Dickerson does pull a risky maneuver when at the halfway mark, what was a mostly atmospheric and chilling horror film suddenly turns into a comedy that offers a pair of decapitated heads bickering back and forth and a villain who drawls out lines like "I've got a natural high, a supernatural high" as if he were attempting a Dirty Harry impression. He also has no idea whether to make Jimmy Bones a bloodthirsty demon or an urban version of The Crow, so he chooses both. Maybe on another night, you would be less forgiving of such scatterbrained material, but on Halloween, this level of nonsensical randomness just titillates our senses. So if you can't get Snoop Dogg and Pam Grier to RSVP to your Halloween party invitation, at least they can still contribute to the festivities in some way.

Borrowing from other films, *Bones* delivers a raining-maggots scene reminiscent of *Suspiria*, a corpse that rebuilds in the same manner as Frank in *Hellraiser,* a secretive connection between the parents of the main characters like the parents in *Nightmare on Elm Street*, and flashback scenes taken right out of '70s blaxploitation flicks. Also unoriginal but impressive are its visualization of hell—a dark and slimy mudslide of squirmy bodies in permanent agony—and its usage of a psychic to preach warnings to the carefree teenagers. Even if these things have been done before, Dickerson directs in a hyper, carefree manner (with the exception of a flashback scene involving the bold, drawn out murder of Jimmy Bones) that makes it clear he just wants the viewers to have fun.

BRIDE OF FRANKENSTEIN (1935)

🎬 **Director:** James Whale
⭐ **Cast:** Boris Karloff, Colin Clive, Valerie Hobson, Elsa Lanchester, Ernest Thesiger, O.P. Heggie
🎞 **Length:** 75 minutes
👤 **Rating:** Not Rated

🗑 **Synopsis:** The monster survives the mill fire from the end of the original and continues to wreak havoc on those who scream at its appearance. Lonely, injured, and despondent, he enters the cabin of a blind hermit and is finally offered safety and companionship. After learning to talk, the monster returns to his creator and demands a mate.

Continuing to fascinate and entrance its viewers after 80 years, *Bride of Frankenstein*, James Whale's follow-up to his 1931 classic, will always be regarded as the best example of a sequel surpassing its predecessor. While it borrows the original's Expressionism style, macabre humor, subversive tones, elaborate Gothic sets, and pathos, Whale has no interest in retelling the same story. Rather than play it safe, he helms the material into territories so bizarre they include a preface that takes us back to Lord Byron's estate where Mary Shelley discusses her new-found fame, an arcane scientist who imprisons miniature humans in glass jars, and Frankenstein's monster learning how to party from an old blind man. Universal wanted *Bride of Frankenstein* simply for financial reasons, but Whale took it as an opportunity to strengthen his skills as a filmmaker.

In a famous scene that was heavily spoofed in Mel Brooks' *Young Frankenstein*, the monster finds his first friend in a blind recluse, whose music causes him to melt into a wide-eyed tranquility. The old man is equally lonesome and forlorn, and thanks the heavens when his friend has finally come, even though he is a hulking mute. They are both outcasts of a prejudiced society, so their friendship is sweet and precious. And since the monster is already dead, he doesn't have to worry about pesky things like lung cancer or alcoholism.

Ernest Thesiger is outstanding as the effeminate mad scientist Pretorius, and Boris Karloff predictably steals every scene, complexly alternating from madness to tenderness, from killing innocent people and hostilely pummeling the water that shows him his reflection to begging for mercy with the faintest of hand gestures and warmly saying to his new friend, "alone bad, friend good."

Lobby card for *Bride of Frankenstein* (1935). Universal Pictures.

THE 'BURBS (1989)

🎬 **Director:** Joe Dante
⭐ **Cast:** Tom Hanks, Bruce Dern, Carrie Fisher, Rick Ducommun, Corey Feldman, Wendy Schaal
⊕ **Length:** 101 minutes
👤 **Rating:** PG

🎬 **Synopsis:** While trying to enjoy a much-needed week off at home, Ray Peterson is constantly distracted by strange happenings in his neighborhood. His friends are convinced that the strange people who have moved next door are part of a Satanic cult, and decide to do a little investigating once an elderly neighbor suddenly goes missing.

The 'Burbs was a childhood favorite that I still quote to this day. But I never recognized its *Pumpkin Cinema* potential until a couple of years ago, when on a dark and drizzly (storms are depressingly rare in Portland, Oregon) October night, I had a few friends over for a movie night. I had only two movies planned because my friends didn't share my creature-of-the-late-night status, but to my surprised delight, the combination of caffeine, sugar, and growing anticipation for Halloween kept them awake enough to request a round three. We had just watched *Trick 'R Treat* and *Re-Animator*, and even though I had plenty of titles to choose from, arriving at a group consensus proved difficult. It seemed like for every option, somebody had either just recently seen it or simply wasn't in the mood. Then someone suggested *The 'Burbs* and we all agreed, even though I was a little hesitant because I never really considered it to be ideal Halloween viewing. But sometimes all it takes is the right group and the right environment to be able to see a film you've had practically memorized since childhood through a fresh set of eyes, to observe and appreciate it in ways you never had before. To my surprise *The 'Burbs* made for a perfect Halloween movie and I will never doubt it again!

With its gossiping neighbors, old man obsessed with keeping his yard the cleanest on the block, and newspaper delivery boy, this film is set in a slice of innocent suburbia so familiar that it's no surprise the same Universal Studios cul-de-sac had just been used for *Still the Beaver*, the follow-up series to *Leave it to Beaver*. It makes you wonder how the Cleavers would have dealt with new neighbors who have strange sounds emanating from the basement at all hours of the night and who seemingly only leave their house to drive bags of garbage to the curb before beating them violently with sticks. The Klopek

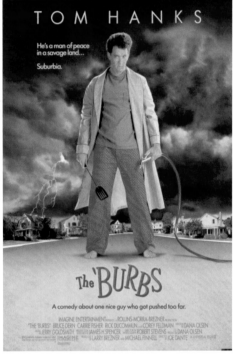

Poster for *The 'Burbs* (1989). Universal Pictures.

Family (no, that is not a Slavic name!), played by the wickedly good trio of Brother Theodore, Henry Gibson, and Courtney Gains (Malachai from the Corn's Children!), make such compelling characters that you really have no idea if they are satanic cannibals or merely misunderstood.

Not only is this one of the funniest movies of the '80s, but it also has honest-to-god creepy moments, such as when Tom Hanks watches out the window in horror as The Klopeks dig in their backyard late at night in the middle of a thunderstorm; I have gotten a chill during this scene every single time, mostly thanks to Jerry Goldsmith's merciless score. Ray then hopes to be comforted by a channel surfing session, only to find *Race with the Devil*, *The Exorcist*, and *The Texas Chainsaw Massacre Part 2*, which later inspires one of the most unsettling dream sequences you'll see in a comedy.

And it wouldn't be a Joe Dante film without a scene-stealing cameo from Dick Miller, and here he plays a garbage man who becomes extremely agitated with Bruce Dern.

THE CABINET OF DR. CALIGARI (1920)

Director: Robert Wiene
Cast: Werner Krauss, Conrad Veidt, Lil Dagover, Friedrich Feher, Hans Heinz Von Twardowski
Length: 69 minutes
Rating: Not Rated

Synopsis: An asylum inmate tells a companion the story of a vengeful magician named Dr. Caligari, who used his hypnotized somnambulist to commit murders, and who was responsible for having him institutionalized.

It's sad but true that not everybody appreciates or enjoys silent films. I was reminded of this when *The Artist* ended up being one of the least-seen films in recent years to completely dominate in awards season. But those of you who appreciate the origins of film history and the different styles of filmmaking, and who don't grow restless at the sight of intertitles, should definitely spare 69 minutes of your October for this nearly century-old icon of German expressionism.

Often regarded as one of the first horror features, *The Cabinet of Dr. Caligari* is easily one of the most influential films of all time, and still feels oddly modern. Not only did it prove that terror can be evoked by peculiar sets and unorthodox camera angles, but it also gave us our first real zombie in Cesare the Somnambulist, who sleeps in a crate and is spoon-fed by his master. The film contains a special twist that was decades ahead of its time. It's the kind of unexpected plot turn that will bend your mind into a pretzel as you try to figure out what's real and what's imaginary.

Adding onto the film's otherworldly feel are the sets, constructed entirely from paper, making the shadows even more striking (especially during a stabbing scene). The buildings all tilt, and the narrow hallways seem like they will crush you if you walk down far enough, suggesting a funhouse-like environment. *The Cabinet of Dr. Caligari* is mesmerizing, disturbing, and surreal, and still packs a powerful punch.

THE CABIN IN THE WOODS (2012)

Director: Drew Goddard
Cast: Kristen Connolly, Fran Kranz, Chris Hemsworth, Richard Jenkins, Anna Hutchison
Length: 95 minutes
Rating: R

Synopsis: Five friends head to a cabin so secluded they are literally blocked from the real world. Unbeknownst to them, they are pawns in one incredibly weird and frightening ritual, beginning with the awakening a family of zombies by reading an old diary out loud. Those who survive this attack have something much bigger waiting for them.

You certainly weren't the only one dismayed by the remaking of countless '70s classics and the many punishing offerings of torture-porn that denigrated the whole genre by going over the line. Joss Whedon was just as upset and he decided to do something about it by imagining his dream horror movie in his head while he was still working on *Buffy the Vampire Slayer*. Together with Drew Goddard, they wrote the entire script to *The Cabin in the Woods* in just three days, and then it was off to beautiful Vancouver, British Columbia for production with an ideal cast, sizeable budget, and a strong belief they were making one of the most important horror films of all time. Their studio, MGM, wasn't as confident and they had trouble grasping both the concept and tone; repeatedly they interfered by attempted to cut out some of the most important scenes and by pressuring Goddard and Whedon to convert the whole movie to 3-D. MGM was hit hard with financial troubles and had to file for bankruptcy in 2010, and even though that meant a release delay so considerable that fans were worried we might have another Warner Brothers/*Trick 'R Treat* fiasco, it allowed *The Cabin in the Woods* to find a much more suitable home in Lionsgate Studio.

Three years after it was filmed, *The Cabin in the Woods* was finally released and became what a huge majority of horror websites and magazines called the greatest genre film of 2012. Goddard and Weddon got to throw in every insane visual and creature they could think of and have each one service the plot. The creative storyline allowed them the chance to pay nods to everything from Japanese horror (where nine-year-old girls get to turn an evil spirit into a happy frog!) to *Evil Dead* to '70s slashers, and lovingly justify all of the most common horror clichés like the creepy gas station owner giving directions to a group of friends that include an athlete, a whore, a scholar, a fool, and a virgin (or as The Director says in the end, "we work with what we have.") It's quite a remarkable balancing act of horror and comedy in a movie that starts out great and keeps getting better and better, and just when we feel it can't possibly offer us any more, a wonderfully familiar face surprises us while exposing yet another shocking layer.

The third act was a thrill to watch in theaters but is even more rewarding at home, when you have a remote control to pause and rewind. These frames beckon to be explored because you surely want to see as much of the angry molesting tree, merman, snowman, dragonbat, sugarplum fairy, psycho clown, dollfaces, sasquatch, werewolf, witches, Cenobite, scarecrow, giant serpent, vomiting infecteds, and impaling unicorn as you possibly can. Any movie would be lucky to have just one of these nighttime army creatures to offer you on Halloween, but *The Cabin in the Woods* uses them all in just a couple of minutes, and it's just perfect.

Poster for *The Cabin in the Woods* (2012). Lionsgate.

It's also refreshing that the stoner not only has the best lines but is also the smartest, toughest son of a bitch in the whole movie. I can only hope that my final words can go something like, "I'm sorry that I let you get attacked by a werewolf and then ended the world."

CASPER (1995)

☒ **Director:** Brad Silberling
★ **Cast:** Christina Ricci, Bill Pullman, Cathy Moriarty, Eric Idle, Malachi Pearson, Joe Nipote
☺ **Length:** 100 minutes
☖ **Rating:** PG

🎞 **Synopsis:** A paranormal psychologist is hired to eliminate the ghosts who haunt a mansion that could contain secret treasures. Once inside, his daughter befriends the ghost of a boy who remembers very little about his childhood. With her help, the ghost hopes to find a way to return to human form, but they must watch out for a sneaky pair of bad guys, who want to steal their discoveries.

It was a risky move to place the portly ghost child who appeared in over fifty animated shorts throughout the '40s and '50s in a feature-length live-action movie, but it just barely prevails despite coming awfully close to self-destructing with an ill-conceived plot development near the climax. Up until this point, Casper the Friendly Ghost behaves and speaks in a way that a hyper 8-year-old would, and has sort of a "big sister/younger brother" relationship with Ricci's character, Kat. So what happens at the Halloween party brings the whole film to an incredulous halt. It would be impossible for them to have even the tiniest bit of romantic chemistry in a scene like this, no matter how capable the actors might be. Even with the lame ending, *Casper* is a film that the whole family can enjoy together on Halloween night.

Children will probably be most entertained by Casper's three loudmouth housemates, whose pranks are actually more cruel than funny. Stretch, Stinkie, and Fatso should have been presented in much smaller doses, because their aggressively obnoxious presence seems to prevent the other characters from really developing. Adults will be more impressed with the elaborate sets, the various bizarre gadgets throughout the mansion, and the many cameos from well-respected movie stars. Somehow this film was able to obtain cameos from Clint Eastwood, Mel Gibson, Rodney Dangerfield, and Dan Akroyd, who reprises his famous role in *Ghostbusters*. Even The Cryptkeeper himself makes an appearance at one point! And we even get to finally find out how the little guy died—not as exciting as a rollercoaster accident or a kangaroo attack, but at least it wasn't something lame like natural causes.

Also, isn't it peculiar that when people in the film die, they return as ghosts with all their physical characteristics in tact, yet Casper just looks like a floating marshmallow?

CAT'S EYE (1985)

Director: Lewis Teague
Cast: Drew Barrymore, James Woods, Alan King, Kenneth McMillan, Robert Hays, Candy Clark
Length: 94 minutes
Rating: PG-13

Synopsis: As a stray cat wanders along the East coast, it becomes a participant in three bizarre, comedic, and chilling scenarios.

Anthology films are intrinsically desirable for Halloween—why choose one scary story when you can have three or four? And as *Creepshow* taught us, Stephen King certainly understands how to write a wickedly good screenplay that juggles multiple stories, and *Cat's Eye* doesn't disappoint. What makes this such a successful Halloween movie is its lightning-quick pace and consistency—each tale starts strong and immediately reels you in, not letting you off the hook until it delivers its ironic, satisfying ending, much like a good episode of *Tales From the Crypt*. And unlike most anthologies, there's no obvious choice for the standout story, making it interesting to predict how your friends will rank the three sequences.

Cat's Eye opens with a steady heartbeat and an extreme close-up of our darling tabby, whose first adventure will be an exciting chase scene with Cujo in New York City. He survives this encounter only to be captured by an employee of Quitters Inc., a company that specializes in unorthodox but highly effective methods of ridding its clients of their nicotine addiction. This tale has a wicked sense of humor and some real Hitchcockian suspense (most notably the scene in the traffic jam when James Woods thinks he has outsmarted Big Brother), and while it's the least horror oriented of the three, it's also the least predictable.

Once the tabby hitchhikes to Atlantic City, New Jersey, he is named Sebastian by a sleazy, obnoxiously wealthy gambler who has won a bet that the cat can cross the busy street without getting run over. Always the gambling man, he then kidnaps his wife's lover, a former tennis pro with an on-off relationship with drugs, and bets that he can't walk along the 5-inch ledge all the way around his architecturally peculiar apartment building, not exactly warning him ahead of time about certain obstacles like bloodthirsty pigeons and water hoses. This segment succeeds with its high stakes, playful attacks on our acrophobia, and comical villain reminiscent of Leslie Nielsen in *Creepshow*. And it's always a pleasure to see the great Mike Starr, who has enjoyed the kind of career that makes IMDb such an entertaining website.

Sebastian then takes a train to Wilmington, North Carolina, where he is adopted by a 9-year-old Drew Barrymore and re-named General—an appropriate name because he soon has to protect the little girl from the vicious 6-inch troll (a great looking creature created by the same man who built E.T.) that sneaks in her bedroom every night while she sleeps. This leads to an epic climax that will satisfy everyone who rooted for Sylvester, Tom, and Scratchy.

CEMETERY OF TERROR (1985)

Director: Rubén Galindo Jr.
Cast: Hugo Stiglitz, Bety Robles, Andrés García Jr., María Rebeca
Length: 88 minutes
Rating: Not Rated

Synopsis: A group of teenagers want to have a little innocent fun on Halloween in a cemetery when they try to use an evil book to bring the corpse of a serial killing Satanist back to life, but they get much more than they bargained for. The foggy graveyard also happens to be the destination for a group of trick-or-treating children.

Poster for *Cemetery of Terror* (1985). Dynamic Films.

Filmed in Texas but aimed at Mexican audiences, *Cemetery of Terror*, which also sometimes goes by the name *Zombie Apocalypse*, is one of the most spirited and entertaining Halloween movies ever, so it frustrates me that something this good could have flown under my radar for so long. Pair it up with *The Midnight Hour* for a Criminally Underrated 1985 Halloween Movie Double Feature.

It begins as three young women express excitement about their amazing Halloween night plans: a rock concert followed by an extravagant jet set party, with celebrities and limousines, unaware that this invitation is all just a ruse by their boyfriends to get them alone in a spooky abandoned house for a night of what Mrs. Doubtfire would refer to as sinking the sub, hiding the weasel, parking the porpoise, a bit of the old Humpty-Dumpty, the bone dance, little Jack horny, baloney bop, and a bit of the old cunning linguistics. The girls are obviously devastated when they see the cobwebbed, dusty house and it's going to take much more than a Boombox playing hilariously unsexy music and a mysterious black book of spells to get them in the mood. Annoyed by the girls' fussiness, the boys decide to spice things up with a trip to the morgue to retrieve a corpse that is needed to execute a certain spell, and they are determined to find the ugliest, most gruesome stiff available. Meanwhile, a Dr. Loomis-like character who looks like a chubby Wayne Coyne is driving to the same morgue to make sure that a certain ugly, gruesome corpse of a demonic serial killer is cremated rather than buried, so it can never walk the Earth again.

The full moon hides and blankets of fog dissolve as a hellacious thunderstorm drenches the six teenagers (and seemingly thousands of crickets and frogs who help make this a really gratifying movie to listen to) gathered at a cemetery to complete the spell. One of them reads from the book, "Make yourself visible, Lord of Darkness, give me proof of your existence!" Before the cemetery turns into a swimming pool like in *The Return of the Living Dead*, the teens return to the abandoned house to have a little fun before their visitor arrives. At this point, we expect the remainder of the film to play out like a traditional slasher even if we have no idea who the inevitable survivor is supposed to be, but the movie shifts gears by introducing us to another group of kids celebrating the best holiday of the year. They are much younger but still on the morbid side, as they hitch a ride with a strange man in a van just so they can start off their night of trick-or-treating at the local cemetery. The particulars of their trick-or-treating agenda are a little unclear because the kids don't carry bags, but instead, lit jack-o'-lanterns with wire handles. With the exception of an adorable airbrushed Michael Jackson jacket and the type of cheap plastic masks with the string that painfully digs into your skin, their costumes aren't anything to brag about, but they clearly have a lot of spirit because as they walk together, they sing a song that goes, "Father, father, today is Halloween." On my third page of scribbled notes, I wrote in big capital letters, "Holy shit, this movie rules!" and while that sentiment could have been applied at any scene, I'm pretty sure it came when zombies (referred to as "creatures of the devil") started rising from the grave to chase the kids who wouldn't drop their precious, protective jack-o'-lanterns that managed to somehow stay flickering.

A CHINESE GHOST STORY (1987)

Director: Siu-Tung Ching
Cast: Leslie Cheung, Joey Wang, Ma Wu, Wai Lam, Siu-Ming Lau
Length: 92 minutes
Rating: Not Rated

Synopsis: A tax collector ventures deep into the woods and encounters wolves, dueling swordsmen, and a mysterious woman, with whom he falls in love. She is a ghost who seduces men for her evil master to feast on, and the only way her spirit can be set free is the possibility of reincarnation.

The opening shots of *A Chinese Ghost Story* provide a perfect Halloween setting in which dead leaves fight with noisy winds at dusk, leading us to a creepy old house that sits next to gravestones. Watching this dazzling thriller from Hong Kong might make you feel a wave of nostalgia, as its basic story shares many similarities with the classic fairy tales from your childhood. On the other hand, the execution is unlike anything you have ever seen. Traditional horror visuals are on board: glowing red-eyed wolves, skeletons that come back to life, monsters lurking in the basement, decapitations, and the universal fear of being alone and lost deep in a forest in the middle of the night. More unusual are the bombastic martial arts battles with aerial swordplay, a tree-demon with a mile-long tongue, reincarnation functioning as a cure, and a main character spontaneously breaking out in a drunken song for no clear reason. It also may very well feature the quickest decomposing of a dead body, including the couple seconds in which we travel down the man's throat and through his stomach.

All of these ingredients are spread throughout a dreamlike, blue-tinted, soft-focused atmosphere where people can leap from tree to tree without the threat of gravity and where even inanimate objects seem capable of keeping secrets. This would be a great film for couples to watch together; it is spooky, but also very endearing, due to the genuine and heartfelt chemistry between the romantic leads.

While being virtually unseen in the United States, it has deservedly achieved such international success that following were two sequels, an animated film version, a television series, and a remake.

CLOWNHOUSE (1989)

Director: Victor Salva
Cast: Nathan Forrest Winters, Brian McHugh, Sam Rockwell, Michael Jerome West
Length: 81 minutes
Rating: R

Synopsis: Three escaped mental patients murder the clowns from a traveling circus and then take their identities. Afterwards, they visit a large house where three brothers are home alone, the youngest of whom has a severe clown phobia.

It's important for a Halloween movie to get off to a strong start and offer tasty treats right away, and this late '80s direct-to-video suburban thriller excites us right away thanks to a title credit for Sam Rockwell! *Clownhouse* was his very first movie and the star of *Moon* showed enormous potential even back then. He plays the oldest of three siblings and often exploits the power of big brother by relentlessly teasing the younger boys and singing fun lyrics like "Casey walking scared, between his legs he has no hair." One of the many things this movie does right is showcase sibling rivalry and adolescent male behavior. Everything they do, from forming alliances to the "I know you are but what am I?" comebacks feels authentic and straight out of your own childhood, so it's easy to empathize when after telling scary stories to each other, they start to hear things that go bump in the night.

It is two weeks away from Halloween and the circus has come to a town that's so Norman Rockwell in presentation that its residents include an Officer Friendly and a Mrs. Applebees. So it's a bit surprising to learn that a mental institution is located nearby and that three inmates would escape as a result of their circus privileges being revoked.

There is a reason why so many haunted houses throw in some clowns and circus themes. Whether it's because of Pennywise or John Wayne Gacy, or their exaggerated expressions that trigger our distrust, or simply the fact that you never know who they really are, coulrophobia is now among the most common fears. If you think their giant shoes are unsettling, imagine if they suddenly appeared next to the table you are currently hiding under. In another chilling scene that perfectly demonstrates the effects clowns have on children, Casey and his brothers are attending a circus show in which acrobats are performing. Casey spots a clown standing at the side of the stage, and the clown stares at him intently before engaging him in a first-rate pantomime act that clearly mocks Casey's nervousness. Then Casey turns around to see the joyous little girl who actually was the proud recipient of the clown's attention; the clown went from threatening to wholesome in a matter of seconds.

It will forever be the fan favorite of the clown subgenre, but *Clownhouse* is much more fun and

sometimes just as scary, as long as you're able to push aside the fact that director Victor Salva later pled guilty to sexually molesting child star Nathan Forrest Winters during production and served 15 months in prison. Although it can be hard to ignore the controversy when the three boys are sometimes not fully clothed, the film gets just about everything else right, and would surely provide 81 exhilarating minutes on Halloween.

Among the many hair-raising moments are a chase scene along the wooded path that leads the boys to the convenience store and the drawing of straws to see which unfortunate sap has to change the fuse in the scary cobwebbed attic with only a lighter to illuminate the way. And the freakiest moment is a blink-and-you-miss-it shot where a fuse creates a strobe effect as one of the clowns sneaks across the room. Have your DVD remote handy because this is a very startling shot you'll want to admire repeatedly!

THE COMPANY OF WOLVES (1984)

🎬 **Director:** Neil Jordan
⭐ **Cast:** Sarah Patterson, Angela Lansbury, David Warner, Micha Bergese, Georgia Stowe
🎞 **Length:** 95 minutes
👤 **Rating:** R

🎞 **Synopsis:** A wise and superstitious grandmother tells young Rosaleen stories of men transforming into wolves and attacking anyone who drifts off the path in the forest. A couple of days later, on her way to Grandmother's house, Rosaleen meets a handsome stranger who decides to go there as well.

Poster for *The Company of Wolves* (1984). Cannon Film Distributors.

This beautifully photographed episodic retelling of "Little Red Riding Hood" intermingles several of the worst nightmares a young child can have, constantly retaining fairy tale authenticity. It juggles psychosexual undertones with Freudian symbolism, and places most of the grotesque imagery in a dark forest where glowing-eyed wolves are hunting. There is even a moment where a little girl running through the forest that encircles her peasant village is confronted by her sinister toys, which have come to life. Much like *An American Werewolf in London* and *The Howling* (both released in 1981), *The*

Company of Wolves is full of impressive special effects, including a couple of great transformation scenes and a moment where the always-captivating Stephen Rea (a Neil Jordan regular) peels off his own skin. There is even a decapitation scene that will catch you completely off guard. Even in the early stages of his career, Jordan was a tremendous talent—here, he knows exactly how to keep us in his hypnotic spell, even when using a complicated dream-within-a-dream narrative.

Sarah Patterson is excellent as the red-hooded girl caught in the throes of puberty's hormonal domination—it must have been daunting to have your first film credit be a starring role in a picture that required wolves to be on set with snipers in case they suddenly snapped (although most of the "wolves" in the movie are actually Belgian Shepherd Dogs with dyed fur). Angela Lansbury is also fantastic as the stern grandmother, and when she tells her "once upon a time" lycanthrope tales, we feel the kind of fanciful excitement we did when hearing our first ghost story. And if the name David Warner doesn't ring a bell for you, then do some research right now and you'll be shocked at just how many valuable contributions he has made to the horror genre (and just about every other genre as well) over the years.

Not only has Jordan directed one of the best werewolf films of all time, but he also graced the vampire subgenre ten years later with *Interview with the Vampire*.

THE CONJURING (2013)

- **Director:** James Wan
- **Cast:** Patrick Wilson, Lili Taylor, Vera Farmiga, Ron Livingston
- **Length:** 112 minutes
- **Rating:** R

Synopsis: Before they embark on their terrifying journey to the Amityville home, paranormal investigators Ed and Lorraine Warren visit an equally spooky Rhode Island farmhouse whose evil presences have latched onto the vulnerable Perron family.

It was extremely rare for two new films spearheaded by the same director and starring the same actor to hit theaters only two months apart, and the fact that their trailers were so similar in tone made things even more interesting. But James Wan managed to hit both *The Conjuring* and *Insidious: Chapter 2* out of the park, each one making over $40 million on opening weekend alone, and ensuring that even if 2013 didn't deliver a lot of theatrical horror releases, at least what we got was mostly high in quality.

While *The Conjuring* doesn't necessarily break any new ground in haunted houses, it borrows wisely from the classics like *The Haunting, The Shining, Poltergeist*, and *The Exorcist*, and at the moment, it holds an 86% on the Rotten Tomato meter, which is almost unprecedented these days for a genre film. Right off the bat it scares the holy hell out of you by presenting quite possibly the creepiest-looking doll ever, which unnerves a pair of young women so much since it's the lead suspect responsible for the "Miss me?" notes that have been suddenly appearing in their home. After the possessed Annabelle earns her rightful place in the dumpster, the two women are awoken to angry knocks at the front door—this is where we become as freaked out as Annabelle's unfortunate owners, and this level of unease doesn't dissipate for the entire running time.

Unlike *Insidious*, there are a few cheap scares in *The Conjuring,* but not for a second do we roll our eyes at the mirror tricks or the birds suddenly and loudly breaking their necks against the windows because Wan has earned the right to scare us any way he pleases by presenting such identifiable characters in awesomely creepy situations, and we're happy to just be along for the ride. After their experiences resulted in one wretched *Amityville Horror* sequel after another, it's nice to see Ed and Lorraine Warren treated as multi-dimensional characters here in such

a sophisticated horror film, and you can't possibly ask for more talented and likable actors to play you than Patrick Wilson and Vera Farmiga (who has been unforgettable as Norma in the absolutely perfect *Bates Motel* on A&E). Paired with a loving couple played by Lili Taylor and Ron Livingston, you have four immensely appealing leads—one of them even gets to flirt with Beelzebub and turn evil in the third act!

We spend most of the time in a Rhode Island farmhouse built in 1863, a dwelling void of coziness and color, but available at a reasonable price since it has hosted numerous acts of terror, starting with a woman (who is a descendant of a Salem witch trial victim) sacrificing her 7-day-old baby in a fireplace, declaring her love for Satan, and then vowing to curse anybody who dares to take her land, right before hanging herself. This farmhouse has all of the haunted house essentials like creaking doors, holes in the walls that lead to secret rooms, lights that swing like pendulums, and a rocking chair that moves on its own. This would be one terrific place for a Halloween party, as would the Warren's house, thanks to a sacred room in their basement that holds all of the cursed items they have acquired from their investigations of demonology and witchcraft. It's easy to understand why their daughter gets curious to go exploring down there, even with the ominous "Danger: Do Not Touch!" signs.

Just listen to the entire soundtrack and it's obvious that this movie has only one goal: to scare the shit out of you, and it succeeds multiple times. Fortunately, Wan had the wisdom and restraint to eliminate a few scary scenes from the script, or else the pacing would have been compromised, we would have been exhausted after an hour, and the most frightening moments (the hide and clap game, the first sight of a demon, something hiding in the darkest corner of Nancy and Christine's bedroom and staring right at them, Judy awakening to a late night thunderstorm and a mysterious figure brushing the hair of a very-alive Annabelle doll) might not have packed such a powerful punch. Pummeling our nerves further is the excellent use of music boxes, empty spaces, matches, ghostly cackles, levitating chairs, and weird little touches, like a sleepwalking girl hitting her head against a wall repeatedly. The only things that would have made this movie better would be to have had one or two less children in the birth control–less Perron family (some of the daughters seem like unnecessary props instead of full characters) and Megadeth's "The Conjuring" play during the end credits.

Even if *The Conjuring* and *Insidious: Chapter 2* (page 83) do in fact happen to be James Wan's horror swan songs, then at least they helped him cement his place in the horror hall of fame, and allowed him to bow out at the top of his game. But considering Wan is still a very young man and has shown the utmost reverence to our beloved genre, it would be shocking if he doesn't dip his toes into the red waters at least one more time. His next project, *Fast and Furious 7*, will probably be the box office champion in 2015, and while that overrated franchise doesn't deserve somebody as good as Wan, it's still inspiring to see someone deserving so sought after in Hollywood. Hopefully this level of success will allow him to make just the kinds of movies he wants, and that can only be a good thing.

CORPSE BRIDE (2005)

Directors: Tim Burton, Mike Johnson
Cast: Johnny Depp, Helena Bonham Carter, Emily Watson, Richard E. Grant, Tracey Ullman
Length: 77 minutes
Rating: PG

Synopsis: A young man practices his wedding vows in a forest and unwittingly becomes a fiancée to yet another girl, who is beautiful but also quite deceased.

Before it was the day for trick-or-treating, bobbing for apples, and costume parties, Halloween was the day for paying respect to the dead. Much like Tim Burton did with *Beetlejuice*, here he once again lifts the veil that separates the living and the dead, but this time the tone is a little more somber. This stop motion animated film might conjure up painful memories of a deceased pet or having your heart broken for the first time, but it effectively taps into that peculiar urge to visit a graveyard on a crisp October afternoon to reflect upon loss and mortality. We haven't the slightest clue of what, if anything, awaits us when our time has come, but one would hope it could be as much fun as how the afterlife is depicted here: a perpetual party where skeletons drink, play pool, and break out into musical numbers in a vibrant jazz club. It is a direct contrast to the world of the living: cold, dreary, where not a single person can crack a smile without looking like they're having a stroke.

It takes about 17 minutes for the film to become noticeably Halloweeny, but it is well worth the wait because before you know it, you're transported to the kind of foreboding forest that Burton is known for, filled with crows, frost, and impossibly twisted skeletal trees. As Victor, a nervous and clumsy sullen young man voiced by Johnny Depp, practices the wedding vows he hopelessly fumbled with during rehearsals, he mistakes a branch for a deceased woman's fingers and is then plunged into the underworld. The exposition for these bizarre circumstances is explained with a magnificent musical number called "Remains of the Day," one of Danny Elfman's finest moments, and also one of the coolest scenes you could possibly hope to witness on Halloween. It was clearly inspired by the Walt Disney-produced animated short from 1929, *The Skeleton Dance*, a delightful musical number featuring four dancing skeletons in a cemetery.

Victor's dilemma becomes even more complicated when he develops strong feelings for the corpse bride, a tortured but ultimately sweet soul who cares enough for her new lover that she reunites him with his childhood dog, Scraps. The way she reacts whenever a talkative maggot shoves her eyeball onto the ground will win you over immediately. At the same time, he yearns to be reunited with his still-living fiancée, Victoria. Because both of these women are as likable as can be, the film becomes sad once again when we realize that one of them will have her heart broken—after all, this is an animated, PG-rated movie, so a necrophilic ménage á trois is highly unlikely. But there are several things to cheer us up, like a cute duet between the aforementioned maggot and a spider, a horny severed hand, and yet another awesome, commanding performance from Christopher Lee. Considering how much undying affection I have for the cult classic *Withnail and I*, it was weird to learn that one of the most despicable bastards I've ever seen in an animated film was voiced by Richard E. Grant!

CREATURE FROM THE BLACK LAGOON (1954)

Director: Jack Arnold
Cast: Richard Carlson, Julie Adams, Richard Denning, Antonio Moreno, Nestor Paiva, Whit Bissell
Length: 79 minutes
Rating: Not Rated

Synopsis: An expedition through the Amazon leads a group of scientists to the horrific "Gill Man," a half-man/half-fish that reacts violently when its territory is invaded. The monster is momentarily captured, but escapes and kidnaps the woman in the crew, with whom he has become infatuated.

It is a shame how so many horror fans have seen every single sequel to *Saw* but not every Universal monster classic. This is easily one of Universal's finest, providing an exhilarating pace, an effectively creepy and unique monster (wearing a convincing rubber suit), a strident score that plays at every single tense moment, and some remarkable underwater scenes.

Lobby card for *The Creature From the Black Lagoon* (1954). Universal International Pictures.

What makes the creature so fascinating is how we never really learn much about it, like we do with Frankenstein, the Invisible Man, Dracula, and the Wolf Man. We never find out how it really spawned from one of Mother Earth's darkest days, how it has stayed alive over the years, and whether it relies on emotions or pure instincts. And unlike the other monsters, this one is just as dangerous in water as it is on land.

In the film's most breathtaking moment, the creature swims directly below Julie Adams, looking up at her longingly and mirroring her strokes. These shots alone allow the viewers to sympathize with it like we have with the other classic monsters. It is also a treat to see the creature in full form for the first time, because director Jack Arnold had teased us and aroused our curiosity with early glimpses of only his arm.

CREEPSHOW (1982)

🎬 **Director:** George A. Romero
⭐ **Cast:** Hal Holbrook, Leslie Nielsen, Ted Danson, Adrienne Barbeau, E.G. Marshall, Stephen King
🎞 **Length:** 120 minutes
👤 **Rating:** R

🎞 **Synopsis:** Paying tribute to the E.C. comics of the 1950s, Stephen King and George A. Romero present us with five different tales: 1) A corpse rises from the grave on Father's Day to get revenge on the woman that put him there, and to finally get the cake that was promised to him; 2) After a hillbilly touches a meteor that crashes near his property, he slowly transforms into a plant; 3) After learning about an affair, a sadistic husband buries his wife and her lover up to their necks in sand, just before the tide comes in; 4) A college professor finds a century-old crate with a really hungry monster inside; 5) A cruel billionaire's tidy apartment is invaded by an army of cockroaches.

With five stories written by Stephen King, directed by George A. Romero, and attributed to the controversial, shocking E.C. comics, it's no surprise that *Creepshow* is considered by most horror fans to be the best horror anthology of all time. King's stories center around universal fears, but we never feel too much discomfort because the film doesn't take itself too seriously. The assortment of monstrosities and oddities are all contained in a fun, colorful piece of work, with lively, stylish direction from Romero, who uses a lot of saturated colors and static shots to make the film look exactly like a comic book at key moments. The stories are all told as a boy's precious comic book gets drenched in a rainstorm after an enraged father tosses it outside, its pages being turned by the wind. The boy and his angry father (played by horror veteran

Tom Atkins) are shown in scenes that bookend the film.

Even though this film is mostly all fun and games, it really knows how to shock and revolt. Your friends will undoubtedly cover their eyes a little, groan in disgust, or laugh hysterically (depending on their level of gore experience) when the fuzzy beast in the crate gobbles up a nerdy college student, or when thousands of cockroaches work together to burst through the neck, stomach, nostrils, and mouth of Upson Pratt, *the* Upson Pratt! This is the kind of movie you really want to experience watching with your friends. Perhaps the best tale of them all is "Something to Tide You Over," where Leslie Nielsen sure isn't the clumsy oaf Frank Drebin of Police Squad that we all know and love. Here, he's a vengeful bastard who cackles uncontrollably and sips champagne as he watches his wife and her lover attempting to hold their breath under impossibly stressful circumstances. My other personal favorite is "The Crate," in which Hal Holbrook's sunny fantasies about being adulated for killing his insufferable wife provide the biggest laughs, shortly before a ferocious throat-ripping monster unleashes the biggest scares. *Creepshow* must also be commended for its ambitious soundtrack that stirs many emotions, its wide variety of locations, and for showing us a follicly-blessed Ed Harris dancing, as well as an overall-clad Stephen King undergoing a plant transformation as he watches Bob Backlund wrestle on TV. King and Romero teamed up again in 1987 for *Creepshow 2*, an underrated sequel that featured by far the scariest segment of either film, "The Raft," based on a King short story from *Skeleton Crew*.

CURSE OF THE DEMON (1957)

Director: Jacques Tourneur
Cast: Dana Andrews, Peggy Cummins, Niall MacGinnis, Maurice Denham, Athene Seyler, Liam Redmond
Length: 95 minutes
Rating: Not Rated

Synopsis: A psychologist is forced to confront his disbelief of the supernatural when a sorcerer tells him that he will be the next victim of a monstrous demon.

You see the demon in the first five minutes of this British thriller, even in a full close-up, as it slowly presses its enormous paw down on its first victim. It is quite a sight, for this is one of the most original and impressive-looking monsters in horror history. You might think that since it arrives so unusually early, the filmmakers didn't have anything else going for them with this project, so you'll be surprised that what follows is a gripping psychological thriller with intelligent dialogue, flawless performances all around, strong direction from Jacques Tourneur, and the kind of climax that will make you giddy. In fact, in the original print, the creature was not shown at all, but producer Hal E. Chester felt the film needed its titular monster front and center, so against the strong wishes of both Tourneur and writer Charles Bennett, new footage was shot and inserted throughout the final print.

This is the kind of film that mostly depends on its soundtrack to induce the chills—at key moments, you will hear loud crashes of thunder, screeching trains, or an exploding orchestra. These are cheap scares but also effective ones, and since the film has so much going for it, you don't feel at all insulted.

The ghosts of Halloween are evident in many scenes, including an annual Halloween magic show that ends in a violent windstorm, a séance on a rainy night, and a man dressed as a clown getting

Poster for *Curse of the Demon* (1957). Columbia Pictures.

attacked by a swarm of leaves that fly like bats. Niall MacGinnis steals the scenes as the goateed black magician who so eloquently says in one scene, "If only we grownups could preserve their (children's) capacity for simple joys and simple beliefs."

Fans of Kate Bush will hopefully recognize a line that is sampled in the title track to her 1985 album, *Hounds of Love*!

DAFFY DUCK'S QUACKBUSTERS (1988)

Directors: Greg Ford, Chuck Jones, Terry Lennon, Maurice Noble, Friz Freleng
Cast: Mel Blanc, Mel Torme
Length: 72 minutes
Rating: G

Synopsis: Daffy Duck inherits a fortune and opens his own ghostbusting company with help from Bugs Bunny, Porky Pig, and Sylvester the Cat.

For those who grew up watching *Looney Tunes*, reserve a night in October for nostalgia as you reacquaint yourself with Daffy Duck, Bugs Bunny, Porky Pig, Sylvester, and Tweety. This was one of Mel Blanc's final performances as the voices for these iconic characters, and even at 80 years of age, he was able to put his whole heart into it and make them sound as youthful and vibrant as ever. Each Porky Pig stutter, Sylvester lisp, and Daffy mispronunciation is played to perfection, which is especially important here since half of the movie consists of classic shorts, with the other half linking them together and expanding them.

In true old-school cartoon fashion, a short preludes the movie; here it is "The Night of the Living Duck," which features Daffy Duck as a horror comic aficionado devouring creepy tales in *Famous Monsters*, *UFO Magazine*, and *Horror D'Oeuvres*. Suddenly, he leaves the safety of his ghoulish bedroom and has to perform stand-up comedy to an audience that consists of Dracula, The Fly, The Invisible Man, The Mummy, Leatherface, Godzilla, and Frankenstein's Monster along with his bride. So right off the bat it's clear that even though this is *Looney Tunes*, it's still quite appropriate for the Halloween season.

The actual movie begins with Daffy as a struggling salesman, his misanthropy at an all time high until he revels at the opportunity to inherit a fortune. All he has to do is make a bedridden bloodhound named J.P. Cubish laugh once, and with the help of hundreds of pies to the face, the old dog laughs continuously for days until he dies. Although Daffy finally is in the lap of luxury, his problems continue, as Cubish returns as a ghost to warn Daffy that unless he displays honesty in his business affairs and uses his wealth for good in this world, his money will suddenly disappear. This results in the opening of Daffy Duck's Paranormalists, an obvious spoof of Ghostbusters, but instead of qualified experts like Egon, Daffy gets stuck with a bunny whose only concern is a vacation in Palm Springs, an

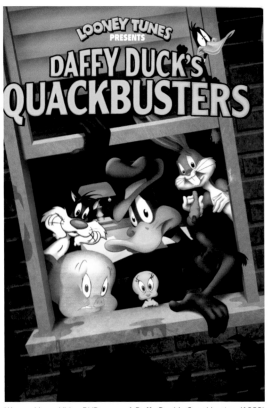

Warner Home Video DVD cover of *Daffy Duck's Quackbusters* (1988).

incompetent pig, and a scaredy-cat. Their various assignments include meeting Count Bloodcount at a castle in Pittsburgh, Transylvania, investigating a haunted motel in Dry Gulch, performing an exorcism on a damsel in distress who appears to be possessed by Zuul, and traveling to the Himalayas to look for the Abominable Snowman, who has the same mannerisms and bunny-obsessions as Lenny from *Of Mice and Men*. However, the funniest segment of the movie belongs to Sylvester and Tweety in a spoof of *Dr. Jeckyl and Mr. Hyde*.

Once the constant curmudgeon Daffy gets publicly humiliated on Zed Toppel's Frightline, his world crumbles all around him in the form of bankruptcy, eviction, and media scrutiny, as well as the continued haunting from Cubish. It's a finale that is a tad too harsh on this beloved character. It just shows you that getting top billing doesn't mean you're guaranteed a happy ending, even in a *Looney Tunes* movie.

DAGON (2001)

Director: Stuart Gordon
Cast: Ezra Godden, Francisco Rabal, Raquel Meroño, Macarena Gómez, Brendan Price
Length: 98 minutes
Rating: R

Synopsis: A boating accident forces a couple to enter a mysterious fishing village for help, but their day keeps getting worse as they are soon running for their lives and about to become a sacrifice for a monstrous god of the sea.

We usually don't get our wishes for a white Christmas or a stormy Halloween, but fortunately our imaginations partnered with the power of cinema can transport us there. And perhaps no movie has as much lightning and torrential downpour as Stuart Gordon's blending of two of H.P. Lovecraft's most respected tales, "The Shadows Over Insmouth" and "Dagon." With *Re-Animator* and *From Beyond* already under his belt, Stuart Gordon had proven that he understands the language of Lovecraft, and here he strikes gold once again.

Once our two very likable protagonists abandon their shipwrecked boat and enter what can only be described as the most inhospitable fishing village on the entire planet, we're right there with them, smelling the unpleasant mixture of saltwater and fish, shivering not only from the rain but also the shifty eyes we get from the mysterious locals. Gordon masterfully keeps the tension escalating slowly and never gives us a chance to catch our breath, so we eventually start feeling like we're also thousands of miles away from home and on the verge of becoming sacrificial meat for a medieval fish god. The chase scenes are almost unbearably suspenseful—revealing one unforgettably creepy location after another—and much of that has to do with the gifted performance of Ezra Godden. His character is very easy to root for; in the beginning of the movie Paul is the bespeckled nerd (surely he wishes he wore contacts for such a rainy nightmare) with the Miskatonic University sweatshirt, bearing an uncanny resemblance to Jeffrey Combs, but after he's put through hell on earth and repeatedly manages to escape from impossibly dangerous situations, he's a Bruce Campbell-esque badass that we want so badly to see make it out of this decrepit fishing village in one piece.

H.P. Lovecraft stories are notoriously difficult to translate into film, and on the rare occasion when it's done right, the filmmakers deserve all the credit in the world. *Dagon* should have been huge, but instead it was denied a theatrical release and premiered on DVD, where the only praise seemed to come from those who read *Fangoria* and *Rue Morgue* on a monthly basis. At least it was recently honored at the annual H.P. Lovecraft Film Festival in Portland, Oregon, where it was well received by a large audience that included Stuart Gordon himself.

Dagon, which excels in presenting a truly horrifying world we haven't seen before, is simply one of the greatest horror movies of the new millennium and those craving a thunderstorm-filled Halloween in Cthulululand would be wise to seek it out. Be warned though: it does contain one agonizing, shocking sequence that will have even the most diehard gorehounds squirming in their seats.

DARK NIGHT OF THE SCARECROW (1981)

⬛ **Director:** Frank De Felitta
⭐ **Cast:** Charles Durning, Robert Lyons, Lane Smith, Larry Drake, Tonya Crowe, Claude Earl Jones
⊗ **Length:** 96 minutes
👤 **Rating:** Not Rated

🗑 **Synopsis:** A group of redneck vigilantes search for a mentally challenged man who they believe murdered a little girl. They find him hiding inside of a scarecrow and fire 17 rounds into him, moments before they learn that he was innocent, and that he had actually saved the girl's life from a dog attack. The men escape judicial punishment but the grieving mother warns them that there are other forms of justice in this world.

TV Guide ad for *Dark Night of the Scarecrow* (1981).

Airing a week before Halloween of 1981, this popular made-for-TV movie was the first to feature a psycho-scarecrow, paving the road for titles like *Night of the Scarecrow*, *Hollowed Ground*, *Messengers 2: The Scarecrow*, *Scarecrow Gone Wild*, and several others. This is by far the classiest of the bunch, relying on atmosphere and paranoia instead of gore and cheap scares.

Early on, I had some reservations about including it because, who wants to spend Halloween watching something as sad as the lovable Bubba Ritter (played by Larry Drake, who you may also know as *Dr. Giggles* and the most terrifying Santa Claus of all time) get unfairly accused of murder right before being murdered himself? But the sting wears off shortly after the courtroom scene and it's a bloody good time watching the good-old boys confront the terrors that await them. It becomes an eerie and exciting whodunit when the men can't figure out who is responsible for placing scarecrows on their property and burying one of their own alive with grain in a silo. The leader of this self-appointed mob—who repeatedly has to persuade his shell-shocked cohorts not to confess to the police—is a mailman

and boarding home resident marvelously played by Charles Durning, whose character is crowded with personal demons that arise with the presence of alcohol and young girls.

Although it is fairly brief, there is a wonderfully spirited scene inside of an elementary school where a Halloween party is underway. A witch is serving punch, pumpkin and skeleton decorations are everywhere, and the kids take a break from bobbing for apples to roam the hallways and play hide-and-seek. Who would blame them for wanting to escape from the grown-ups dancing to country music? Other festivities include a cornfield hosting a cicada sing-along and a tractor running over numerous pumpkins.

DAWN OF THE DEAD (1978)

Director: George A. Romero
Cast: Ken Foree, David Emge, Gaylen Ross, Scott H. Reiniger, David Crawford
Length: 127 minutes
Rating: X

> **Synopsis:** After a plague brings dead people back to life with a hunger for human flesh, a group of people escape Philadelphia in a helicopter and seek refuge in a shopping mall.

Made ten years after Romero's *Night of the Living Dead*, this sequel brings more humor to the table, but retains the original's social commentary and revolting images. George Romero's camera lingers upon some of the vilest, in-your-face effects from Tom Savini's legendary repertoire, playfully testing us on how much we can stomach. It is such a well-liked movie that I don't expect anyone to complain that I broke my two-hour time limit rule.

Like the original, the villains here aren't just the zombies, but also the sickest sides of human nature because once again, the hope of working together to save themselves is undermined by greed, power, and selfishness. Romero proposes some interesting questions about what happiness is to modern Americans. All traces of their former lives lie in bleakness, but our protagonists can see their dreams and fantasies within the walls of a shopping center, and even though it's flooded with zombies, they cannot resist the temptations of capitalism. The zombies stick around because they recall the mall playing an integral part in their past lives. They clumsily play with hockey equipment on a skating rink and stumble on escalators just because all they can really do is act on instinct.

A shopping mall is really the perfect location for a horror film; its overbearingly bright lighting, elevator music playing at the most inappropriate times, countless effective hiding places, and rows of stores that seem to go on forever give the building a baleful personality of its own.

This was followed by *Day of the Dead*, which succeeds in making the zombies even more sympathetic. But that film is marred by too many unpleasant, obnoxious characters that scream all their lines at the top of their lungs, and compared to the graveyard and farmhouse in the original and the shopping mall in *Dawn,* its locations are drab and dull.

DAWN OF THE DEAD (2004)

Director: Zack Snyder
Cast: Sarah Polley, Ving Rhames, Jake Weber, Mekhi Phifer, Ty Burrell, Michael Kelly, Kevin Zegers
Length: 100 minutes
Rating: R

> **Synopsis:** A nurse awakens to see her idyllic neighborhood in ruins and her friends and neighbors ravenously feasting on each other. She escapes and finds shelter in a shopping mall with other survivors, including power-hungry security guards. They soon learn that no matter how many precautions they take, the zombies always manage to find a way inside.

Let's face it: when it was first announced that George A. Romero's chopping mall classic was part of the long list of horror remakes, we all expected the worst. We felt a little better when it was given an R rating and when no WB stars or teen icons appeared in the cast. We felt even more relieved when the terrifying trailer became available. Horror fans turned up in mobs for the opening weekend and made the reinterpretation of *Dawn of the Dead* the number 1 movie at the box office, finally putting an end to the winning streak of another bloodbath, *The Passion of the Christ*. It went over extremely well with the public and managed to be just the kind of film that the horror community desperately needed. Even more surprising was its clear favorability with film critics, something that big-budgeted Hollywood horror films seldom receive.

While nowhere near as gory and satirical as the original, this still offers impressive doses of blood and humor. The zombies here have learned some tricks from 28 Days Later's "infected," and now have the ability to run, making things even more hopeless for those trapped inside the mall. This completely changes the dynamics in the war between the humans and the dead. In the original, the survivors were able to destroy individual zombies as easily as stepping on ants, but to defeat just one of these new, highly caffeinated and steroid-abused zombies is an enormous task.

The cast members, led by art-house icon Sarah Polley, are all in fine form. She and Jake Weber are especially intriguing, and they have romantic chemistry that is far quieter and more subdued than found in most disaster movies. Perhaps we could have learned more about them if there weren't so many damn people showing up at the mall! Obviously, the biggest flaw in this film is the amount of mallrats: at least four of them serve no purpose to the plot whatsoever.

The character of Andy (played by Bruce Bohne) evokes genuine compassion from the viewers, giving us opportunities to recuperate from the intense zombie attacks. He is gun store owner who is trapped, alone, and hungry. To pass the time, he plays chess with Ving Rhames: they sit on their respective roofs and communicate by using binoculars and posterboards. They play another game together that involves spotting zombies below that resemble celebrities and using them for shooting practice. These characters are obviously very crafty, so you would expect them to find a much better way to transport food over to Andy than simply speculating that zombies won't fancy the brain of their beloved pet canine.

First-time director Zack Snyder deserves much credit for crafting one of the all-time scariest movie openings and for reminding us that remakes don't always have to tarnish the legacy of the original. Unfortunately, for every *Dawn of the Dead*, there are about 20 worthless remakes on the level of *A Nightmare on Elm Street* and *13 Ghosts* (oh, I'm sorry, *Thir13en Ghosts*, ugh).

DEAD ALIVE/BRAINDEAD (1992)

Director: Peter Jackson
Cast: Timothy Balme, Diana Peñalver, Elizabeth Moody, Ian Watkin, Brenda Kendall, Stuart Devenie
Length: 97 minutes
Rating: Not Rated

Synopsis: A Sumatran rat monkey is transported from Skull Island to a New Zealand zoo, much to the misfortune of an overbearing old woman spying on her son. She stands too close to its cage, gets bitten, dies, and rises from the grave as a hideous, bloodthirsty zombie. Her son still tries to protect her, even though she is feasting on the locals and sabotaging his one chance at love and happiness.

Those with a fondness for glorious gore-o-ramas need to check out what Peter Jackson was doing years before his triumphs in Middle Earth. Five years after his unflinching debut, *Bad Taste*, he returned to the land of exaggerated gore and silly dialogue with *Dead Alive,* also known as *Braindead* in some countries, which still holds the record for using more fake blood than any other movie. Here is a film that has layers

upon layers of blood, guts, intestines, and eviscerated bodies that are so chopped up they are merely slush. The characters have a tough time escaping from the zombies because they keep slipping on the mass of goo that permeates the floor. You will see a zombified woman tear off a large chunk of skin as she is applying her make-up, syringes thrusting through eyeballs and nostrils, zombies having sex, a priest getting impaled on a gravestone, a man biting through human intestines, a zombie baby using a severed human leg as a weapon, horny zombies chewing on each other's lips, torsos being ripped in half, zombies munching on their own ears, severed heads being sliced and diced in blenders, a man using a lawnmower to make zombie stew, and the nastiest scene you'll ever see involving custard. This is not a film for the squeamish, but for everybody else, it's a hilariously sick adventure that, despite its uncompromising level of gore, somehow escapes offensiveness.

One of the best scenes presents a priest who "kicks ass for the lord"; as he is demonstrating his impressive karate skills to dismember a pack of hungry zombies, he makes the mistake of allowing a head that he recently kicked off its body to sail upward and land on his shoulder. In another hysterical scene, a nerdy mama's boy takes a zombie baby to the park in a stroller.

Beware of the 85-minute R-rated version, in which heavy editing leaves most of the action scenes dry and incoherent.

DEAD OF NIGHT (1945)

Directors: Alberto Cavalcanti, Charles Chrichton, Basil Dearden, Robert Hamer
Cast: Michael Redgrave, Mervyn Johns, Googie Withers, Sally Ann Howes, Basil Radford, Ralph Michael
Length: 102 minutes
Rating: Not Rated

Synopsis: An architect arrives at a remote farmhouse and swears that all of its inhabitants, who he has never met, have been in his reoccurring nightmares. Perplexed and intrigued, everybody shares their own personal encounter with the supernatural. Once small details from his nightmares come into play, the architect knows he must leave the house or something horrible will happen.

If *The Twilight Zone*, *Night Gallery*, or *The Outer Limits* is your cup of tea, then this influential British anthology of creepy tales would make a suitable Halloween companion. Like the aforementioned projects, *Dead of Night* relies on a palpable sense of dread, where the characters experience unexplainable things that cause them to question their own sanity.

This quintet of tales, which would all be ideal for a campfire setting, consists of: 1) An injured racecar driver sees something troubling when he looks out of his hospital building: a hearse, whose driver beckons

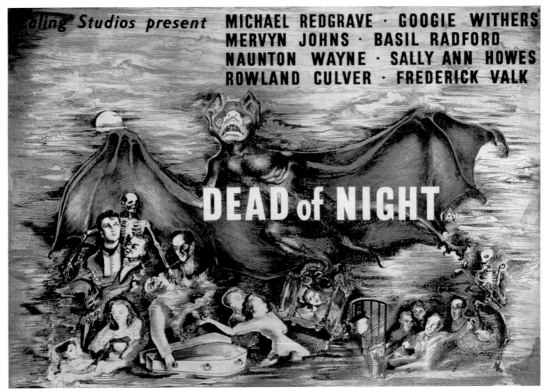

Poster for *Dead of Night* (1945). Ealing Studios.

him inside. Despite its extremely brief length, it delivers one of the film's most suspenseful moments. 2) While children play a game of Hide and Seek at a Christmas party, a teenaged girl encounters a little boy who was supposedly murdered 40 years ago. This is easily the weakest of the five, but it is also short and it does keep the viewers involved. 3) A recently-purchased antique mirror may contain the spirit of a vengeful murderer as it reflects its own twisted history when a man stares into it. This skillfully directed segment constantly makes us question the husband's mental health as he stares at a background that should not be there. Who ever thought a simple image like a Victorian room with a fire burning could be so unsettling? 4) Two feuding golfers strike a bet over a woman that leads to a suicide and subsequently, to a haunting that goes hilariously wrong. Directly contrasting the tales that sandwich it, this episode of silliness offers persistently quirky and wry British humor, as well as visuals like a golfer struggling against a possessed golf ball. Many will agree that it's out of place, but its light-heartedness should win you

over. 5) A boozing ventriloquist and his tormenting dummy can't seem to stop the act even when the show is over. It is the most popular of the five tales, and also the most influential, obviously inspiring *Magic* and plenty of others.

For the film's initial US release, tales 2 and 4 were cut due to concerns over the running time (even back in 1945, producers believed American audiences were too dumb to appreciate European classics). This was an obvious blunder, causing viewers to wonder what the hell two central characters were even doing in the movie.

What elevates *Dead of Night* above the standard horror anthology is how it successfully utilizes such an intriguing set of circumstances to keep the viewers guessing; we are just as baffled as the characters. This strategy could have easily backfired if it had a weak ending, but it most certainly does not! It's an intelligent, ambitiously surreal freakfest of a conclusion that manages to exceed dangerously high expectations.

DEMONS (1985)

🎬 **Director:** Lamberto Bava
⭐ **Cast:** Urbano Barberini, Natasha Hovey, Paola Cozzo, Karl Zinny, Fiore Argento
🎞 **Length:** 88 minutes
👤 **Rating:** Not Rated

🎞 **Synopsis:** A group of people, seemingly chosen at random, receive free passes to see a horror film at a newly renovated theater in Berlin. But the grisliness on the big screen is nothing compared to what's transpiring in the theater, where one by one the audience members transform into bloodthirsty demons.

While it's certainly no *Purple Rose of Cairo* or *Matinee* in the art-imitating-art field, *Demons*—which takes place in the mysterious Metropol movie theater—does an admirable job in using the magic of the cinema to influence and mirror the real world. The odd assortment of theater attendees is watching a violent horror film about teenagers exploring an old chapel and finding the tomb of Nostradamus. They open the grave to find a mask that turns whoever wears it into an instrument of evil. A similar mask is displayed in the theater lobby, and a prostitute can't help but to try it on, which results in a small cut to her face. While she inspects it in the bathroom, the throbbing,

bubbling gash grows and then explodes in a burst of custard-like ooze. Then the real fun begins.

If your idea of Halloween excitement resembles riding a motorcycle inside a theater while slicing away at demons with a Katana sword to the sounds of Accept's "Fast as a Shark," or snorting coke through a straw in a coke can, or not asking any questions when a helicopter crashes through the ceiling for no reason whatsoever, then *Demons* will charm the pus out of you. Even though it's far from perfect, a movie featuring clumsy dialogue, hide-and-seek with demons, and a soundtrack of European metal, Mötley Crüe, and Billy Idol is such an easy thing to embrace.

From the deepest red and blue palates to the outlandishly detailed gore and hilariously overdubbed dialogue, *Demons* is as stereotypically Italian as it gets, and that makes sense because this movie is basically a collaboration of some of Italy's most respected horror filmmakers. The director is Mario Bava's son, who learned the tricks of the trade while working as a personal assistant to his father for several films. Dario Argento co-wrote the screenplay as well as produced, and Michele Soavi not only served as assistant director, but also played two different characters.

Another horror movie set in a movie theater that is totally deserving of your time is *Popcorn* (1991), in which a rowdy crowd dressed in costumes is attending a scary movie marathon, having a wonderful time with the '60s schlock being shown as well as all the gimmicks made popular by William Castle. Since there's a good chance you'll never get to attend a horror festival with a giant mechanical mosquito hovering over the crowd, aroma-rama nose guards, electrical buzzer seats, and a nurse making you sign a document so they can't be sued if you have a heart attack, you can at least watch people enjoying it. There is even some really fun Reggae music, which I found mystifying until I learned that the film was shot in Jamaica.

DOLLS (1987)

🎬 **Director:** Stuart Gordon
⭐ **Cast:** Stephen Lee, Carrie Lorraine, Ian Patrick Williams, Guy Rolfe, Hilary Mason, Carolyn Gordon
🎞 **Length:** 77 minutes
👤 **Rating:** R

🎞 **Synopsis:** Six travelers arrive at an English mansion when a thunderstorm immobilizes their vehicles. They are given food and shelter by an elderly couple, who share their home with hundreds of dolls. Only those who are still kids at heart have a chance of surviving the night.

Even though this is a killer doll film with an executive producer credit going to Charles Band, this is not a Full Moon production, so don't think for a second that it is on the level of garbage like *Dollman vs. Demonic Toys* or the hundreds of *Puppet Master* sequels. Released even before *Child's Play* made killer doll films trendy, *Dolls* is a much more elegant and absorbing film than you would expect, but certainly not without a nasty mean streak, flaunted when the pint-size monsters take mini-saws to the ankles of the female victims.

After the two outrageously gory H.P. Lovecraft adaptations, *Re-Animator* and *From Beyond*, it was surprising to see Stuart Gordon construct a rather simple and strangely moralistic Brothers Grimm-esque fairytale where bad people are destroyed and good people receive an important life lesson. At one point, he even takes us inside a little girl's fanciful imagination, where her giant teddy bear (looking like it escaped from Bjork's "Human Behavior" video) gobbles up her greedy father and wicked stepmother.

The bulk of the film takes place inside a house straight out of the spookiest of fairy tales—claustrophobic hallways seemingly go on forever, intermittently illuminated by candles and assailing lightning; it would be the perfect place to host a Halloween party. As young Judy is told early on, it's the right place to be if you have an active imagination. One of the rooms hosts genuinely sweet characters conversing about toys in ways that are every bit as warm and sweet as in the *Toy Story* trilogy, all while in another room, armies of dolls bite, stab, saw, bludgeon, drill, and shoot characters that have refused to surrender to the good will that toys provide.

Blending the magic of childhood with graphic acts of violence is a delicate balance, but then again, that was what made certain classic fairy tales so enjoyable. At one point, Judy is reading *Hansel and Gretel*, certainly made more exciting by the strobe light the storm provides, unaware that her no-good father and cartoonishly evil stepmother are planning on abandoning her. Adding to her vulnerability are the house's owners, an elderly couple (wonderfully played by Ian Patrick Williams and Carolyn Purdy-Gordon) who are generous hosts and skilled dollmakers but whose demeanor indicates there's a slight chance that they're planning to eat her for breakfast. And even though she lost her best friend Teddy Bear in the rainstorm, she has found a new friend in Ralph, played by the wonderful actor Stephen Lee. A refreshing contrast to the selfish parents and obnoxious hitchhikers, this is one of the most lovable characters imaginable, employing a child-at-heart attitude and endearing sense of humor. Whether he is subtly realizing that Judy's crazy stories about dolls coming to life might have some validity, playing with the toys with the same enthusiasm as a child on Christmas, or desperately trying to defend himself against Judy's enraged father, Lee hits all of the right notes and steals every scene he's in.

Affirming this as a perfect Halloween companion is its brisk running time and a finale that is both sweet and sinister. And since the ending contains the two biggest laugh-out-loud moments ("THE KILLER DOLLS!!!" and "P.S. I took the hitchhikers with me"),

we finish the movie feeling happy, fulfilled, and energized enough to keep the Halloween festivities going until the sun comes up.

DONNIE DARKO (2001)

Director: Richard Kelly
Cast: Jake Gyllenhaal, Jena Malone, Drew Barrymore, Mary McDonnell, Beth Grant, Patrick Swayze
Length: 113 minutes
Rating: R

Synopsis: A disturbed and delusional high school student named Donnie is visited by a giant bunny rabbit who tells him that the world will come to an end in 28 days, which is also Halloween. The rabbit leads Donnie on a path of destruction where he rebels against the conservative authorities who rule his high school, and on a path of discovery where he delves into the studies of time travel.

Every now and then, a very special movie gets unfair treatment at the box office and with critics. It usually comes and goes without anybody noticing and remains a hidden gem. This was supposed to happen to *Donnie Darko*, but the tiny crowds who first saw it in the initial theatrical run and those curious enough to rent it refused to stay quiet. It took another couple years of surviving on video shelves and occasional midnight "cult" showings for the word-of-mouth to significantly spread, and then it was unstoppable. It has earned many dedicated websites from worshipping fans, endless debates on its ambiguity, a second theatrical release four years after its initial run, and very successful DVD and soundtrack sales. It may have even increased sales for bunny rabbit ears and skeleton bone shirts.

The film begins harmlessly enough, with gentle pans of Virginian mountains and typical family dinner arguments. Things get darker when the titular character gulps anti-depressants and verbally abuses his mother. Nothing can quite prepare us for what happens next, and then we're treated to a myriad of genres and complex themes that grow stranger with each scene. As the events unfold, it is really difficult to fully grasp what is happening, and by the end,

you'll wonder if it's like a David Lynch film where you're not supposed to know what's happening or if it's something that will become clearer with repeated viewings. Regardless of where you stand, it's a fascinating piece of work that knows a lot about its various subjects, such as time travel, the elusiveness of dreams, and the complications of adolescence.

This instantly had "cult classic" written all over it because of its trippy and hallucinatory images, references to '80s pop culture (there are hilarious lines about the Smurfs and Kelly Bundy, for example), and the kind of rebel-yell moments that would make angst-ridden teenagers applaud. Jake Gyllenhaal makes Donnie Darko a hero, somebody whose life is spiraling out of control but who is still intelligent enough to fight back against hypocrisy in his suburban high school. There is also a soundtrack that children of the '80s (or anyone with good taste) will enjoy.

Patrick Swayze and Beth Grant have a lot of fun with their ridiculous Bible-thumping characters and provide the film's biggest laughs. Mary McDonnell is also fabulous as a mother who seems like a broad stereotype at first, but then fleshes out into one of the most honest and likeable characters (she shares a particularly bittersweet moment with her son). There are also strong supporting performances from Noah Wyle and the always-entrancing Maggie Gyllenhaal.

Horror fans will smile when the cute couple of Donnie and Gretchen go see *The Evil Dead* on one of their first dates. Richard Kelly stated in an interview that in the original script, they were going to see *C.H.U.D.*, but finding out who owns rights to the film was proving to be a lengthy process. Luckily for him, he came into contact with Sam Raimi, who offered him the use of *The Evil Dead* for free.

DOUBLE, DOUBLE, TOIL AND TROUBLE (1993)

Director: Stuart Margolin
Cast: Mary-Kate Olsen, Ashley Olsen, Cloris Leachman, Eric McCormack, Meshach Taylor
Length: 96 minutes
Rating: G

Synopsis: Desperate for financial hope, the Farmer Family visits their wealthy, vindictive Aunt Agatha. Two twin sisters discover that Agatha is a witch and has used a moonstone to cast an eternal curse on her sister. With the help of a homeless man and a miniature clown, the girls hope to rescue their Aunt Sophia from Agatha's evil wrath.

OK, am I really doing this? Fine, let's get it over with. First off, this is entirely humorless, probably even for Olsen Twins standards. Every single joke and attempt at comedy falls so flat that it's not even accidentally amusing. It was made for TV and it sure looks like it. On the other hand, it genuinely cares about Halloween, and it succeeds in putting the girls in a Halloween adventure that involves imagination, danger, and mystery. There is a pumpkin-carving contest, a black cat, fall foliage, and a spirited speech from Oscar the Clown (played by horror veteran Phil Fondacaro) about the magic in the air as Halloween approaches. There is also a spooky "gathering" scene with a bubbling caldron and singing witches, as well as a talking crow that has the same kind of attitude as Peter Lorre had in *The Raven*.

The role of the wicked witch has been played time and time again, and Cloris Leachman (who plays both aunts) doesn't add anything new to the part, but she is so good at it.

DRACULA: PRINCE OF DARKNESS (1966)

Director: Terence Fisher
Cast: Christopher Lee, Barbara Shelley, Andrew Keir, Suzan Farmer, Francis Matthews
Length: 90 minutes
Rating: Not Rated

Synopsis: After ignoring the dire warnings of a cleric, two couples traveling Eastern Europe find themselves stranded by their coachman as night approaches.

Hammer films from the '60s are always conducive to the Halloween spirit, with their angry skies, lavish gothic sets lit to perfection to make shadows look as ominous as possible, and eccentric characters drawn to the dark side. *Dracula: Prince of Darkness* is a sequel to *Horror of Dracula,* and even though it does introduce elements that Dracula fans are all-too-familiar with—like a driver refusing to budge his horses one more inch closer to the legendary castle of Count Dracula as nighttime is approaching, and the use of the hapless insect-munching servant to the Count—it has an excellent pace and enough fresh ideas to really stand out in the crowded family of Dracula films.

A prologue opens the film where we see the Count's somewhat amusing demise in the original film, where he's reduced to a pile of ashes, and it takes another 45 minutes before we get to see Christopher Lee's resurrection, but the build-up is so masterfully executed that we thank the Count for taking his sweet time. After the eccentric old cleric (played in a commanding presence by Andrew Keir) warns the four travelers to stay away from the castle, only Barbara Shelley's Helen heeds his warnings, and it's very exciting to watch her clash with her companions as they become pawns in a bizarre series of circumstances: stranded by their driver, they are later greeted by horses pulling an empty carriage, and once the passengers settle in, the horses serve as soulless chauffeurs as they ignore all directions and head right to the castle. One character remarks how eerie the castle appears and another replies, "Well, let's find out just how eerie." Then we enter one of the greatest looking castles in movie history.

As the characters explore the castle to see dinner waiting for them and their luggage mysteriously placed in the bedrooms, we're treated to a series of magnificent sets and helpful ingredients for a late October night: candles flickering, curtains blowing in the noisy wind, echoing footsteps, thunder. Just as much attention to detail is placed in the eventual rebirth of the Count, where Helen's husband is hanging upside down, his blood spilling onto a pile of ashes that slowly morph into a skeleton in a series of nice-looking dissolves aided by a strong pool of mist. Once we see Christopher Lee, we're reminded just what an amazing presence he has always been, but it's kind of distracting how we keep waiting for that captivating baritone of his to utter a line that never comes. It's pretty damn mystifying Christopher Lee goes through the entire movie without muttering a single word of dialogue (a result of Lee being quite unhappy with the script), but it's commendable how the film doesn't depend on him to do so; he is still a dominant presence when he allows his minions to do all the talking for him. Also refreshing is how Dracula's obligatory demise isn't a result of garlic, sunlight, a crucifix, a stake to the heart, or holy water.

ERNEST SCARED STUPID (1991)

Director: John R. Cherry III
Cast: Jim Varney, Eartha Kitt, Austin Nagler, Shay Astar, Jonas Moscartolo, John Cadenhead
Length: 91 minutes
Rating: PG

> ## "You will die for the disgrace of your forefathers!" "I didn't have four fathers! I only had one father and I didn't know him that well!"

Synopsis: While playing in a tree house, good-hearted but dimwitted Ernest P. Worrell accidentally releases an evil troll that had lain imprisoned for 200 years. The troll then terrorizes the streets of Brairville, Missouri, on Halloween, transforming children into miniature wooden statues.

Yeah. Get used to jokes like these. This is so moronic that you could easily lose all of your friends if you make them watch it on Halloween night, but if your house is crawling with little kids or those who are very, very, very young at heart, then this should keep them entertained. It is understandable why so many kids were drawn to Jim Varney's low-brow character—he's a loveable doofus with a clown-like demeanor and whatever he lacks in wisdom, he makes up for with imagination and loyalty.

Not only does the majority of the film take place on Halloween, but it is also loaded with fog, lightning, and surprisingly creepy-looking monsters. And during the opening credits, Ernest mugs to the camera between shots from classic (and not so classic) horror films. *Ernest Scared Stupid* can also boast about containing something that no other film has: a villain that proudly proclaims, "Not even milk can stop me now!" Even though 31 probably isn't the ideal age to become introduced to Ernest, I was charmed by his character enough that I decided to check out *Ernest Saves Christmas* last December. I didn't laugh much at all at either film, but their holiday spirit was contagious.

THE EVIL DEAD (1981)

Director: Sam Raimi
Cast: Bruce Campbell, Ellen Sandweiss, Hal Delrich, Betsy Baker, Theresa Tilly
Length: 85 minutes
Rating: NR

Synopsis: Five friends travel to a remote cabin, and in its cellar, they find an old tape recorder and the "Book of the Dead." They play a tape that explains demon resurrections, and in the process, an evil is unleashed that possesses the vacationers and turns them into demons.

The character of Ash sure has come a long way. We think of him as a fearless, wacky, chainsaw-wielding superhero who spews one-liners in the face of evil, and serves as a microcosm for all that is good in the world. However, in the first half of *The Evil Dead*, he is a scared sweetheart who speaks softly, is often frozen in fear, and can't find the strength to pull the trigger on his rifle. While revisiting this hugely popular movie, you immediately get the sense of youthful energy and it makes you thankful that the group of inexperienced but highly passionate filmmakers was so damn uncompromising. The demons shown here are truly original: they look like zombies that suffer from constant muscle spasms, have the ability to float above ground, can talk like the greatest death-metal vocalists without moving their mouths, and are impossibly strong. They are also vicious little monsters—their fingertips are like acid when placed on human skin, and they refuse to stay down. In an exceptionally gory scene, the character of Scotty chops up one of his friends with an axe, yet the severed parts still shake aggressively.

There are numerous moments that could easily make your guests scream out loud, so it's a great film to watch on Halloween when you want the room to stay alive and bustling. A high tolerance for gore is essential though, as there are a handful of moments that define the word "disgusting," but with the exception of an oddly tasteless tree-raping scene, everything is done in high-spirited fun.

Among the many nice touches are a possessed Linda singing to Ash, a film projector that plays itself while blood is spilling out from every nook and cranny, and the presence of fog in the outdoor scenes that is so strong, it looks like you're soaring through clouds in an airplane. This twisted work of art was followed by the even sillier *Evil Dead II* and the epic *Army of Darkness*.

EVIL DEAD II: DEAD BY DAWN (1987)

Director: Sam Raimi
Cast: Bruce Campbell, Sarah Berry, Dan Hicks, Kassie Wesley, Denise Bixler, Richard Domeier
Length: 84 minutes
Rating: R

Synopsis: A vacationing couple enters a cabin and unknowingly plays a tape recorder that releases a satanic force. When his girlfriend is turned into a revolting creature, Ash must uncover the secrets of the Necronomicon in order to save his life.

For this project, Sam Raimi took the energy and charm from the first *Evil Dead* and multiplied it by a thousand. Everything, from the acting to the special effects, is more over-the-top, more elaborate. The grisliness comes almost immediately, as we see a woman get demonized, decapitated, and deposited under ground, all before the five-minute mark. Raimi dictates the action so rapidly, you might start to wonder if you accidentally pressed fast forward on the remote control.

The camerawork is notably impressive in the point-of-view shots of the sinister force chasing the unlucky vacationers. Despite all the technical virtuosity, cult-star Bruce Campbell steals the show, reprising his role from the original as the chainsaw-armed stud who resembles a comic book hero. His delivery and facial expressions are intentionally overdone, adding to the film's goofy tone. In one of the most hilarious scenes, he has to battle his own hand, which has become possessed.

Poster for *Evil Dead 2* (1987). Rosebud Releasing Corporation.

If you have protection and don't mind being drenched in gallons of blood or having the occasional eyeball fly into your mouth, then this cabin would make the perfect Halloween setting. It has a piano that plays itself, mirrors that cause reflections to become violent, and the capability to make every single thing inside shake forcefully. It is also surrounded with skeleton trees that can come to life!

Evil Dead 2 also has one of the strangest endings of all time—the kind of groovy ending that you couldn't have predicted in a million years.

THE EXORCIST (1973)

🎬 **Director:** William Friedkin
⭐ **Cast:** Ellen Burstyn, Linda Blair, Jason Miller, Max von Sydow, Lee J. Cobb, Kitty Winn, Jack MacGowran
🎞 **Length:** 121 minutes
🎭 **Rating:** R

🎞 **Synopsis:** A film actress's 12-year-old daughter becomes inhabited by a demon who calls himself the Devil. When countless doctors fail to cure the girl, her desperate mother turns to a pensive priest and one of the only people in the world with actual success in exorcisms.

Based on the popular novel from William Peter Blatty, *The Exorcist* gave the horror genre a much-needed return to critical respect and universal appreciation. To watch this film on any October night will provide you with one of the most intense and unforgettable cinematic experiences you will ever have. Its ability to shock, disturb, enchant, entertain, and paralyze you with fear doesn't go away with repeated viewings—

Film still for *The Exorcist* (1973). Warner Bros.

no matter how many—so this is one title that you need to have in your movie collection.

Over the years, the most grotesque shots, like Linda Blair vomiting "Satan Soup," have unfortunately undermined the film's more intellectually stimulating and emotionally involving aspects. Those who see *The Exorcist* for the first time will be surprised by its lengthy prologue in Iraq where Max von Sydow ends up standing face to face with a statue of the devil under blinding sunlight, by the importance placed on Father Damien Karras's troubling family life, by its ability to portray a girl so innocent and loveable that we can't possibly imagine a scenario where she could scare anybody, and by the circumstances in which a certain character takes possession of an ancient artifact. They might also be caught off guard by the kind of explicit language that would give your religious grandmother a heart attack.

The disgusting visuals and blasphemous verbal attacks wouldn't be nearly as effective if we didn't care for the characters. Ellen Burstyn and Linda Blair play such a likeable, pleasant mother/daughter pair in the first half, so when the devil complicates their loving relationship, it's not only entertaining to watch, but is also tragic and poignant. Jason Miller is equally sympathetic as the soft-spoken priest who is slowly losing both his mother and his faith. Aspiring

screenwriters should study the leisurely scene in which he meets Lieutenant William Kinderman on an autumnal afternoon; their dialogue is so natural and rich, and each word is absolutely necessary.

Halloween night is supposed to give you a good scare, and you are not going to find a movie scarier than *The Exorcist*. Whether it's the quiet tension, creepy religious undertones, vicious sound effects, the use of Mike Oldfield's "Tubular Bells," the still awe-inspiring special effects, or the devil's dirty deeds, this is a movie that gets to you, like it's declaring a duel with your soul.

Its popularity resulted in a slew of exorcism/Satan pictures (not to mention two sequels and two prequels) all around the world, including *Seytan* (1974) from Turkey and *Alucarda* (1977) from Mexico, which had been suffering from a horror drought. The exceptionally well made *Alucarda* has all the ingredients of a good Halloween movie—spooky organ music, nuns whose garments resemble mummy wrappings, cobwebs, a cemetery, Satanic possession in a convent orphanage that looks more like the Cryptkeeper's lair, and a plethora of blood, fire, and nudity—but it's so experimental that for as much as *The Exorcist* frightens you, *Alucarda* just weirds you out.

FINAL DESTINATION (2000)

Director: James Wong
Cast: Devon Sawa, Ali Larter, Kerr Smith, Kristen Cloke, Seann William Scott, Tony Todd
Length: 98 minutes
Rating: R

Synopsis: A teenager who has boarded a plane on a class trip to France has a vivid premonition that the aircraft will explode shortly after take-off. He and a few others leave and return to the airport, making them the only survivors when the plane does, in fact, explode. By barely avoiding the tragedy, they have cheated Death and interrupted its grand design, so it proceeds to take their lives away, one by one.

"In death, there are no accidents, no coincidences, no mishaps, and no escapes," a mortician (played by *Candyman*'s Tony Todd in all of his baritone glory) says to a couple of the students who managed to extricate themselves from an ill-fated airplane, and who believe that Death is on an obligatory path to claim the lives it feels entitled to.

Refreshingly original and playfully morbid, *Final Destination* is a teen thriller that excites its viewers not by endless cat-and-mouse chases, but by forcing them to fantasize about all of the sensational ways certain characters will die; scenes patiently unfold, with the camera pointing to seemingly simple objects that could somehow pose a threat. And yet each time we're caught completely off guard—one death in particular had entire theater audiences jumping out of their seats in disbelief, with choruses of deafening laughter following. Another impressive death is total silliness, and captures one's attention the same way falling dominoes do. *Final Destination* is smart in how it personifies the Reaper not by a black cape and a scythe, but by a subtle mist or a cool breeze that floats through open windows and under doors, creating one of the more elusive movie villains.

As a film for Halloween night, it works for just about every type of movie fan, even those without a proclivity for the genre. But only horror fans will smirk at the characters' last names, which include Chaney, Browning, Murnau, Waggner, and Hitchcock. Director James Wong absolutely dominates in the opening scenes, creating a tense atmosphere where, at an airport on a rainy night, superstitious Alex sees one ominous sign after another—the departure time is the same as his birthday, the cargo vehicle that passes under the walkway is numbered 666, a John Denver (who died in a plane crash) song is playing throughout the airport—setting off his internal alarms until we witness one of the most exhilarating and horrifying plane crashes ever depicted on film. Wong maintains a firm grip on the material until the teenagers (who apparently never learned to look both ways before crossing the street) keep blabbering complicated dialogue about how they can use their original seating charts on the plane to figure out who is next to die, and about how if they cheat Death once again, they can save their own lives. The latter thought doesn't make much sense at all, because wouldn't that just enrage Death even more? Or maybe Death just embodies a "fool me once, shame on...shame on you. Fool me, ya can't get fooled again" attitude.

Initial audience testing proved that the public admired the film mostly for its lurid fascination and elaborate, adrenalin-fueled deaths, and as a result, several existential and sentimental scenes were cut, and a new, high-powered ending was added to give the target audience more of what they craved.

FLESHEATER/REVENGE OF THE LIVING ZOMBIES (1988)

Director: Bill Hinzman
Cast: Leslie Ann Wick, Bill Hinzman, John Mowod, Kevin Kindlin, Denise Morrone
Length: 88 minutes
Rating: Not Rated

> **Synopsis:** A Halloween hayride takes a group of friends to an area where their boozing and lusting will be interrupted by brain-munching zombies.

From the outset, equipped with lengthy stationary shots that serve no purpose and howlingly horrific acting, we know what we are in store for, and pray that it maintains this level of amateurish nonsense to assure us 88 fun-filled minutes. Helmed by the late Bill Hinzman, who served as assistant cameraman in Romero's *Night of the Living Dead* and who also played the part of the graveyard ghoul, reprises his role and proves that zombies understandably do not show signs of aging, even after 20 years. He also takes the liberty of ripping off everything from the bickering characters trapped in a farmhouse to the flannel-shirted good old boys who use their rifles to hunt the walking dead, yet it is hard to ridicule him when *Flesheater* is so much fun.

Whether you are asking yourselves why in the world an editor would allow a 30-second stationary shot of a farmer simply dusting off a pentagram or are laughing at the gratuitous nudity and violence, this is a Halloween film that you should watch with several friends, especially if they are gore-hounds (there is a remarkably high body count and several outrageous killings) or capable of shouting out witty commentary.

Halloween is represented here by caramel apples, costumed kids, seas of foliage, and a party, which despite taking place in an ugly, dank setting that resembles a garage or a basement unsuitable for socializing, would be worth attending for the presence of the host, the hilariously drunk Count Dracula, played by Andrew Sands (who also served several production responsibilities).

You really cannot ask for anything more from a film that immediately promises "evil which will take flesh and blood from thee and turn all ye unto evil."

1408 (2007)

Director: Mikael Håfström
Cast: John Cusack, Samuel L. Jackson, Mary McCormack, Tony Shalhoub
Length: 104 minutes
Rating: PG-13

> **Synopsis:** A writer known for his series on the most haunted hotels in America gets more than he bargained for when he stays at a notorious room in New York City's Dolphin Hotel, which allegedly nobody has been able to survive in for more than an hour.

Just the first few minutes will show why this brilliantly executed Stephen King adaptation is conducive for Halloween night. The rain is pouring down impossibly hard as a drenched man checks into a hotel in the middle of nowhere to do research for his latest book, yet another entry in his haunted hotel series. This man is Mike Enslin, a moody introvert harboring the pain of recently losing his young daughter to cancer and separating from his wife. He spends his nights alone in different hotel rooms, narrating to his hand-held recorder much like Dale Cooper did in *Twin Peaks*. He wants nothing more than to finally get a glimpse of another world, or even the faintest hint of paranormal activity, but despite the hotels' grisly past and eccentric owners, he never finds anything, and this repeated disappointment only adds to his cynicism. But this all changes once he travels to New York City for a one-night-stay in room 1408 at the Dolphin Hotel.

For the majority of the film, it is just John Cusack in a hotel room; however, this is the trippiest room you've ever seen—it has the ability to transform, manipulate, and psychologically torture its inhabitants by preying on their specific weaknesses. It plays like a good old-fashioned haunted house nightmare, borrowing elements of everything from *The Shining* to *The Twilight Zone.* Cusack gives an absolutely spellbinding performance in what is essentially a one-man-show, and despite the character's flaws, you're rooting for him every moment. He is a multi-dimensional character, and the more we learn about him, the more fascinating and sympathetic he becomes. Samuel L. Jackson is also memorable as The Dolphin

One of five postcards included in the 2-Disc Collector's Edition DVD for *1408* (2007). Dimension Films.

Hotel's manager, which in the Stephen King short story, was a short, elderly British gentleman. This was a wise casting decision because it makes the room seem even more ominous; when Sam Jackson refuses to step inside, you know that it's one evil room.

Topnotch scares abound in *1408* and are more on the psychological side of the spectrum, but it certainly has its fair share of indelible images, such as the pantomime exchange with the strange silhouette at the hotel across the street, the walk across the ledge that will be unbearably tense for those who suffer from vertigo, the encounter with an unfriendly ghost in the air ducts, and the repeated use of The Carpenters' "We've Only Just Begun," one of the most creative uses of music in a horror film.

Because it places pathos-loaded characters in some incredibly heartbreaking situations, *1408* isn't the giddy, carefree Halloween adventure that other films in this book are. But it's easy to look past this minor inconvenience because not only is it scary as hell, it's also perhaps the greatest horror film of the first decade in this millennium.

FRANKENSTEIN (1931)

☗ **Director:** James Whale
★ **Cast:** Colin Clive, Mae Clarke, Boris Karloff, Edward van Sloan, Frederick Kerr
⊛ **Length:** 70 minutes
🧍 **Rating:** Not Rated

🗑 **Synopsis:** A talking bag of turnips auditions to befriend a ballerina with bwarzenblassphobia (fear of radishes) just in time for Thanksgiving dinner. You know what Frankenstein is.

Sparked to life by a competition among literary friends to see who could come up with the best horror story, the Frankenstein monster has been one of horror's biggest icons for almost two hundred years, and still stands tall and proud even after being dragged through the mud with schlock like *Frankenstein Meets the Spacemonster* (1965), *Jesse James Meets Frankenstein's Daughter* (1966), The *Erotic Rites of Frankenstein* (1972), *Frankenstein's Great Aunt Tillie* (1984), and *I, Frankenstein* (2014).

Mary Shelley was only twenty-one when *Frankenstein: or, the Modern Prometheus* was published, unleashing the crime against nature that was as sympathetic as a Titan tied to a rock who has his liver pecked away by an eagle on a daily basis. Its first dramatic interpretation, a play titled *The Man and the Monster; or The Fate of Frankenstein*, took place at the Royal Coburg Theatre in London in 1826, and then came a short film called *Frankenstein* (1910) and the 1915 feature *Life Without Soul*, which is unfortunately a lost film. Despite having the luxury of learning from other people's mistakes, it was still a mighty feat for Universal to do justice to Shelley's novel; for one, its initial make-up tests with then-star Bela Lugosi—who was already apprehensive due to the fact that his Monster had not a single line—provoked ridiculous bafflement rather than shrieks. But the film that reunited director James

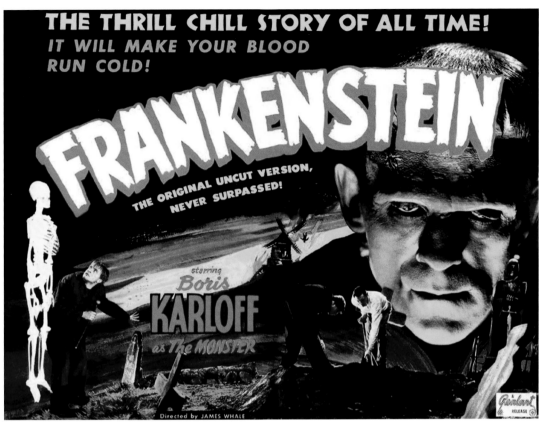

Lobby card for *Frankenstein* (1931). Universal Pictures.

Whale with leading man Colin Clive (whose careers were launched from the successful 1930 war movie *Journey's End*) turned out as perfect as just about anything can be, and yet it only improved over the decades with the restoration of key lines and scenes that were previously censored.

Assuming you were smart enough to take off work and school on November 1st so you can pull a Halloween all-nighter, and assuming you are smart enough to have seen this timeless classic in its entirety multiple times, I recommend watching this as one final festivity as that pesky November sun creeps closer and closer, because even if you fall asleep, there's something sentimental and magical about those thunder claps and the crackling of electricity that could actually conjure up all the great pumpkins and the Samhain saints to your dreamland, especially considering your final visions on this holiday included a grey-skied funeral procession with a grim reaper statue, a clumsy hunchback stealing an abnormal brain, and an apparatus levitating our most sacred of monsters above the watch tower to the "electrical secrets of heaven" that are strikes of lightning. It's important to end Halloween on the best possible note, and I prefer to have characters like Henry, Dr. Waldman, and Baron wishing me goodnight with lines like "Have you never wanted to do anything that was dangerous? Where should we be if nobody tried to find out what lies beyond? Have you ever wanted to look beyond the clouds and the stars or to know what causes the trees to bud and what changes a darkness into light? But if you talk like that, people call you crazy. Well, if I could discover just one of these things, what eternity is for example, I wouldn't care if they did think I was crazy" or "Oh, in the name of God! Now I know what it feels like to be God!"

FRIDAY THE 13TH

Friday the 13th (1980)
⊟ **Director:** Sean Cunningham
★ **Cast:** Adrienne King, Betsy Palmer, Jeannine Taylor
⊛ **Length:** 95 minutes

Friday the 13th Part 2 (1981)
⊟ **Director:** Steve Miner
★ **Cast:** Amy Steel, John Furey, Kirsten Baker
⊛ **Length:** 87 minutes

Jason Lives: Friday the 13th Part VI (1986)
⊟ **Director:** Tom McLoughlin
★ **Cast:** Thom Mathews, Jennifer Cooke, David Kagen
⊛ **Length:** 86 minutes

Friday the 13th Part VIII: Jason Takes Manhattan (1989)
⊟ **Director:** Rob Hedden
★ **Cast:** Jensen Daggett, Peter Mark Richman, Kane Hodder
⊛ **Length:** 100 minutes

If one of your Halloween cravings is to watch teens get hacked and slashed at a summer camp, then the *Friday the 13th* series should immediately come to mind, and in my opinion, four out of the twelve entries are especially good for this occasion.

The original *Friday the 13th* borrowed important elements from previous classics, such as the lengthy "psycho point-of-view" opening shot from *Halloween* and the surprise "gotcha" ending from *Carrie*, but in the wake of its enormous success, it would receive countless imitators of its own. Irrespective of an impressive Tom Savini body count, there isn't much that stands out about *Friday the 13th* until the bloody murder mystery is solved, and then the film really comes alive. For the final 20 minutes, the villain and the final girl embark on an exciting game of hide-and-seek that has the girl hide, get found, knock down the villain, run away, and repeat. It's especially exciting because for once, both of the combatants are of equal strength, and while they take advantage of an arsenal of weapons, they will still resort to clawing, biting, and pulling hair.

But most likely you'll be craving a *Friday the 13th* film for a particular hulking, unstoppable, fast-walking, machete-wielding Jason, and there are many sequels to choose from. Even though it doesn't make a lick of sense when you try to dissect the timeline, and even though its opening scene caused many fans to feel ripped off, *Friday the 13th Part 2* still holds up quite well today because of its surprisingly likable characters, well-executed action scenes, smart editing, and the most attractive girls in the entire series! But be warned, Jason looks like the maniac from *The Town that Dreaded Sundown* and doesn't acquire his iconic hockey mask until the next entry.

In my opinion, *Jason Lives: Friday the 13th Part VI* is easily the greatest film in the whole franchise, and in many ways it feels more like a throwback to Universal monster movies than a standard '80s slasher. In the first 5 minutes alone, Jason receives an awesome lightning bolt resurrection in a graveyard, punches out the heart of Horshack from *Welcome Back, Kotter*, and poses in a James Bond-style title sequence, all but assuring us that this will be the film that gets the *Friday the 13th* series back on track after the (somewhat unfair) backlash that came with the imitation-Jason in *Part V*. Even with all its Gothic flavors, heavy doses of humor (that hilarious survivalist paintball fight would have felt so out of place in the previous entries), and elaborate death scenes, *Jason Lives* takes the time to flesh out its principal characters and give them interesting personalities. Be sure to pay close attention to all of the subtle references to horror icons—I counted Carpenter, Karloff, and Garris, but there were probably several others.

Another one of the better entries is *Friday the 13th Part VIII: Jason Takes Manhattan*, which seems to take a lot of flak from people only because the title can be considered dishonest since most of the action takes place on a cruise ship. I, for one, was so happy to see Jason finally escape Camp Crystal Lake and stretch out his legs on such a colorful, flashy setting like a fancy yacht. But I would have traded New York sewer baby Jason for a scene in which he yells, "I'm walkin' here! I'm walkin' here! Up yours, you sonofabitch!" at a cab driver.

FRIGHT NIGHT (1985)

Director: Tom Holland
Cast: Chris Sarandon, Roddy McDowall, William Ragsdale, Stephen Geoffreys, Amanda Bearse
Length: 105 minutes
Rating: R

> **Synopsis:** A teenaged boy believes that Jerry Dandridge, the suave, handsome man that recently moved in next door, is a vampire. When he can't get his mom or his friends to believe him, he turns to hammy, washed-up actor Peter Vincent, who played a fearless vampire killer in old horror films. Once the boy's girlfriend is kidnapped, he and Peter have to destroy the vampire by dawn, or lose her forever.

Lobby card for *Fright Night* (1985). Columbia Pictures.

At a time when predictable slasher films were everywhere, Tom Holland put mainstream horror back on track with *Fright Night*, by far the greatest and most entertaining vampire film of all time, using ingredients that made *Nosferatu* and *Dracula* so successful, but throwing in plenty of fresh ideas. It's one of those movies that will make you feel every possible emotion, and despite the radical shifts in tone, it flows magnificently well and never hits one wrong note.

It has goofy comedy (such as when Charlie Brewster repeatedly makes a fool out of himself while trying to reveal the vampire's identity), edge-of-the-seat suspense, atmospheric locations, tear-jerking demises, moments of genuine sincerity (the relationship between Charlie and Peter Vincent is especially moving), hypnotic eroticism (the vampire and Charlie's girlfriend share an extremely passionate, sexy moment, even without showing us any nudity), and mesmerizing special effects. Also noteworthy is the convincing dialogue, a soundtrack that consists of totally awesome '80s synth-pop, and a hypnotic and beautiful score by Brad Fiedel. And if that wasn't enough, there is even an autumnal presence in all of the exterior scenes, so this is easily one of the most perfect movies to watch on Halloween night, especially if you appreciate the eccentricities of the '80s.

As impressive as the creature effects and vampire attacks are, this is a movie you will mostly remember for its fascinating characters. Roddy McDowall is both uproarious and sympathetic as the aging, conceited has-been who can't even afford to pay his rent. He hams it up with lines like "Stop, spawn of Satan!" and also acts as the father figure to young Charlie. Chris Sarandon gives the performance of a lifetime as sexy vampire Jerry Dandridge; he has so much fun with this role, but also successfully conveys the loneliness and pain of being undead. Equally unforgettable is Stephen Geoffreys as Evil Ed, evincing depth and sophistication in what could have been just a comic relief/ sidekick role. William Ragsdale (from '80s sitcom *Herman's Head*) and Amanda Bearse (who went on to play Marcy Darcy in the hit show *Married With Children*) are also outstanding as the teen lovers. Jonathan Stark is also very good as Jerry's snarky roommate; a homosexual relationship between the two characters is suggested.

If for some insane reason you haven't seen *Fright Night* yet, then slap yourself in the face, put this book down, and go buy, rent, or stream it immediately! And if you accidentally choose the pathetic remake, then you deserve what you get for ignoring my all-time favorite movie (well, OK, tied with *Psycho*) for so many years!

THE FUNHOUSE (1981)

Director: Tobe Hooper
Cast: Elizabeth Berridge, Cooper Huckabee, Miles Chapin, Largo Woodruff, Kevin Conway, Sylvia Miles
Length: 96 minutes
Rating: R

Synopsis: Four teens decide to spend the night inside the funhouse of a traveling carnival. Once inside, they witness the vicious murder of a fortune teller and accidentally make their presence known. This sends a carnival barker's severely-deformed son after the teens, who are shocked to discover that all of the doors have been locked.

The Funhouse doesn't get enough respect because, with the possible exception of *Something Wicked This Way Comes*, no movie has done a better job in showcasing our fascination with carnivals. Gene Siskel even declared it one of the most underrated horror movies in a special episode of *Siskel & Ebert* in 1988 titled "Hidden Horror."

One of the ways to rejuvenate a banal subgenre is to place the characters in interesting and unusual settings, and Tobe Hooper knows why carnivals simultaneously entice our curiosity and make our skin crawl. Much like the group of friends that run into the cannibalistic Sawyer clan in Hooper's first film, the unforgettable *The Texas Chainsaw Massacre,* the four affluent teenagers in *The Funhouse* find themselves completely out of their familiar, relaxed suburbia when they enter the world of the carnies. In a delightful montage, the teens enjoy a variety of carnival rides, but then are beckoned to a darker world by various seedy barkers to view animal mutations, magic shows, female strippers, and freak shows. Much like *Chainsaw*, Hooper takes his time in delivering the carnage—we haven't even seen the funhouse yet, and it *is* most definitely worth the wait. To spend the whole night in this funhouse, full of cobwebs, ghoulish décor, and mannequins that stare and cackle like the ones in David Schmoeller's *Tourist Trap*, would be scary as hell for anyone, but to be trapped in there with a homicidal maniac with an appearance so disturbing he has to wear a Frankenstein's monster mask (a creature he has a lot in common with) in public is something you would spend years in therapy for if you somehow happen to survive the night. In another interesting angle, unlike most slasher movies, the villains' motives are clear to us even before the bloodshed begins; we know why they have to hunt down the teens, and this makes both sides appear equally desperate.

The pace is so deliberate and the suspense so ruthless that when a character clumsily drops his lighter at a crucial moment, we feel like we're right up there with him. When the game is over and the inflatable fat woman laughs for the last time, we feel a sting that stays with us throughout the remainder of the night.

The best line is undoubtedly, "You made me drop my cotton candy, you freak!"

GHOSTBUSTERS (1984)

Director: Ivan Reitman
Cast: Bill Murray, Dan Aykroyd, Harold Ramis, Sigourney Weaver, Ernie Hudson, Rick Moranis
Length: 108 minutes
Rating: PG

Synopsis: After a university puts the kibosh on their experiments, three parapsychologists start their own ghost-extermination business. They are successful, but an uptight environmentalist shuts down their machinery and causes all hell to break loose in New York City. Meanwhile, a local art deco apartment building is hosting demons who await the revival of their demigod, Gozer.

Ghostbusters is one of those rare multi-million dollar budget adventures in which its heart and humor are just as potent as the special effects. When I watched it as a child, I was mostly attracted to the various gadgets (especially the proton guns), the Ectomobile, the spectacular special effects, and the pesky spirits, but now I am just as impressed with the quirky one liners and sexual innuendos.

The actors all perfectly understand the nature of their characters and they feed off each other's performances well, providing some hilarious ad-

Poster for *The Funhouse* (1981). Universal Pictures.

Lobby card for *Ghostbusters* (1984). Columbia Pictures.

libbing. Best of all, every character is funny, but they don't know they are funny, so it never looks like they are showing off or begging for laughs. In the exclusive club, Bill Murray plays a boyishly charming, wise-cracking ladies man; Dan Aykroyd is an arrogant know-it-all who never stops talking; Harold Ramis is an always-professional, no-nonsense megageek; and Ernie Hudson is a religious man who didn't even believe in ghosts prior to joining the Ghostbusters. They are all flawed, but earn our affection immediately and keep it for the whole duration. Also endearing are Rick Moranis as an overbearing health-nut who always manages to lock himself out of his apartment and Sigourney Weaver as the bewitching love interest of Murray who has the unfortunate task of living in an apartment where the eggs cook themselves on the kitchen counter and whose refrigerator is a conduit to another world.

The opening scenes take place in the maze-like basement of the New York Public Library, a wickedly good place for suspense, where your footsteps echo and anything could be right around the corner. When a ghost chases an elderly librarian, she runs down the claustrophobic aisles enclosed by towering bookshelves and has no idea which direction to turn, even though she has probably worked there for decades. Moments later, the Ghostbusters investigate the library and meet up with a floating apparition who is reading a book. Every single aspect of this scene is perfect: the Ghostbusters have never seen a real ghost before, so they have no idea how to handle the situation. When Murray tries to make contact, the ghost just places a finger to her mouth and ssssh's him, sending a breeze through his hair. What happens next is something that would have traumatized me as a child if it hadn't been so damn fun! Another legitimately creepy moment comes when Weaver is attacked in her armchair by dogs from hell.

Ghostbusters also benefits from a nostalgic, synthesized soundtrack (including a Halloween mix CD staple), creepy demon voices provided by director Ivan Reitman and Paddi Edwards, futuristic set pieces, and the mother of all climaxes! The Ghostbusters vs. The Marshmallow Man is one of the most enamoring confrontations for anybody alive in the '80s. You know a villain is memorable when it destroys a city with a big smile on its face.

THE GHOST AND MR. CHICKEN (1966)

🎬 **Director:** Alan Rafkin
⭐ **Cast:** Don Knotts, Joan Staley, Liam Redmond, Dick Sargent, Reta Shaw
🎞 **Length:** 90 minutes
🧍 **Rating:** G

🎟 **Synopsis:** A timid and cowardly typesetter for a small town newspaper is finally given the chance to write a feature article, but first he must spend the night alone in the sinister Simmons mansion on the 20th anniversary of its legendary murder-suicide.

Promotional photo for *The Ghost and Mr. Chicken* (1966). Universal Pictures.

At around midnight, the monotonous drizzle that had been greeting Portland for four days straight was finally gaining strength and reminding me of the kind of Midwestern October downpour I cherished growing up. I figured it would be an excellent time to light a couple of candles promising fragrances of autumn leaves and cinnamon apples and watch *The Ghost and Mr. Chicken*, a film that I had heard only complimentary things about for years but for some odd reason never saw. My pen was getting a workout just within the first minute of the film because I had to take note of the lightning, the playfully eerie score by Vic Mizzy (who also wrote the classic *Addams Family* theme), the house that looked so uncannily like Norman's that I immediately pictured Mother's silhouette in the upstairs window, Don Knotts's always engaging presence, and a sign welcoming me to Rachel, Kansas: Home Plate for Wheat and Democracy. Eighty-nine minutes and three pages of enthusiastic scribbles later, I wrote something that I hadn't ever said before, "They don't make 'em like that anymore."

Expanded from the *Andy Griffith Show* episode "The Haunted House," *The Ghost and Mr. Chicken* was Don Knotts' first film since leaving Mayberry, North Carolina. He fortunately took all of Barney Fife's mannerisms with him: the nervous twitches, the bug-eyed double takes, the shy stuttering, the phony machismo, the whiny pleas, and everything else that made him the relatable underdog everyone loves to root for. We get a sense of his sympathetic buffoonery right away when he proudly displays the Press badge he obviously made for himself and proceeds to take photographs of a man who was supposedly just murdered. After taking down witness testimony, he drives to the Rachel Courier Express and excitedly boasts about this huge scoop, only to be interrupted by the deceased man walking in, drunk with a bandage over his head. "But you're supposed to be dead!" We get a sense right away that this isn't the first time Luther Heggs has done a sad Charlie

Brown walk to extricate himself from a chorus of laughter and mocks.

The most Halloweenish moments arrive when we take a tour of the dreaded Simmons House with Luther. This house is every bit as foreboding as the rumors proclaimed, so we don't blame Luther one bit for wanting to end the night as quickly as possible; after a brief tour, he zips himself up in a sleeping bag and trembles the night away. But by then he has already witnessed a front door that opens and closes by itself, a trap coal chute, rocking chairs that never stop, creaking stairs, a record player that chooses only the most stressful moments to start playing, hidden passageways, furniture veiled in cobwebs, mannequins, and a bloody fingertip–stained organ that plays by itself at the stroke of midnight.

By the time he wakes up the next morning, the horror elements of the movie disappear, as the rest of the story focuses on Luther's new-found fame in his small town, a possible courtship with a woman he has secretly loved, and a lawsuit against the newspaper filed by the heir of the Simmons house. But the laughs don't disappear, as just about every scene made me laugh so hard I surely would have awakened my neighbors if the rain hadn't drowned me out. I especially loved the most awkward lunch date ever, Luther's unbelievably bad public speaking skills (made even worse when a gust of wind blows away all of his papers), the scenes with the Psychic Occult Society of Rachel that looks more like a church ladies league, and Luther's nervous dialogue to the girl of his dreams—a typical line goes something like, "My mother liked good food. She always used to say 'I'd rather eat good food than bad food any old day of the week.'" Attaboy, Luther! And attaboy, Don Knotts, the world misses you terribly!

GINGER SNAPS (2000)

Director: John Fawcett
Cast: Emily Perkins, Katharine Isabelle, Kris Lemche, Mimi Rogers, Jesse Moss, Danielle Hampton
Length: 108 minutes
Rating: Not Rated

Synopsis: On the night she has her first period, a teenaged girl is attacked by a strange creature. She survives, but later undergoes physical transformations and a craving for animalistic sex and tearing living things to pieces. Her younger sister desperately searches for a cure before Halloween night, when the next full moon will arise.

Those who believe that the werewolf subgenre has for the past couple of decades fallen into a pit of tired clichés and formulaic mediocrity need to give this Canadian teen thriller a chance. It throws the majority of old Hollywood lycanthrope rules out the window and uses the curse of the wolf as a metaphor for menstruation. Ginger and Brigitte are sisters and best friends, practically inseparable and completely uninterested in others. They spend most of their time thinking about death and planning their own suicides. For a school project, they photograph each other in various mock deaths that are so gruesome and disturbing, they are immediately sent to the guidance counselor. They are social outcasts who not only rebel against everything in their suburban hell, but also against nature, because even though they are both high school students, neither of them has begun menstruating. What makes them different from most teen females in horror films is how comfortable they are with their outcast roles. So when the older sister, Ginger, begins to change, Brigitte doesn't know what would be worse: her sole companion turning into a bloodthirsty werewolf or a blossoming, nubile young woman who will go to desperate measures just to fit in. The screenplay, written by a woman, has dialogue so graphic regarding female cycles that males will probably squirm uncomfortably in their seats, but this mostly just occurs in the first half. The early moments also unfortunately include cruel treatment of dogs and too much vomiting, but patience shall be rewarded in generous proportions in the second half.

Ginger Snaps is loaded with jolting acts of violence (the werewolf attacks are pure savagery), but all of the blood and guts serve a more important purpose than to gross us out. It makes Brigitte's situation all the more distressing, because not only does she have to worry about Ginger befalling an eternal curse, but she also has to clean up her messes (in the form of half-devoured bodies) in order to protect her from the authorities. There is a moment near the climax where we see nothing but total darkness and the only audible thing is heavy breathing from a frightened character. With each second that passes, our nerves get increasingly frenzied to the point where we are breathing just as hard as she is.

GOTHIC (1986)

Director: Ken Russell
Cast: Gabriel Byrne, Julian Sands, Natasha Richardson, Myriam Cyr, Timothy Spall, Alec Mango
Length: 87 minutes
Rating: R

Synopsis: On June 16, 1816, a group of intellects meet at poet Lord Byron's home for a hallucinatory night full of substance abuse, orgies, ghost stories, hide and seek, and personal hysteria. As they descend deeper and deeper into madness, Mary Shelley conjures up the story of Frankenstein.

You could chop up *Gothic* into a thousand pieces and re-arrange them in any order, and it wouldn't make much difference. This is as incoherent and difficult as they come and would not gain structure from repeated viewings. It's a very easy task to abandon narrative conventions by presenting a succession of increasingly weird visuals, but to make the audience entertained and intrigued requires a great level of skill and ambition. As usual, director Ken Russell defies the line between reality and fantasy and gives us one hell of a nightmare. This psychedelic, masochistic freakfest would heavily appeal to fans of *Rocky Horror Picture Show* and/or David Lynch; everybody else should proceed with caution.

The distinguished characters of Mary Shelley, Lord Byron, and their companions are all eccentric and drugged out of their minds, but their non-slurred speech mimics Gothic romantic literature. They also overreact to everything and turn on each other in an instant. Not for one second do they seem like real people, capable of functioning in the outside world and forming meaningful relationships. They are the fragments of our craziest dreams, doing and saying things with no rhyme or reason to them. It's interesting how they all separate and explore the mansion by themselves on multiple occasions and always find ways of running into each other when somebody is desperate for companionship and on the brink of total insanity. Their encounters get more extreme, violent, and wacky each time.

If for some reason you want an unusual and unconventional Halloween, I'm sure a combination of hallucinogenic drugs and Ken Russell's *Gothic* would do the trick.

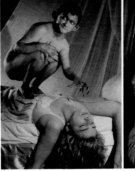

Les Fiches de Monsieur Cinema card for *Gothic* (1986)

THE GRANNY (1995)

📽 **Director:** Luca Bercovici
⭐ **Cast:** Stella Stevens, Shannon Whirry, Ryan Bollman, Patricia Sturges, Sandy Helberg
🎞 **Length:** 87 minutes
👤 **Rating:** R

🗑 **Synopsis:** Wheelchair-bound Granny drinks an elixir from the fountain of eternal youth, but she neglects the essential cleansing ritual. Soon after being pronounced dead, she awakens to wreak havoc on her greedy, foul family, who forged her will and stole the inheritance.

You know a film has ventured into insane territories when a woman becomes so aroused while looking at a closet full of fur coats that she precedes to pleasure herself until a few of the fur coats come to life and chew her face off. Or when a severed head gets frustrated at his body for his terrible sense of direction. The second half of this direct-to-video schlock-fest consists of one jaw-dropping scene after another, hitting its peak at an outrageous dinner scene that would whet the appetites of Leatherface and his family.

Employing the same pacing and comedic timing that made cult-favorites like *The Boneyard* so enjoyable, *The Granny* has a mostly stagnant first half—it relies on its quirky characters to illustrate that this family cannot wait to tear each other apart. Director Luca Bercovici cleverly saves the bloodshed for when an angry rainstorm furthers the off-kilter atmosphere, and after he establishes that Granny's relatives, a ruthless pack of conniving vultures, deserve to be beheaded, castrated, or even murdered by killer fur coats. For such a low-budget, direct-to-video bloodbath, it is surprising how much the actors seize the material and manage to stay in character when Granny is spitting at them some of the worst one-liners of all time. After spending a life actively watching professional wrestling, Granny returns from the grave with a Krueger-like attitude, growling lines like "I'm going to eat you for lunch" while she does her business.

Even most of its fans will probably put *The Granny* in the "it's so bad, it's good" category, which is unfair because it achieves everything it set out to do. It is stupid and sickening, but that is what it wants to be. And there is occasionally a detectable clarity to the filmmaking (especially in a scene where a little girl is fleeing through a path trying to dodge clutching branches, a trip made even trickier by blinding rainfall) that reminds us that even the stupidest and silliest of films require a certain degree of skill and style to work. The film's only blatant miscalculation is its failed attempt to make the stunning Shannon Whirry appear plain and dull just by giving her glasses and a ponytail holder, because after all, the visually impaired obviously can't get by in modern America without constant ridicule.

HALLOWEEN (1978)

Director: John Carpenter
Cast: Jamie Lee Curtis, Donald Pleasence, Nancy Loomis, P.J. Soles, Charles Cyphers, Kyle Richards
Length: 90 minutes
Rating: R

🍿 **Synopsis:** A man who was institutionalized for the brutal murder of his older sister on Halloween night escapes and returns to his hometown of Haddonfield, Illinois. Meanwhile, a group of teenaged girls try to enjoy their Halloween night, oblivious to the fact that they are being stalked.

Press kit photo for *Halloween* (1978). Compass International Pictures.

If you are reading this, then the chances are high that you've seen a little film from the '70s called *Halloween*. It has become so revered by both critics and the horror community that it would be impossible to say anything about it that you haven't heard a thousand times already, so I will not waste your time. Instead, I will offer a couple of suggestions to those who practically have the movie memorized by now.

You don't have to watch it sitting down in a dark room. In October, the Halloween spirit should be with you at all times, and this movie can generate it almost instantly. Have it playing when you are carving a pumpkin or putting up decorations, and allow its creepy soundtrack and hammy Dr. Loomis dialogue to give you extra energy. Just have it handy, so whenever you are doing something like cooking dinner and want to instantly feel even more enthused about the wonderful day that is approaching, all you have to do is press a button.

Of course, in addition, you should also actually *watch* the film once a year, because it's a complex piece of filmmaking that manages to elicit fear and suspense even though by now we know exactly what is going to happen. Try watching it with a lit pumpkin and a bowl of its oven-fresh seeds in the room to further spice up the ambience. Then you will be able to see, hear, taste, and smell Halloween all at once.

HALLOWEEN II (1981)

Director: Rick Rosenthal
Cast: Jamie Lee Curtis, Donald Pleasence, Charles Cyphers, Lance Guest
Length: 92 minutes
Rating: R

Synopsis: Laurie Strode is hospitalized and still very vulnerable because until the psychopath with the butcher knife and William Shatner mask is pinned, Festivus is not over.

Even though Halloween was quite eventful for the residents of Haddonfield in John Carpenter's original classic, the night was still young when Michael Myers fell off the balcony after getting shot numerous times by Dr. Loomis. Trick-or-treating time may have expired but costumed adults are still roaming the streets, making it easy for Michael to blend in, just as long as he avoids the many television news crews gathered at the crime scenes. *Halloween II* is a direct continuation, so you can't ask for a more appropriate double feature than these two. The first time I saw it, I felt let down that such a huge majority of the movie takes place inside a dimly-lit hospital, but once I revisited it on the night before Halloween, I realized that this was a really solid follow-up—maybe it took another movie titled *Halloween II* to make me finally appreciate what director Rick Rosenthal, and writers John Carpenter and Debra Hill achieved here.

Halloween II couldn't have possibly gotten off to a better start, as a shocked Dr. Loomis inspects the area where Michael Myers should be lying dead. Crickets, wind, and police sirens fill the soundtrack before Carpenter's cold, calculated synthesizer kicks in. The neighbor, who assumes Dr. Loomis is playing

a joke, says that he's been trick-or-treated to death tonight, and then Loomis responds with, "You don't know what death is." What follows is one of the coolest title sequences ever, in which the camera slowly zooms in on a flickering jack-o'-lantern until we can practically smell the candle as it tries to singe the orange flesh. The jack-o'-lantern suddenly splits open to reveal that it's been hiding a skull!

With the sight of a little boy who has bitten into chocolate caramel razorblade goodness, you can tell that this movie intends to be much more graphic than the mostly blood-free original; the needle thrusting and hot tub dunking are among the many gruesome highlights. And even though the dim lighting is far-fetched for hospital scenes, when it's accompanied by the chilling soundtrack, you get some of the eeriest scenes of the whole series. The pacing could have been a little better (it takes so long for the security guard to find Michael that it's surprising that more clichéd black cats didn't jump out at him), Jamie Lee Curtis isn't given nearly enough to do (for the final thirty minutes, she's basically just crawling around and looking sleepy), and I wish more scenes could have taken place outside of the hospital, but it's still easy to see why this movie has enough fans to warrant two separate Blu-Ray releases within a span of one year. There's the 2011 30th Anniversary Edition that is worth owning solely for the *Terror in the Aisles* special feature, and there's also a Shout Factory Collector's Edition with a stunning transfer and a second disc full of special features.

HALLOWEEN III: SEASON OF THE WITCH (1982)

Director: Tommy Lee Wallace
Cast: Tom Atkins, Stacey Nelkin, Dan O'Herlihy, Michael Currie
Length: 98 minutes
Rating: R

Synopsis: While investigating the mysterious death of her father, a woman gets trapped inside the Silver Shamrock Novelties factory and learns of their sinister plot to murder children all over the country by implanting microchips in their masks that will activate on Halloween night.

Universally maligned by critics and moviegoers at the time of its release, it recently celebrated its 30-year anniversary with a Collector's Edition Blu-Ray (courtesy of some of horror's best friends these days, the fine folks at Scream Factory) that reminded many people that it's not such a bad movie after all. Its several special features help clarify some of the "what if" questions that have always plagued it, and earned it such bitterness and resentment. What if the intended original director, Joe Dante, stayed with the project? Would he have turned this into the kind of crowd-pleasing horror-comedy that he is known for? Would the film have a better reputation if it were just titled Season of the Witch? Could more involvement from John Carpenter have helped its chances? What if this movie had been promoted differently to reduce the harsh backlash from those who were dismayed to see so many masks, but not a single one resembling William Shatner?

When asked about a possible third Halloween installment, John Carpenter and co-writer of the original Debra Hill expressed interest, but only if they were allowed to venture outside of the Michael Myers mythology and slasher formula. It was their intention to wisely turn Halloween into an anthology series where every year we would be treated to a new feature film, each one completely separate from the other entries except for taking place on October 31st. What stings the most is realizing all that could have been had Halloween III been better. We could have gotten so many imaginative and scary Pumpkin Cinema shoo-ins (which might have cemented Halloween as the greatest horror series ever) instead of offensively idiotic subplots later on involving Michael Myers and his dorky "Thorn" cult. There was simply too much on the line and this movie had neither the big scares nor humor to appeal to large audiences. Instead, what we got was a slow-paced science-fiction brooder with cold, futuristic synthesizers, robots disguised as humans, a cartoonish villain who wants to take over the world with a convoluted and incoherent plan, and parallels of advertising and mind control. The only thing cheering us up is that infectious Silver Shamrock jingle set to the tune of "London Bridge is Falling Down." It's an adorable sight to see two children wearing scary Halloween masks sitting close to the television and bobbing their heads back and forth to "Two more days 'til Halloween, Halloween, Halloween, two more days 'til Halloween, Silver Shamrock." Also respectable is the self-referential nods to the original and its willingness to a show something as grisly as a pumpkin mask dissolve over a kid's head like acid and then a variety of creepy crawlies spill out of its eye holes! These deaths are much more creative than anything Michael Myers could do with that butcher knife.

There is a delightful montage towards the end that should please anyone who was mesmerized by the VHS cover, in which a trio of trick-or-treaters are silhouetted against a falling orange sky: little ghouls and goblins roam the streets in New York, California, and many places in between, and their costumes are both nostalgic and creepy. The evil Mr. Cochran wants to turn these children into piles of mush to get revenge on the current state of Halloween. Desperately wanting a harvest festival for the ancient Celts like the last great Samhain of 3,000 years ago, he believes that bringing back sacrificial traditions will control the environment once more—this for some reason has something to do with the planets being in alignment and a piece of Stonehenge being stolen. Stonehenge is only slightly less silly here than it was in This is Spinal Tap and Troll 2.

Poster for *Halloween III: Season of the Witch* (1982). Universal Pictures.

Poster for *Halloween 5: The Revenge of Michael Myers* (1989). Galaxy International Releasing.

HALLOWEEN 4: THE RETURN OF MICHAEL MYERS (1988)

☒ **Director:** Dwight H. Little
★ **Cast:** Danielle Harris, Donald Pleasence, Ellie Cornell, Michael Pataki, Beau Starr, Sasha Jenson
⊕ **Length:** 88 minutes
👤 **Rating:** R

🎬 **Synopsis:** After being institutionalized in a comatose state for ten years, Michael Myers awakes and escapes, just in time to visit his hometown on Halloween and stalk his young niece.

Even though the original plan was to follow Part II with a set of completely unrelated sequels, *Halloween III*'s failure at the box office and with the critics put the kibosh on originality. So instead, executive producer Moustapha Akkad decided to satisfy the public's appetite for more butchering from the William Shatner-masked psychopath.

The opening shots, an awe-inspiring chain of authentic harvest celebration, triumph in casting the appropriate mood. Partnered with a minimalist soundtrack, these shots take us to a lovely cornfield at twilight, with fluttering homemade ghosts and devoted scarecrows that grin at a vast emptiness. Director Dwight Little quickly replaces these graceful ideas with plot devices and clichés we have all seen hundreds of times, yet he succeeds in keeping the momentum going by providing a dynamic cat-and-mouse chase between Michael Myers and his long-suffering psychiatrist, Dr. Loomis, now with facial scarring and a cane. *Halloween II* suffered by tiring the viewers with endless scenes in a dimly lit hospital, but *Halloween 4* never stays still, and offers a generous supply of locations in both day and night scenes.

The second half brings the film down a few notches when it introduces yet another team of inebriated hillbillies, armed with flannel and rifles. And a scene in which young Jamie gets separated from her foster sister while trick-or-treating should have been one of the most unforgettable moments in the entire series—it is appropriately subdued and slightly foreboding, but it's over in an instant and we are not as scared for the targeted little girl as we should be; this was Little's chance to artistically present Halloween night as both a magical and galvanizing presence, like he did for the daytime shots during the open credits. More satisfying is a later scene where Michael stalks his victim on a rooftop and a hilariously ironic ending—one that wouldn't have worked if Danielle Harris and Donald Pleasence hadn't given such engaging performances—perhaps the most pleasing ending to any *Halloween* film.

HALLOWEEN 5: THE REVENGE OF MICHAEL MYERS (1989)

☒ **Director:** Dominique Othenin-Girard
★ **Cast:** Danielle Harris, Donald Pleasence, Ellie Cornell, Wendy Kaplan, Matthew Walker, Beau Starr
⊕ **Length:** 96 minutes
👤 **Rating:** R

🎬 **Synopsis:** Ever since she murdered her foster mother, young Jamie Lloyd has been receiving professional help at Haddonfield Children's Clinic. She has developed a psychic link to her boogeyman uncle and can sense his inevitable return. Halloween is approaching and the murders have started again.

Released only a year after Part 4 and featuring primarily the same characters, this fifth installment had every potential to be worthless and forgettable. But once we witness an awesome title sequence in which a pumpkin is brutally massacred and an early death that is so startling we think that it has to be a fluke or a dream sequence, we have reason to believe that this inexperienced director is up to the task of improving on the previous sequels.

You might find yourself wondering why you are so entertained because you have seen it all before:

Michael Myers hunts horny teenagers, killing some and chasing the others while the wacky Dr. Loomis tries to stop him and John Carpenter's score plays again and again. What makes this distinctive are the atmospheric locations and the clever use of editing, which brings a new intensity to all of the clichés we've gotten so used to. There is also another gifted performance from young Danielle Harris, who is mute for the first half of the film. You take a big risk whenever you have a little girl be the star of the film, but Harris proves once again to be just as capable, vulnerable, and likeable as Jamie Lee Curtis was in the original. She has some great moments with Donald Pleasence, whose beloved character has officially lost his marbles.

The playful suspense fortunately overtakes the mean-spirited idea of putting the unstoppable killing machine against two 9-year-old kids, so things never get too out of hand. But what really hurts *Halloween 5* are the obligatory promiscuous teenagers who are so annoying this time, we start to lose patience when their scenes in a barn go on and on without any stabbing.

HALLOWEEN H20: 20 YEARS LATER (1998)

🎬 **Director:** Steve Miner
⭐ **Cast:** Jamie Lee Curtis, Josh Harnett, Adam Arkin, Michelle Williams, L.L. Cool J, Jodi-Lyn O'Keefe
🎞️ **Length:** 85 minutes
👤 **Rating:** R

🗑️ **Synopsis:** Laurie Strode, the survivor of the first two films, has changed her name so that her knife-wielding brother won't be able to find her. She is teaching at the prestigious private school that her teenaged son attends. On the 20th anniversary of the horrors that befell her, she is paranoid that Michael Myers will return once again.

With the moronic and goofy *Halloween 6: The Curse of Michael Myers*, it looked like the series was finally ready to be dead and buried, but executive producer Moustapha Akkad refused to throw in the towel on his moneymaking maniac. *Halloween H20* goes back to the basics, pretending that the previous four entries never existed and containing many throwbacks to the original. It also recruited original star Jamie Lee Curtis and her mother, the legendary actress Janet Leigh (who hadn't been in a theatrical film since *The Fog*), and a team of likeable, attractive supporting players. This helps to somewhat fill the void left by the passing of Donald Pleasance.

The first few shots consist of knives stabbing through pumpkins and dead leaves plastering wet streets, and every now and then we're treated to a nice touch, such as curtains fluttering like ghosts in the wind. This is really a no-nonsense film (evident from its breakneck pace and short running time) that just wants to be frightening and to make the *Halloween* series worthy again. The scariest moments come when Michael confines two teenagers to a small gap between a gate and a locked front door, swinging his knife but barely missing, when somebody simply tries to remove a corkscrew from a garbage disposal, and when an elevator comes into play.

Fans of the original will chuckle when Laurie Strode reacts to a closet during a chase scene with Michael. While this film doesn't break any new ground, it includes the kind of classy, shocking ending to allow this respectable horror series to die with dignity. But that dignity was stolen with yet another sequel, the truly disastrous and despicable *Halloween: Resurrection*.

HALLOWEEN NIGHT (2006)

Director: Mark Atkins
Cast: Derek Osedach, Rebekah Kochan, Scot Nery, Jared Cohn, Sean Durrie, Alicia Klein, Amanda Ward
Length: 85 minutes
Rating: NR

Synopsis: A horribly disfigured maniac escapes from a mental institution and interrupts a Halloween party taking place in the house where, as a kid, he witnessed the rape and murder of his mother.

Fangoria editor Michael Gingold based this fright flick very loosely on an elaborate Halloween party he hosted that coincided with the escape of a dangerous man from a nearby asylum. Admittedly, this is a standard slasher movie, but it has more plot than most of its direct-to-video cohorts, and it benefits from strong performances from the entire cast, top-notch kills, clever uses of everyday items such as cell phones and laptops to enhance suspense, erotic lesbian scenes, and characters that love Halloween so much they don't even take off their beloved masks when they drive.

Beginning with a vulgar prologue that depicts the rape and murder of a woman while her son hides in the same room, *Halloween Night* at first doesn't seem like the fun-loving Halloween companion we expected, but soon we skip to the present where college students prepare for the ultimate Halloween party. Our curiosity rises with each scene because legendary prankster David teases us with a few clues on how he plans to scare the pants off of his party guests.

Even though it wants you to believe this is a true story, it makes no attempt to sustain credibility when the body count becomes so high that we begin to wonder how in the world so many gruesome deaths can go unnoticed, and when a severely burned man can walk around so vibrantly and gracefully while looking like a corpse exhumed after a hundred years.

It's not a perfect film, but it deserves to have a sacred word like Halloween in its title.

HALLOWEENTOWN (1998)

Director: Duwayne Dunham
Cast: Debbie Reynolds, Kimberly J. Brown, Judith Hoag, Joey Zimmermann, Robin Thomas
Length: 84 minutes
Rating: G

Synopsis: While listening in on a private conversation between her mother and grandmother, morbid 12-year-old Marnie Cromwell discovers that she comes from a long line of witches. Later that night, she and her two siblings follow their grandmother to her home, located in Halloweentown, a mortal-free world, where every day is Halloween. Together at last, the Cromwell witches prepare to defeat the evil forces that are attempting to take over both Halloweentown and the world of mortals.

This made-for-Disney movie will delight kids and those who are still kids at heart. Its wholesomeness is enhanced by a likable cast, a cheery color scheme, and positive messages about accepting your loved ones for who they are, even if their lifestyles contradict your own. Even the obligatory mega-villain exudes likeability—his over-the-top, Mr. Burns evilness makes us smile, though we still can't wait for one of the gigantic pumpkins to fall on him.

Halloweentown cannot compete with Jack Skellington's world in *The Nightmare Before Christmas*, but it does manage to use its resources to create a special, whimsical town that often looks as edible as Willy Wonka's factory. A hefty portion of the film's budget obviously went to the costumes, which are inspired, colorful, and even quite ghastly. There are pumpkinheads, vampires, ghosts (who are tired of the endless stereotypes about them), and just about every other monster you can imagine. Perhaps the most animated resident of Halloweentown is a wise-cracking skeleton whose lack of eyeballs doesn't hamper his cab driving skills.

Kimberly Brown's Marnie Cromwell has more attitude and verbal hostility than most pre-teen protagonists in family films, but that's understandable considering her mother's lifelong household ban on Halloween. She's still a good kid, though, and it's absolutely precious how she looks at her broom as if it were a beloved pet. At the heart of the film, Debbie Reynolds steals every scene as the larger-

than-life grandmother, who arrives unexpectedly at the Cromwell house on Halloween with a giant suitcase filled with candy, decorations, costumes, and even pentagrams. She is determined to give the Cromwell kids the Halloween they deserve, despite her daughter's sternness. She also gives the kids plenty of good advice, like "Being normal is vastly overrated."

Whether it is reiterating the fact that the apple filled with razorblades is a myth or simply portraying trick-or-treaters having the time of their lives, director Duwayne Dunham's passion for Halloween is unquestionable. This was followed by three sequels, 2001's *Halloweentown II*, 2004's *Halloweentown High*, and 2006's *Return to Halloweentown*.

THE HALLOWEEN TREE (1993)

Director: Mario Piluso
Cast: Leonard Nimoy, Ray Bradbury, Alex Greenwald, Edan Gross, Andrew Keegan, Kevin Michaels
Length: 90 minutes
Rating: Not Rated

Synopsis: Four children embark on a magical journey in order to rescue their friend from the ghosts of Halloween past. They travel back to the origins of All Hallows' Eve, and explore how the holiday is celebrated all over the world.

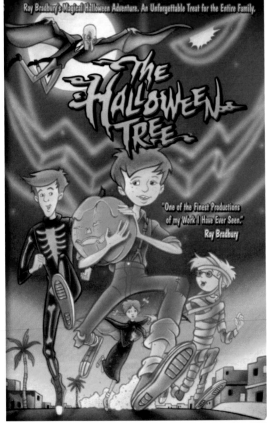

This marvelous adaptation of the timeless Ray Bradbury children's novel would be a worthy movie to show elementary school classes whenever October 31st falls on a weekday. Bradbury narrated this film himself and he does a wonderful job in vocally retaining the passion of his literature. Everybody involved with this project seems to truly believe that Halloween is the greatest day of the year. In *The Halloween Tree*, you will see all of the visual ingredients: kids trick-or-treating, good costumes, cute neighborhood decorations, a haunted house, a never-ending supply of jack-o'-lanterns, thunderstorms, fluttering ghosts, a black cat, a full moon (even sometimes shown with a skeleton grin), witches on brooms, gargoyles, graveyards, a swarm of hungry bats, clouds that morph into something scary, cobwebs, mummies, candy, and even a corpse sitting at a dinner table.

It might make you a bit nostalgic because it will remind you what it was like to be a kid on Halloween night. You stepped outside and the wind seemed to speak to you, telling you that just about anything could happen on this night. You were innocent,

Turner Home Entertainment VHS cover for *The Halloween Tree* (1993).

naïve, and you wanted to be spooked. The amount of excitement overwhelmed you to the point where you would have to run from house to house at a lightning quick pace, trying to collect as much candy as possible. Halloween will never quite be the same again, but the day belongs to everybody, and adults can enjoy a movie like this just as much as kids can, just as long as they still maintain a love and appreciation for October.

The children in *The Halloween Tree* are very likeable, as they only want to save the life of their good friend, who has made every previous Halloween so memorable for everybody. With the leadership of the bizarre and untrustworthy Mr. Moundshroud, they travel on kites and broomsticks to Paris, Mexico, and Egypt to find the answers they need, and in the process, learn that variations of Halloween are celebrated all over the world.

It's probably best to watch this a couple of days before Halloween, preferably alone, and you will be rewarded with the Halloween spirit while you still have plenty of time to make the most of it.

HAUNTED (1995)

🎬 **Director:** Lewis Gilbert
⭐ **Cast:** Aidan Quinn, Kate Beckinsale, John Gielgud, Anthony Andrews, Alex Lowe, Anna Massey
🎞️ **Length:** 108 minutes
👤 **Rating:** R

🎬 **Synopsis:** Professor David Ash is invited to an English mansion to investigate the spirits that are allegedly tormenting an elderly woman. There he meets and falls in love with a beautiful young woman, much to her older brother's dismay. David later finds himself seeing the same things as the elderly woman, and is forced to question his beliefs regarding the existence of ghosts.

Artisan Home Entertainment DVD cover for *Haunted* (1995).

If you are with your significant other and want a rainy and romantic October night, then this James Herbert adaptation would be a fine companion; it's an interesting love story with enough twists to keep you both intrigued. It's also one of the most gorgeous-looking horror films out there. It has that kind of quiet Gothic elegance that tempts you to press pause just so you can examine the entire screen, patiently taking in every precious detail. Practically every shot is full of beauty, grace, and mystery, but perhaps the most enchanting of all is when a small cloud of dust spins rapidly in front of Professor David Ash, then rises and morphs into a ghostlike blur, floating further and further away until it dissolves into the moonlit lake.

The soundtrack mirrors the film's subdued poignancy; set in England in the 1920s, *Haunted* has the kind of simple but effective sound effects reminiscent of the black and white haunted house thrillers. The wind whistles against windows, the doors slowly creak open, the rain creates a mood of both romance and apprehension, and Debbie Wiseman's music is tender and heartbreakingly beautiful.

Not only does *Haunted* look and sound great, but it has eccentric characters, smart dialogue, and an exhilarating climax. Aidan Quinn and Kate Beckinsale are very engaging leads, and Anthony Andrews is outstanding as the creepy and glum older brother, Robert.

THE HAUNTING (1963)

🎬 **Director:** Robert Wise
⭐ **Cast:** Julie Harris, Claire Bloom, Richard Johnson, Russ Tamblyn, Lois Maxwell, Fay Compton
🎞 **Length:** 112 minutes
🎭 **Rating:** Not Rated

🎃 **Synopsis:** A psychologist investigates an old New England mansion with a 90-year history of scandals, murders, and suicides. He hopes to find proof of the existence of ghosts and possibly a key to another world, and brings with him a pair of women who have personal experience with the paranormal. Once inside the walls of Hill House, they get more proof than desired.

One of the greatest haunted house films of all time, *The Haunting* has just about everything one could hope for in a psychological thriller, and it remains the kind of exceptionally eerie film that is intimidating to watch alone. It was probably therapeutic for the soul for Robert Wise to follow up a movie this brooding with *The Sound of Music*!

The Haunting leaves just about everything to the imagination: the only seen horrors in this 90-year-old deranged mansion that was born bad include a bending door and a shaking spiral staircase. It achieves a primal terror through atmosphere, sound effects, lighting, strong performances, and effective voice-over work that confirms that a certain character officially has bats in her psychologically tortured belfry. This character is Eleanor, a mousy, awkward, and depressed young woman still reeling from the death of her invalid mother. Keeping her spirits solid is the belief that Hill House is her Shangri La, the place she was always meant to be, and because of that, nobody will dare throw her back out into that cold, dark world full of burdens and bickering. There is a scene in which she lies in bed, trying to keep calm while a commanding pounding noise seems to get louder and louder. She is so scared amongst the booms that she has to grip the hand of her roommate. Director Robert Wise keeps the camera on her for so long, you begin to question whether the hand she is holding belongs to her roommate after all. Just thinking of what could be lying in bed beside her is enough to send intense shivers up and down your spine. It's hard to argue with the character of Luke Sanderson when he says that the house ought to be burned down and the ground sowed with salt. He is played by Russ Tamblyn, who also had a big part in Robert Wise's *West Side Story*, and who you also may know as Dr. Jacoby from *Twin Peaks*.

And if all that wasn't enough, the setting takes place in October in New England! At one point, Richard Johnson's character warns the others that they must expect every night in this house to be Halloween. Also be sure to read the hair-raising novel the movie was based on, Shirley Jackson's *The Haunting of Hill House*, preferably while drinking a pumpkin spiced latte!

HAUSU/HOUSE (1977)

🎬 **Director:** Nobuhiko Obayashi
⭐ **Cast:** Kimiko Ikegami, Miki Jinbo, Kumiko Ohba, Ai Matsubara, Mieko Sato
🎞 **Length:** 88 minutes
🎭 **Rating:** Not Rated

🎃 **Synopsis:** A teenage girl named Gorgeous brings along six of her friends for a summer vacation at her aunt's house. There's just that small issue of the aunt being deceased and the house being hungry for youthful girls.

While American audiences were having their minds blown by David Lynch's feature film debut, *Eraserhead*, in 1977, another equally unconventional film by a new director was screening in Japan and changing the rules of what the art of cinema could accomplish. But unlike the midnight stoner art-house crowds at *Eraserhead* screenings, *Hausu*'s adoring audiences consisted mainly of children. Published reviews were

Promotional art for *Hausu* (1977). Toho Company.

unusually sparse for Nobuhiko Obayashi's candy-colored, trippy horror-fantasy because this is the kind of film that leaves even the most veteran of moviegoers flabbergasted. It is a whirlwind of hallucinations, an incomprehensible magical journey that uses every cinematic trick in the book—superimpositions, freeze-frames, stop motion animation, color tints, and chroma key compositing—to achieve the effect of an 88-minute dream sequence, the most incredible dream you've ever had. This psychedelic haunted house fantasy was made with innovation and energy front and center, not realism. If you want a WTF Halloween like no other, than join the seven giggly Japanese schoolgirls with names like Fantasy, Gorgeous, Melody, and Kung Fu, as they travel through *Wizard of Oz*–like painted backdrops to a house with a huge tongue and insatiable appetite. Awaiting your arrival will be the evil spirit of an old woman and her laser-beam-eyed cat, Blanche.

The Japanese film studio Toho was eager to capitalize off the American success of *Jaws* so they hired Obayashi to write a script with the same level of excitement. He asked his daughter, who was around 10 years old at the time, what would be as frightening as the killer shark in Amity, and that inspired a flurry of childlike wonder unable to filter out the strangest and most inexplicable things: a futon monster, a piano that devours people, pulling up a severed head from a well instead of a watermelon, and being attacked by your own reflection. He mixed these ideas with several others, some equally absurd and others influenced by his direct connection to the atomic bombing of his hometown of Hiroshima, into a script that was unlike anything the studio executives had ever seen. They liked the script but were unable to find a director willing to take it, and were reluctant to consider Obayashi, whose prior experience included only commercials and short films. He campaigned relentlessly for years until the public's enthusiasm for *Hausu* became too passionate to ignore.

Whether you are straight-edge or would like nothing more than to drop acid and frolic into a hybrid of *Scooby Doo* and *Alice in Wonderland*, *Hausu* is something everyone needs to experience.

73

HÄXAN: WITCHCRAFT THROUGH THE AGES (1922)

Director: Benjamin Christensen
Cast: Maren Pedersen, Astrid Holm, Benjamin Christensen, Oscar Stribolt
Length: 91 minutes
Rating: Not Rated

Synopsis: Half documentary, half dramatization, this silent film attempts to explain the mystery of witchcraft from a historical and cultural point of view.

In recent years many theaters across the country have held special October screenings of the 1922 Danish/Swedish silent film *Häxan* with a live music group providing their own soundtrack. Just last year alone, Pacific Northwesterners could go to various theaters to enjoy live performances from Funerary Call, Sarah Angliss, and Jaggery and Walter Sickert & The Army of Broken Toys, all while gazing at witches, demons, devils, and torture chambers that have been immortalized on celluloid for over 90 years now. It's an event as conducive to the Halloween atmosphere as attending a live concert for Ghost B.C. (who also hail from Sweden).

Häxan was summoned after writer and director Benjamin Christensen extensively studied *The Malleus Maleficarum*, a 1486 how-to-condemn-and-sacrifice-witches guide for dummies written by German Catholic clergyman Henrich Kramer. This fiction/documentary hybrid presents seven chapters of moving pictures, beginning with a 13-minute lecture (which even has its own classroom pointer stick to emphasize details on paintings, drawings, and sculptures) about how primitive men blamed everything that was incomprehensible to them on sorcery and evil. Be on the lookout in chapter 1 for a creature that bears an uncanny resemblance to that despicable oaf, Jar Jar Binks. Our first glimpse of live action takes us to the Middle Ages, as women visiting a sorcerer receive a special ointment that allows them to fly through the night air to participate in the Witch Sabbath. Much of the film supports an inter-title that reads, "During the witchcraft era, it was dangerous to be old and ugly, but it was not

safe to be young and pretty either" when an elderly beggar is captured and questioned by the Inquisition judges. At first, she refuses to admit to something that isn't true, but once the many torture devices come into play, her confessions become so expansive that she accuses other women in town of worshipping Satan, starting a vicious cycle of ignorance, paranoia, violence, and murder. Normally this sort of material would be too punishing and unjust for a Halloween movie, but a comical interpretation of Lucifer and the scatterbrained arrangement of scenes are just a couple of reasons why *Häxan* couldn't be further removed from the cruelty in similarly-themed films like *The Pit and the Pendulum* (1991).

Masters of illusion Jean Cocteau and Georges Méliès obviously taught Christensen a thing or two about special effects, for the sights of illuminated witches flying through dark clouds, piles of coins blowing through an open door, and the depictions of Hell still manage to look impressive in the era of *Gravity* and *Life of Pi*. *Häxan* was a hit in its native countries, but it would take decades to find audiences in many other parts of the world, and when most people finally did get to see it, it was heavily censored. Considering how it was made less than thirty years after a stationary shot of a train coming closer and closer to the camera caused people to faint, the ratings board clearly didn't think the public was quite ready for an old witch breaking off the finger of a corpse, witches-in-training lining up to literally kiss Satan's ass, a baby being tossed into a boiling pot, demons forcing people to dance over a cross, a nude woman sleepwalking through the forest, or the devil seducing someone while her husband sleeps beside her. It's extraordinary and oddly inspiring that a movie like this could have even existed back in 1922 and that so many people flocked to see it, helping to lay the foundation of a long-term, healthy relationship between Satan and the box office.

HELL NIGHT (1981)

Director: Tom DeSimone
Cast: Linda Blair, Vincent Van Patten, Kevin Brophy, Jenny Neumann, Peter Barton
Length: 101 minutes
Rating: R

Synopsis: Four pledges have to spend the night in a mansion with a gruesome past for their initiation, which doesn't sit well with the mutant psychopaths living in the basement.

With the possible exception of *The Funhouse*, another underrated gem from 1981, it's hard to think of a better slasher movie for Halloween than *Hell Night*—a fitting title since so many misguided groups throughout history have considered Halloween a night of pure evil. I usually always take lots of notes while watching movies for this book, but this time I only wrote a single line, back when the opening credits were still rolling: the utterly brilliant and insightful observation, "awesome party with fires, motorcycles, and hundreds of extras." Then the pen went down and wasn't picked up again simply because I didn't want to take my eyes off the screen or separate myself from the story for a second. I had been in a slump due to the previous five movies I watched being huge disappointments, but this won me over so much that I wonder just what the hell was wrong with the 10-year-old version of me who felt rather indifferent towards it.

A plot where people have to spend the night in a creepy old house as part of a fraternity initiation is certainly nothing new, but never has the task seemed this perilous and unenviable, due to the fantastic back story of one of the creepiest looking houses to ever exist. At the gates, the president of the fraternity tells the story of Raymond and Lillian Garth, who wanted nothing more than to bring one normal child into the world but instead only produced hideous freaks that never saw the light of day. After Raymond suddenly slaughtered his entire family one night before killing himself, nobody has lived inside the Garth Manor. The most unsettling piece of the puzzle for the four unfortunate souls about to enter is that the police were not able to find all of the bodies. It's also not an unusual plot piece to have the fraternity members try to sabotage the pledges' chances by filling the house with ghoulish props and traditional haunted house sound effects, but these affluent kids up the ante with convincing projections of walking corpses.

It doesn't take long for the body count to rise, and that sets off a spine-tingling chase between deformed mutant cat and horny boozed-up mice in a ghastly, inescapable abode that features a hedge maze and winding underground tunnels. Adding to the viewers' enjoyment is crisp, beautiful photography, unbearably tense synthesized music, eerie and autumnal Gothic atmosphere, and characters that are a tad more interesting than the ones you're used to seeing in '80s slasher pictures.

HOCUS POCUS (1993)

Director: Kenny Ortega
Cast: Bette Midler, Omri Katz, Sarah Jessica Parker, Kathy Najimy, Thora Birch, Vinessa Shaw
Length: 96 minutes
Rating: PG

Synopsis: In Salem, Massachusetts, three witches were executed, and 300 years later, on Halloween night, a teenager named Max lights a candle that brings them back to life, and they are absolutely famished for some adolescent souls.

Hocus Pocus is a flawed movie for sure but it's hard to think of a more popular Halloween movie from the past 20 years that people insist on watching every year, which is understandable considering how it's a Disney film that takes place on Halloween in the most Halloweenish of towns, Salem. There are some really nice touches for the biggest adorers of All Hallows' Eve: both the children and the adults appear to have a blast trick-or-treating, there is a Halloween party filled with suburban parents that miraculously looks

Walt Disney Company press photo for *Hocus Pocus* (1993).

like fun, and multiple scenes in a foliage-covered cemetery. But the biggest factor that has us returning to this flick year after year with a wide grin is Bette Midler's irresistible performance as the buck-toothed Winifred Sanderson, the leader of the witch trio. The divine one has stated in interviews that it was her favorite performance, and that she would have been happy playing this part for the rest of her life, even though the flying scenes caused her some physical discomfort. It's nice to know she had as much fun filming it as we have watching it.

Hocus Pocus is funniest whenever the 17th-century witches react to present life—they are terrified of buses, untrusting of streets, and have no idea why their master has given them a chocolate-covered finger of a man named Clark. They are much more in their comfort zone when dealing with a talking black cat and the corpse of Winifred's former lover. This

zombie is played by Doug Jones, a high-in-demand actor who has become the master of prosthetics thanks to roles in films like *Pan's Labyrinth* and *Hellboy*. One of the film's biggest laughs comes when he tells Winifred to go to hell, to which she replies, "Oh, I've been there, thank you. I found it quite lovely," right before she flies towards him on her broom and kicks his head off. If only our teen heroes could have provided this much entertainment; compared to the witches, they are boring and obnoxious. It's difficult to sympathize with Max when his shoes get stolen by the blonde grunge guy and "Ice," considering how in the previous scene, he had the gall to suggest that Halloween is a conspiracy invented by the candy companies and then rudely ask out a fellow student right in front of the whole class (in which the dearly departed comedic actress Kathleen Freeman plays the teacher).

Disney could have had a real box office blockbuster

on their hands, but they foolishly chose to release this movie in July! Why is it so hard for these people in Hollywood to understand that Halloween movies should be released in October? Also somewhat baffling is how this PG-rated movie brings up the subject of virginity in scene after scene, surely resulting in parents having to explain to their children several years earlier than expected the importance of abstinence.

HOLD THAT GHOST (1941)

🎬 **Director:** Arthur Lubin
⭐ **Cast:** Bud Abbott, Lou Costello, Joan Davis, Richard Carlson, Evelyn Ankers, Marc Lawrence
🎞 **Length:** 86 minutes
👤 **Rating:** Not Rated

🎬 **Synopsis:** Two bickering gas station attendants inherit an old, creepy, motel from one of the town's most notorious gangsters. They visit their new property and find themselves stranded with a few other strangers when their cab driver abandons them. Everybody tries to make the most out of the situation, but they soon discover that they are not the only ones inside.

Poster for *Hold That Ghost* (1941). Universal Pictures.

This was only the fourth film Abbott and Costello ever made together, and it remains their greatest achievement. It shows them at the top of their game, demonstrating superb comedic timing and priceless chemistry. It also introduced the idea of putting this dynamic comedy pair into spooky situations, paving the way for their encounters with Frankenstein, Dracula, and the Wolfman (1948), Boris Karloff (1949), the Invisible Man (1951), Dr. Jekyll and Mr. Hyde (1953), and the Mummy (1955).

Because of a couple of overlong musical numbers in the opening scenes, *Hold That Ghost* gets off to a slow start (even though it's always a pleasure to see and hear The Andrews Sisters), but patience is rewarded, for once everybody gets deserted on a dark and stormy night, every scene that follows overflows with comedic gold. The house is a menacing presence, with dead bodies stored in closets, gutters that collapse under heavy rain, rooms that transform with a simple tug of a coat hanger, and the kind of stark shadows that black and white cinematography captures so well. Also effective is a soundtrack that attacks you in key moments, so this film should give you the chills that you are supposed to feel on Halloween night.

Some of the film's highlights include Costello struggling to make a bed, a clumsy dance-off to "The Beautiful Blue Danube," a priceless argument regarding the meaning of "a figure of speech," a bedroom that repeatedly transforms into a gambling parlor, and the usage of a sink to play "choo-choo train." *Hold That Ghost* is a light-hearted treasure that is essential for fans of this unforgettable, irreplaceable duo. Be sure to look out for *The Three Stooges*'s Shemp Howard, who makes an appearance as a diner employee.

HOUSE (1986)

Director: Steve Miner
Cast: William Katt, George Wendt, Richard Moll, Kay Lenz
Length: 93 minutes
Rating: R

Synopsis: A horror novelist struggling with the sudden disappearance of his son, the end of his marriage, and traumatic memories of the Vietnam War returns to his childhood home, where he is confronted by an entirely new set of horrors.

Written by the same talented man who gave us *Night of the Creeps* and *The Monster Squad*, directed by the same man who helmed the first two *Friday the 13th* sequels, and with a cast that includes *Night Court*'s Richard Moll and *Cheers*'s George Wendt, this mid-80s horror-comedy—which has a playful spirit without skimping on the horror—is a crowd-pleaser for so many reasons.

While revolving around pretty deep themes like a little boy's disappearance, an elderly woman's suicide, and the post-traumatic stress disorder caused by the Vietnam War, this is a movie that at its core just wants us to have a good time, so it pulls no punches with its goofy-as-hell creature effects, hilariously out-of-place pop songs, and outrageous sight gags. Even among all of the silly shenanigans is a level of artistry that makes this house fascinating to explore; closets and mirrors become portals to other universes, axes and knives float through the air, chimneys function like vacuums to suck humans up, and from a certain window, it becomes the classic gothic haunted mansion, teetering upon a hostile sea. The characters are also extremely likable and good-natured, especially William Katt, who you most likely remember as Carrie White's studmuffin prom date.

So if you are entertaining a group of friends who happened to grow up in the 1980s, then this will make you feel right at home. It was followed by *House II: The Second Story* (one of the most clever sequel titles ever), the completely unrelated *The Horror Show* (titled *House III* in some countries for some mystifying reason), and *House IV*, which features the greatest haunted pizza scene you'll ever see.

HOUSE OF FRANKENSTEIN (1944)

Director: Erle C. Kenton
Cast: Boris Karloff, J. Carrol Naish, Lon Chaney Jr., John Carradine, Anne Gwynne, Glenn Strange
Length: 70 minutes
Rating: Not Rated

Synopsis: On a stormy night, Dr. Gustav Niemann and his hunchbacked companion escape from an asylum. They hope to get revenge on those who have wronged them, as well as continue the work of the legendary Dr. Frankenstein by resurrecting Count Dracula, the Wolf Man, and Frankenstein's Monster.

This third sequel to the James Whale classic steers the series in a new direction by uniting the most popular Universal monsters for the first time. Even though this has Frankenstein in its title, the Monster (who we don't even see until the third act) receives less screen time than Dracula and the Wolf Man. In

Promotional print for *House of Frankenstein* (1944). Universal Pictures.

fact, the first 30 minutes play like a traditional vampire tale, involving a man who decides to release the wooden stake from Dracula's heart, causing him to rise from his coffin once again. There is even a scene where he flies as a bat and enters a woman's bedroom to feast on her as she sleeps. Although John Carradine does a fine job as the count, Bela Lugosi is sorely missed. Karloff isn't the Monster either, but he does star as the mad scientist this time around.

House of Frankenstein is tremendously ambitious and inventive for a sequel #3, but it offers nothing that will linger in your memory afterwards. It appropriately opens with a rainstorm, as the carriage of Professor Lampini's Chamber of Horrors rolls into town, carrying the skeleton of Dracula inside. The other monsters are shown much later, in a frozen limbo, in a marvelous scene inside an icy cavern.

Also noteworthy are the unusually complex relationships between the characters, especially a love triangle with the hunchback, a circus dancer, and the Wolf Man. And with the help of a brisk running time, this not only strengthened the *Frankenstein* franchise, but also proved that classic monsters could work together in a film.

HOUSE ON HAUNTED HILL (1959)

Director: William Castle
Cast: Vincent Price, Carol Ohmart, Richard Long, Alan Marshal, Carolyn Craig, Elisha Cook
Length: 75 minutes
Rating: Not Rated

Synopsis: An eccentric, sardonic millionaire invites five seemingly random people for a party in a mansion with a murderous past. He promises to give $10,000 to whoever can survive the night.

As gimmick-maestro William Castle's *House on Haunted Hill* opens, we just stare at a black screen as a chorus of scary sounds sets the mood: piercing screams, ghostly moans, maniacal laughter, rattling chains, creaking doors, etc. Soon after, the always-commanding Vincent Price stares at us and invites us to a party with food, drinks, ghosts, and perhaps even a few murders. The house contains secret passageways, ceilings that drip blood, severed heads kept in storage, chandeliers that have a tendency to fall, an organ that plays by itself, and even an acid-filled pit. At one point, one of the party guests has just become separated from the rest of the group. She wanders aimlessly through the creepy old house with only a flickering candle to guide her way. She inspects the walls carefully, and then something happens that ranks among the most bloodcurdling moments in film history, sure to send the Tingler down your spine. Another moment that will give you that ultimate Halloween rush is when the Vincent Price skeleton says "Come with me, murderess, come with me" as it places its phalanges against the screaming woman, paralyzed with fear.

Price with his devilish charm and Carol Ohmart in full femme-fatale mode are wickedly good as a

Press kit photo for *House on Haunted Hill* (1959). Allied Artists Pictures.

married couple whose relationship has all come down to who can out-scheme the other. Also impressive is Carolyn Craig as the target for many of the house's most-heinous oddities—the poor dear sees one mentally traumatizing thing after another, so she spends a significant amount of time screaming her lungs out. We are tempted to join in when we realize how unsatisfying the ending is, but up until then, the film has worked on every level.

Audiences in 1959 were lucky enough to witness one of Castle's most interesting gimmicks: "The Emergo." A pulley system was constructed in theaters that allowed a plastic skeleton to soar over the crowd at a key moment in the film. This allegedly worked well until boys decided to bring their slingshots to theaters to attack the poor defenseless skeleton!

HUMANOIDS FROM THE DEEP (1980)

🎬 **Director:** Barbara Peeters
⭐ **Cast:** Doug McClure, Ann Turkel, Vic Morrow, Cindy Weintraub, Anthony Pena
🎞 **Length:** 80 minutes
👤 **Rating:** R

🗑 **Synopsis:** A small fishing village is terrorized when scientific experiments result in a violent breed of half-men, half-fish who have an insatiable appetite for buxom young women.

Blood, boobs, and beers are everywhere in this Roger Cormon-produced exploitation cult hit where, once again, scientific experiments result in mutant freaks preying on a small town. Before it turns into a gory and perverted update on *The Creature from the Black Lagoon*, the picture starts with an incredibly well-staged salmon fishing misadventure where a little boy gets gobbled up by fish monsters as hapless adults watch in horror. You just know a movie means business when the monsters have lots of fresh meat to choose from, including a verbally abusive, piece-of-scum father, and they sink their teeth into the sweet, innocent child instead. The movie takes on a nasty, somewhat frustrating tone when the next couple of victims are even more sympathetic and when an upsetting racism angle is introduced; however, it

doesn't take long until you're once again laughing and munching on candy without a care in the world.

From the goofy Tea Party–like caricatures that populate this small town to the horny teen that uses his ventriloquism skills to get his ladies in the mood, *Humanoids from the Deep* is heavy on the comedy and most of it works quite well. Also working quite well are the many ample bosoms that constantly struggle to stay confined to their tiny bikini tops (as the camera lingers hungrily on them), a delicacy that attracts the humanoids just as much as the horny teens. But while the Black Lagoon's creature retained a tragic forlornness to his female human attraction, the humanoids are unrestrained, animalistic, and unwilling to take it slow.

The movie isn't all b-movie campiness, as director Barbara Peeters demonstrates real skill behind the camera and gives us one of the most adrenaline-heavy climaxes in horror history—seriously, what better place for an attack of this magnitude than at a carnival? If only more Halloweens could involve sea humanoids ravaging in a blood-soaked orgy atop a moving carousel, then the world would be a much better place.

IDLE HANDS (1999)

🎬 **Director:** Rodman Flender
⭐ **Cast:** Devon Sawa, Seth Green, Elden Henson, Jessica Alba, Vivica A. Fox, Jack Noseworthy
🎞 **Length:** 90 minutes
👤 **Rating:** R

🗑 **Synopsis:** A teenaged pothead discovers that he is the maniac who has been killing people all over town when his devil-possessed right hand hacks up his parents and best friends. This makes things complicated when the girl of his dreams finally starts to notice him.

We horror fans hold films like *Evil Dead 2*, *Re-Animator*, and *The Return of the Living Dead* on a special kind of pedestal because it's such a rarity to find a film capable of scaring us silly while also provoking giggles loud

enough to startle pets and neighbors. To find just the right meaty area of comedy and horror is a delicate dance and nine times out of ten, the results are disjointed and tone-deaf. That's why it's so disheartening when a horror-comedy comes along that knocks everything out of the park, only to be greeted by empty theaters and little fanfare. Much like the equally-underappreciated *Slither*, the highly-ambitious *Idle Hands* serves up the most outlandish of situations, yet takes itself just serious enough to keep us on edge and make us honestly care about what happens to its characters. Just after the first few seconds of the kickass title sequence you can tell that this movie means business, and the opening

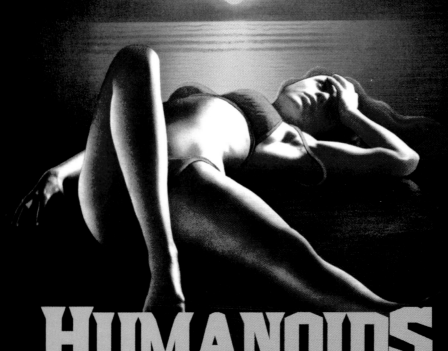

VIC MORROW
DOUG McCLURE

HUMANOIDS
FROM THE DEEP

THEY'RE NOT HUMAN. BUT THEY HUNT HUMAN WOMEN
NOT FOR KILLING. FOR MATING.

New Horizon's Roger Corman Classics DVD cover for *Humanoids from the Deep* (1980).

scene—featuring a rare un-comedic appearance by the great Fred Willard—is so full of shocks and suspense that you wonder if the filmmakers might have thrown all their eggs into one basket. But rest assured because the film never loses its incredible pace or subversive attitude.

Devon Sawa plays a likeable stoner who takes way too long to notice that he has been possessed, with all of the evil confined to one body part, resulting in first-rate physical comedy routines and a hilariously distracting make-out session with Jessica Alba. His best friends also smoke a tremendous amount of weed to the point where they have a "no hard feelings" reaction to getting impaled and decapitated. You'll also see a cat licking a detached eyeball, a severed head finishing a sentence post-decapitation, a knitting needle stabbing through a

man's ear and out the other, a hand being chopped off, a punk-rock singer (played by Dexter from The Offspring) getting scalped so severely that his brains are exposed, another head splattering against a window, and the kind of humongous human-blending electrical fan that only seems to exist in fictional schools. Despite all of this, you will probably still have to look in the comedy section to find this in video stores, a testament to the poor treatment from its marketing team. But perhaps the worst omen for the film came in the form of the Columbine Massacre, which not only postponed its release date to show sensitivity towards the victims, but also limited an audience craving a story in which a teenager goes on a killing spree.

If it's 4:20 in October and you want to shout at the devil, you really can't do much better than *Idle Hands*.

IN THE MOUTH OF MADNESS (1994)

Director: John Carpenter
Cast: Sam Neill, Julie Carmen, Jürgen Prochnow, David Warner, John Glover, Charlton Heston
Length: 95 minutes
Rating: R

Synopsis: Insurance investigator John Trent is hired to look into the strange disappearance of Sutter Kane, an enormously popular writer whose horror novels are believed to have caused an epidemic of paranoid schizophrenia among his less stable readers. While driving through New Hampshire, Trent finds himself stuck in Hobbs' End, a fictionalized town in Kane's latest book where monsters lurk everywhere and nothing is what it seems.

It has become notoriously difficult to translate the literature of H.P. Lovecraft onto the big screen, so John Carpenter did not receive enough credit with what he accomplished here. While not based on any specific Lovecraft tale, *In the Mouth of Madness* manages to visualize the mood, atmosphere, and hushed apocalyptic doom that make the literature so haunting and visceral, while also making many references to specific stories of his and using direct quotes. It is a dreary and complicated film with a nonlinear structure and an unsteady line between reality and fantasy, which might be too confusing for a Halloween flick if it wasn't so engrossing and downright bloodcurdling. Horror films typically use every level of the fright-o-meter to slowly build tension and make the viewers increasingly vulnerable to the biggest chills, but with this project, Carpenter

Les Fiches de Monsieur Cinema card for *In the Mouth of Madness* (1994).

only concerns himself with the highest point in the meter, which results in so many moments of paralyzing fear, it might be hard to catch your breath.

There is no question who the character of Sutter Kane is based on. Carpenter also delves into Stephen King territory by symbolizing the apocalypse and human extinction in the form of a small ghost town in New England.

Sam Neill gives a great performance and, unlike Jack Nicholson in *The Shining*, doesn't succumb to insanity too quickly. Horror vet David Warner is also in fine form, and that's no surprise considering his previous experience with Lovecraftian mythos (*Necronomicon*, *The Unnamable II: The Statement of Randolph Carter*). Also look for the late, great actress Frances Bay (*Blue Velvet*, *Happy Gilmour*), who doesn't exactly play the sweet old granny that she was known for.

As *In the Mouth of Madness* gets weirder and weirder, it raises more philosophical questions like "are we mere fragments of a higher power's imagination?" or "does art imitate life or does life imitate art?" but it provides no easy answers. It doesn't let you off the hook either, because the ending is both ambiguous and maddening. Then the wildly out of place '80s metal song that plays over the ending credits disorients you even more. It is a thinking man's horror film, but it's also for anybody who simply enjoys a good scare.

INSIDIOUS(2010)

Director: James Wan
Cast: Rose Byrne, Patrick Wilson, Lin Shaye, Barbara Hershey, Ty Simpkins
Length: 103 minutes
Rating: PG-13

Synopsis: Soon after a family of five moves into a new house, the oldest son slips into a coma and the mother experiences terrifying visions. Believing the house is haunted, they once again move, but the problems follow, and they learn that there is a lot more to their son's condition than just a coma.

Director James Wan and writer Leigh Wannell took the horror genre by storm in 2004 with their indie hit *Saw*, which spawned several (mostly unnecessary) sequels and countless torture-porn imitators. They teamed up again for *Dead Silence*, an admirable but flawed murder mystery involving the ghost of a murdered ventriloquist. When they decided to tackle the haunted house subgenre with *Insidious*, these two young men really proved that they are the real deal, and the horror community will no doubt be salivating over their future projects for quite some time.

The past several years have been a cynical time for old-school horror fans; Hollywood only seems concerned with either ruthlessly remaking and butchering our beloved classics or spewing out sequels to franchises that have long overstayed their welcome. Wan and Wannell are obviously diehard fans of the genre and with *Insidious*, they gave horror fans a real gift: an original haunted house-supernatural flick that deserves to go down as one of the scariest motion pictures of all time.

On Halloween night, you need a good scare, and no film in the past ten years except for Neil Marshall's blood-soaked nightmare in the caves of hell, *The Descent,* can rival *Insidious* in terms of sheer spine-tingling terror. You won't find any false scares here—no shrieking cats being thrown into the frame or clichéd tricks with mirrors—because every single spook is handled with so much precision and expertise that when discussing the movie afterwards with your friends, you will each have a different take on the scariest moment. The ghost standing behind the curtains in the baby's room, the black-veiled hag who has haunted Patrick Wilson's character since childhood, the demon pacing back and forth on the balcony, the creepy voice in the baby monitor, the little boy dancing to Tiny Tim's "Tiptoe Through the Tulips" (a song you will never be able to hear again without getting chills), the smiling mannequin family in The Further, the fire-faced apparition suddenly appearing at the kitchen table, and several other moments will do wonders to your heart rate. *Insidious* also works so well for a Halloween movie because in its third act, where a devoted father attempts to astro-project to a netherworld to rescue his comatose son, you feel like you are wandering through one of the trippiest haunted houses ever, filled with fog, endless pools of darkness, and every now and then, insanely horrifying images.

However, these supremely executed scares wouldn't be nearly as powerful had it not been for the knockout performances by the entire cast, especially Rose Byrne, who at one point begins to wonder if the

FROM THE WRITER AND DIRECTOR OF **SAW**
AND THE PRODUCERS OF **PARANORMAL ACTIVITY**

THE FURTHER YOU TRAVEL, THE DARKER IT GETS.

A JAMES WAN FILM

Poster for *Insidious* (2010). FilmDistrict.

universe is doing whatever it can to mentally destroy her. These are not your typical haunted house movie characters whose troubles would be over if they only had the common sense to get the hell out; rather, this is an intelligent, loving, and extremely sympathetic family you can relate to throughout the film.

Much like *1408*, this is an atmospheric and classy thriller that earned huge box office success and positive reviews, proving once again that a horror movie does not need violence, gore, or an R-rating to be a classic.

Even though *Insidious* ended on such a perfectly heart-stopping note, James Wan and Leigh Whannell delved deeper into The Further for *Insidious: Chapter 2*, which appropriately hit theaters on Friday the 13th of 2013 and surpassed another fantastic supernatural film, *The Exorcism of Emily Rose,* for the highest September opening for a horror film. It answered many of the questions proposed from the original and while it's not as frightening, *Chapter 2* is a hell of an entertaining sequel.

Insidious: Chapter 2 reunites the entire cast (fortunately the two Lambert boys don't seem to have aged a day in three years) for events that take place directly after Renai's upsetting discovery of a certain photograph, a corpse, and a husband that doesn't seem quite like himself. There were a few goofy choices, like dubbing in Lin Shaye's voice for flashback scenes and having a paranormal expert rely on Boggle™ techniques, and the comic relief of Specs and Tucker is amped up a little, but none of that interferes with the story or lessens the impact of the biggest scares: an army of demons summoned beside Dalton's bed, a demented hospital patient with grabby hands, and the revelation that Lorraine was stuck in an elevator with a recently deceased. Instead of the Darth Maul fire-faced demon (one of the only things that didn't quite work from the original), here we get something much more intimidating: a psycho bitch whose parenting techniques rival *Carrie*'s mom, and who has a clever connection with the old hag in black. But by far the film's biggest strength is Patrick Wilson's slow and fascinating deterioration into totally unhinged, Jack Nicholson-in-*The-Shining* level of madness.

INVASION OF THE BODY SNATCHERS (1956)

Director: Don Siegel
Cast: Kevin McCarthy, Dana Wynter, Larry Gates, Carolyn Jones, King Donovan, Virginia Christine
Length: 80 minutes
Rating: Not Rated

Synopsis: Seeds drifting through space take root in a quiet town in California, producing pods that duplicate the residents and take over their bodies while they sleep. When the town's doctor discovers that he could be the last citizen unchanged, he attempts to warn the neighboring towns before the alien race completely takes over.

It seems like an ordinary day for a small town doctor until a young woman reports that her uncle is no longer her uncle and a little boy is certain that his mother is no longer his mother. Adding to his confusion are numerous patients who made urgent appointments but then canceled with no explanation. When he is called by a friend who discovers a body in his home that looks human but has no defining features like fingerprints or hair, Dr. Bennell suspects that these bizarre occurrences reflect a much larger problem than what a psychiatrist previously described as mass hysteria caused by worrying about what is going on in the world.

Whether you choose to delve into the script's allegorical ambiguity or just take it at face value, *Invasion of the Body Snatchers* is a thoughtful, taut, and well-crafted adaptation of Jack Finney's novel. It teases with the notion of what life would be like without love, emotions, or individuality. One by one, Dr. Bennell loses his close friends to the aliens that strip away their identities, but retain their appearances, memories, and voices. They tell him in monotonous dialect that they were wrong for fearing this inevitable takeover, and warn him that it is only a matter of time before he falls asleep and surrenders to the pod that is ready to take over his body. Don Siegel directs with confidence and throws suspense and intrigue into each scene. When Bennell and his love interest have to walk the streets pretending to be among the clones, you will most likely be too spellbound to oblige the interrupting trick-or-treaters.

The studio executives chose to bookend the film with scenes of Bennell telling his harrowing story to a team of shrinks in order to bring in a glimmer of hope. This was a wrong move, but Siegel's film is so harrowing it would have taken a lot more than wimpy executives to weaken it.

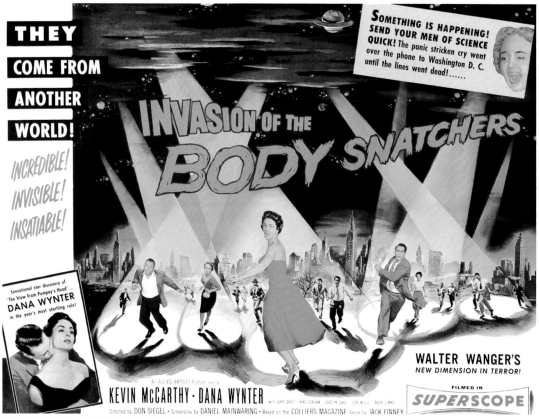

Lobby card for *Invasion of the Body Snatchers* (1956). Allied Artists Pictures.

INVASION OF THE BODY SNATCHERS (1978)

Director: Philip Kaufman
Cast: Donald Sutherland, Brooke Adams, Leonard Nimoy, Jeff Goldblum, Veronica Cartwright
Length: 115 minutes
Rating: PG

Synopsis: Wispy alien spores travel through space and land in San Francisco. Soon after, frantic residents are complaining that their loved ones haven't been themselves lately. When a health inspector catches a glimpse of pod creatures that resemble his friends, he discovers that cloning has spread throughout his city, and he has no way of knowing who he can trust.

Even with its star-studded cast, it would be easy to overlook this film while browsing through video stores because it is but one of several remakes of Don Siegel's sci-fi classic. Those willing to give it a chance will be relieved by how it not only catches up to advanced technology and special effects like most remakes do, but how it also expands on ideas and scenarios implied by the original. The remake shifts the action into a large city, but it still preserves the same claustrophobic dread and allegorical interpretations, as well as the same resonating paranoia that will have you cautious the next time you pass a stranger on the street. Those in love with the original will also enjoy a cameo from Kevin McCarthy in which he reenacts the fanatical "You're next!" scene.

Philip Kaufman seduces us into the film and constantly has us guessing which characters have already been duplicated. Adding to the tension are subtle touches, such as a cracked windshield and prolonged telephone busy signals that disorient the viewers. Donald Sutherland gives one of his best performances as Matthew Bennell, who, even in the most hopeless, sleep-deprived scenarios, refuses to let go of his personality and allow an emotionless minion to masquerade forever in his skin.

The gloriously icky special effects come into play when a character literally crumbles to pieces, when a group of undefined bodies metamorphose around a sleeping Bennell, and when a clone is viciously impaled by a spade.

Since this film is so disciplined and powerfully executed, it is surprising when it contains one of the goofiest, most out-of-place sight gags ever caught on celluloid. Just when we are trapped in a vortex of fear, Kaufman breaks the mood by showing a half-man/half-dog crawling towards our heroes as banjo music fills the soundtrack. What the hell?

Not only is Kaufman's *Invasion of the Body Snatchers* a contender for greatest remake, but also for the most chilling ending in a horror film.

JACK-O (1995)

Director: Steve Latshaw
Cast: Linnea Quigley, Maddisen Krown, Gary Doles, Ryan Latshaw, Catherine Walsh
Length: 88 minutes
Rating: R

Synopsis: Three teen delinquents explore a cemetery on Halloween and disturb the grave of a warlock who was murdered a long time ago, so of course he rises from the grave as a towering pumpkin-headed demon to get revenge. As the nursery rhyme goes, "Mr. Jack will break your back, cut off your head with a whack, whack, whack. The pumpkin man will steal your soul, snap it up, and swallow it whole."

The father in this so-bad-it's-good movie tells the babysitter that working on his annual haunted garage for the trick-or-treaters helps keep him young, and I have a feeling watching movies like *Jack-O* on Halloween might do the same for me. There's something about these cheesy, horribly-acted, low-budgeted Ed Wood-ish thrillers that is healthy for the heart, and an occasional dose is even more beneficial than vitamins.

It not only stars scream queen Linnea Quigley, who is introduced with an obligatory shower scene, but it brings two famous actors back from the grave to earn two final film credits by using previously unseen stock footage of John Carradine and Cameron Mitchell, playing a warlock and a creature feature TV host, respectively. Normally I would have qualms about criticizing the acting ability of a little kid,

but it becomes easier after learning that he's the son of the director. He plays the fifth generation descendent of the man who killed the warlock, and in the capricious rules of *Jack-O*, is the only one that can put the pumpkin demon to rest for good. You and your friends will be howling in laughter when you see how he reacts as Jack-O tries to bury him alive! Even though he looks bored out of his mind in every scene, we'll still root for any kid that wears a Jason mask like a hat during Halloween day, and at night protects his precious bag of candy even as he's being chased around the neighborhood by a scythe-swinging willow-the-wisp.

Despite the many shortcomings, this ends up being one of the most Halloween-friendly horror movies you'll ever see, thanks to scenes involving trick-or-treating, horror movie marathons, spook houses, and a creature with a glowing pumpkin as a head (only looking scary when shrouded in storm clouds and fog). There's even some excellent comic relief at the expense of a couple who spend their Halloween night watching a Rush Limbaugh/Glenn Beck–type analog and berating the trick-or-treaters for expecting their free handouts. While everyone else dies at the slice of a scythe, this woman dies while preparing a slice of toast—being electrocuted until she turns into a skeleton. I recommend checking out the 10th anniversary DVD because it also contains one of the most interesting commentary tracks you'll ever hear.

American Home Entertainment VHS cover for *Jack-O* (1995).

KENNY & COMPANY (1976)

Director: Don Coscarelli
Cast: Dan McCann, A. Michael Baldwin, Jeff Roth, Reggie Bannister
Length: 90 minutes
Rating: PG

Synopsis: A 12-year-old boy learns many lessons while preparing for Halloween, as he deals with a neighborhood bully, his first school crush, and the loss of his dog. But on Halloween night, he sets his problems aside and goes on a spooky adventure with his friends.

John Carpenter gets all the credit for immortalizing our favorite holiday on the big screen, but another master of horror attempted this a couple of years prior, but unfortunately his Halloween-themed movie received only a couple of screenings and spent decades in total obscurity until Anchor Bay dug it up and finally gave it the DVD release it deserved. If you want a nostalgic family film that will transport you right back to your childhood, or if you want to experience the launching pad to *Phantasm*, then devote some October time to this early Don Coscarelli movie, which even starts off with an animated jack-o'-lantern title sequence. There are various Coscarellis all over the credits because, with such a miniscule budget, the writer/director/editor/cinematographer had to enlist his family for help and even shot several scenes in the family home.

At only 21 years of age, he could still vividly recall what it was like to be a kid so he successfully fills *Kenny & Company* with little slices of life from a child's perspective, and mostly ignores a plot-driven narrative. There are isolated scenes of Kenny and friends prank calling, petting the family dog while laying on the grass watching the clouds, skateboarding down streets where the danger is not cars but a neighborhood bully, eating snow cones, making a dummy to place in the middle of streets, and looking for a toy to bring to a birthday party, but all of these events encompass the exciting three day stretch before Halloween night, when a child's imagination and energy level peaks. After about an hour, it's time for the three boys to show off their costumes (which they have already tried on a couple of times, like most kids do) and run into the night where an adventure devoid of parents and responsibilities awaits them. The most interesting of the three costumes belongs to the title character, a homemade bear outfit that people keep mistaking for other animals; there is even a point-of-view shot which reminds us how much louder breathing is under a mask. Armed with weapons that make them feel braver, they go trick-or-treating and eventually find that special house in the neighborhood with an impressive garage of horrors. When Coscarelli saw how audiences reacted to this scene with a collective shriek, he realized how much fun it was to frighten people, so he decided to go a few steps further with *Phantasm*. According to the commentary track on the DVD, the original plan for a follow-up was going to be *Something Wicked This Way Comes* (which would have also starred Michael Baldwin and Dan McCann), but they were unable to acquire the rights.

For *Phantasm* fans, it's a real treat to see Michael Baldwin and Reggie Bannister together in an innocent classroom setting where they just have to dodge spitballs instead of brainsuckers. Good ole Reggie is as loveable as ever playing what Kenny described as the best teacher he's ever had, someone who can relate to children and who even plays football with them during recess. *Kenny & Company* is light-hearted, breezy, and so damn sweet, but it does take some unexpected turns when 12-year-old Kenny has to learn about death—everyone who had a pet as a child should prepare to get a little misty-eyed. The gorgeous flower power soundtrack also adds a layer of sadness throughout the movie, so it's probably best to watch this in the weeks leading up to Halloween instead of on the day itself.

KILLER KLOWNS FROM OUTER SPACE (1988)

Director: Stephen Chiodo
Cast: Grant Cramer, Suzanne Snyder, John Vernon, Royal Dano, John Allen Nelson
Length: 86 minutes
Rating: PG-13

Synopsis: A spaceship lands in Santa Cruz, carrying mutant clowns intent on capturing humans. With the help of the only police officer that believes him, a teenager enters their lair in hopes of rescuing his abducted girlfriend.

C'mon, everyone needs a little killer clowns from outer space in their lives at some point—it's a wonderful visual that immediately excites the imagination. Director and co-writer Stephen Chiodo—who insists that no drugs were involved in the making of the movie—got the idea when thinking how terrifying it would be to drive at night, look over, and see a clown staring back at you because nothing is more alarming than seeing a clown somewhere it shouldn't be. The movie's execution isn't quite as effective as its concept; it's just another brainless goofy spoof on '50s sci-fi flicks, but it is worth recommending for its lightning quick pace, witty characters, bizarre sets, and good uses of pie-throwing and shadow puppets. The clowns make decent baddies simply because they are so ugly and are able to show a malevolent side to popcorn and cotton candy. There is even a cotton candy cocoon clearly inspired by *Invasion of the Body Snatchers*!

As you would surely surmise from the title, the characters in this movie are about as bright as a burnt-out marquee, and would seem right at home in a *Police Academy* film. Two guys are so one-dimensional that all of their lines and actions revolve around their love of ice cream. The best thing this film has going for it is the awesome set piece of the circus tent–shaped spaceship. Inside, you'll find revolving doors, bright colors, interesting decorations like candy cane-striped poles, and a funhouse-like atmosphere. To see the protagonists wander deeper and deeper, only to run into "another door!" and eventually, the leader of the clowns, is engaging. Until every town has its own *Killer Klowns from Outer Space*–inspired haunted house, this movie, flawed as it is, fills a void. A 3-D sequel has been planned for many years by the Chiodo brothers but frustratingly they haven't found studio support despite the original's long-lasting popularity on DVD. It would look a lot more like *Jaws 3-D* than *Avatar*, but it would almost guarantee a good time at the movies!

LEMORA: A CHILD'S TALE OF THE SUPERNATURAL (1975)

Director: Richard Blackburn
Cast: Cheryl Smith, Lesley Gilb, Richard Blackburn, William Whitton, Maxine Ballantyne, Hy Pyke
Length: 113 minutes
Rating: PG

Synopsis: A female vampire uses an infamous gangster as a pawn to lure his angelic, innocent daughter to her lair. The girl is then transferred to a nightmarish world in order to see her father one last time.

Stick it to the Catholic League of Decency, who gave this vampire cult classic the harsh Condemned rating, and spend a chilly October night with Lemora. The repressed sexuality and religious hypocrisy that fuses through this Southern Gothic, Prohibition-era retelling of *Little Red Riding Hood* was obviously too much for them to handle, and as a result the film received the most limited of distribution.

Bravely veering into taboo subjects like lesbianism and pedophilia, it does a magnificent job of conveying loss of innocence as the porcelain girl, named Lila, temporarily leaves the constant comfort of her lifelong church for a quest of self-discovery. As she enters the outside world for the first time, the grownups all breathe down her neck, especially the older men who gawk at her with sexual predation. In the film's best scene—a recipe of Lovecraftian elements—she's the sole passenger on a train that aimlessly drifts through an enchanted forest inhabited by snarling, fanged brutes. If only more haunted hayrides could be this stimulating. She is on her way to the mysterious town of Astaroth (named after a Crowned Prince of Hell in demonology) to see her injured father but learns that he is being held captive by a seductive vampiress.

The film unfolds like the trippiest of fairy tales, where all traces of convention and logic concede to atmospheric visuals and well-crafted scares. The unearthly chuckling from Lemora's freaky children and the old hag's arcane song to Lila will simultaneously inspire a chill and make you wonder what the hell is going on.

MAY (2002)

Director: Lucky McKee
Cast: Angela Bettis, Jeremy Sisto, Anna Faris, James Duval, Nichole Hiltz
Length: 93 minutes
Rating: R

Synopsis: May is a shy, awkward, and unstable young woman who has been lonely all of her life. When her search for a perfect friend goes terribly wrong, she decides to create a perfect friend by sewing together her favorite body parts from those who have wronged her.

Let's face it, not all Halloweens can be winners. Perhaps your friends ditched you at the last minute, right around the time neighborhood hoodlums were destroying the jack-o'-lanterns you slaved over. Or maybe you're just simply under the weather at the most inconvenient of times. After all, the month-long anticipation of Halloween night brings almost impossibly high expectations. If, by some unfortunate chance, you find yourself in a melancholy mood and want a film that understands that not every Halloween can be all fun and games, then you should befriend *May*. It will evoke a strong, contemplative reaction because it is uncompromising in its weirdness, and it's like nothing you have seen before. It's the kind of movie that ends with a silent and stunned audience, all trying to comprehend what they have just seen. Even if you aren't sure if you liked it, it nestles in your memory for days and slowly but surely, earns your appreciation.

The film has been compared to *Carrie* because of the uncanny similarities between the title characters (the enormously talented Angela Bettis even starred in a made-for-TV remake). They have both been social outcasts all of their lives—strange, morbid, and pathetically sympathetic. They both face disappointment and heartache every day, until one tragic circumstance pushes them over the edge. *May* has also been compared to *Frankenstein* because of the gruesome procedure that May goes through to make a friend who won't betray her.

Bettis's performance as the veterinary surgical technician with some of the poorest social skills ever is one of a kind, and she and director Lucky McKee would work together again in *The Woman, Roman,* and *The Masters of Horror* episode "Sick Girl." The always-reliable Jeremy Sisto is also wonderful as her morbid dream boy who at first is intrigued by her weirdness (May has a great reaction when she watches his hilariously gory student film), but eventually realizes that her elevator doesn't go all the way to the top.

Usually, a film this melancholy and low-key wouldn't be at all conducive for Halloween, but its third act takes place on Halloween night and it really delivers the festivities. And Lucky McKee deserves lots of praise because there aren't many filmmakers that could make an ending like *that* work. His follow-up feature, the witchcraft-laden *The Woods,* is another quiet film that bares an effective balance of beauty and blood.

THE MIDNIGHT HOUR (1985)

☗ **Director:** Jack Bender
★ **Cast:** Lee Montgomery, Jonna Lee, Shari Belafonte, LeVar Burton, Cindy Morgan, Jonelle Allen
⊛ **Length:** 94 minutes
⚑ **Rating:** Not Rated

🎃 **Synopsis:** Before attending a Halloween party, a group of teenagers break into Pitchford Cove Witchcraft Museum and recite a spell that brings the dead back to life. Later in the night, while his friends are becoming transformed into vampires, werewolves, and zombies, bookworm Phil falls in love with a cheerleader who passed away in the 1950s.

Oct. 26–Nov.1 1985 *TV Guide* ad for *The Midnight Hour* (1985).

The teenagers in this made-for-TV movie love Halloween and know how to make the most out of it. In the final period of the school day, they play hangman on the chalkboard with puzzles like "Ghouls just want to have fun," and one of them presents a report to the class about the origins of the holiday. In order to get the best possible costumes, they resort to sneaking into a witchcraft museum to borrow things for the night. Discovering that they still have plenty of time before the party, they immediately journey to a cemetery. These are the kind of people you would be wise to befriend around the time the leaves begin to fall. Despite their unlawful shenanigans, they really aren't the loud, obnoxious imbeciles that we usually see in '80s Halloween-themed thrillers. *The Midnight Hour* is sweet-natured and wholesome in how it presents a likeable group of suburban friends so eclectic they include the school jock, the ultra-dweeb, and African-Americans.

Among the many little touches that help make this such an outstanding film for Halloween night are a newspaper boy delivering his papers wearing a skeleton mask, a teenager dressed as a vampire scaring two little girls just because he can, a boy dressed as a mummy dousing himself with ketchup and eggs for a more disgusting look, and another party-goer constantly scratching his head due to his itchy wig. Whereas most TV movies play it safe to reach a specific demographic, director Jack Bender reaches deep into his bag of treats and presents something tasty for everyone. You will see a cheerleader zombie whose wild ways forlornly hint about how she died, a vampire bite that lasts long enough for multiple bottles of red wine to spill, a spellbinding zombie resurrection that actually begins inside their coffins, a sex-starved partier being seduced by his girlfriend's voodoo-vixen ancestor, a recently demonized alcoholic father (played by *Inva-*

sion of the Body Snatchers star Kevin McCarthy) trying to gobble up his son, an endearing romance between a loner and the aforementioned cheerleader zombie, a hilarious musical number reminiscent of "Thriller," werewolves roaming suburban streets, a thirsty midget zombie diving into a punchbowl, ingenious Halloween costumes, a couple trapped in a crypt, etc.

Anyone who was elated with *Donnie Darko*'s soundtrack might be tempted to sing along to the impressive assortment of pop numbers that fit perfectly with Bender's innocent, whimsical tone. Brad Fiedel, who wrote such a beautiful score for *Fright Night* (released the same year,) also contributes to the superb soundtrack.

Jonna Lee and Lee Montgomery lead the strong cast as doomed lovers whose romance gets increasingly complicated and complex as the sun prepares to welcome November. It certainly isn't the most accessible movie to rent, but once Phil's 1956 Cadillac exits the cemetery gates, prompting the ending credits to fall on a full moon, you'll realize it was well worth the time and effort spent to track it down.

MONSTER HOUSE (2006)

Director: Gil Kenan
Cast: Mitchel Musso, Sam Lerner, Spencer Locke, Steve Buscemi, Maggie Gyllenhaal, Jason Lee
Length: 91 minutes
Rating: PG

Synopsis: Three kids discover that the creepy old house in their neighborhood is actually alive, and will gobble up anything and anyone that gets too close. That puts the whole town in danger because Halloween is approaching, and the house seems hungry for some trick-or-treaters.

Poster for Monster House (2006). Columbia Pictures.

Here is an original, twisted fable that deserves to be partnered with *The Nightmare Before Christmas* for an ultimate, all-ages Halloween double-feature. Using a process called "performance capture," the cast members had to act out every scene with approximately 150 markers attached to their faces and bodies; these dots were able to record nuances of the actors' facial expressions and body movements. There were about 200 different cameras recording the actions, allowing this digitized information to be converted to 3-D animation. This new form of animation (which gained attention with producer Robert Zemeckis's own creepy masterpiece, 2004's *The Polar Express*) obviously requires much more work from the actors, who in traditional animated films just had to sit comfortably in a private booth and read into a microphone. And right away we can tell that this is one good looking movie, the kind that should be watched in theaters and big screen televisions and not on airplanes or laptops. *Monster House* opens with an arresting tracking shot that follows a leaf's journey as it breaks off its branch and sways freely in the wind until it's caught in the wheel of a girl's tricycle. From there, we learn what happens when mean old Mr. Nebbercracker catches you standing on his lawn.

Kids who were lucky enough to have a mysterious house in their neighborhood will identify the most with this story. The house could have had a dark past or a frightening owner who was rumored to be a witch, or maybe it just looked uninviting and freakishly out of place. This was the house that kids dared each other to approach on Halloween, even if just to ding-dong-ditch; by escaping unharmed, you would be idolized by your peers. But only the bravest or dumbest of kids would ever ding-dong-ditch the Monster House, a ferocious beast that lures children inside by presenting their favorite childhood toys that were long ago snatched away by the house's owner.

This film knows a lot about what it was like to be a child and it may remind you of getting in trouble for not calling home when you were staying over at a friend's house, of having power struggles against authoritative babysitters, of using star-69 to catch prank-callers, debating over who called first dibs over a girl, and having the ultimate thrill as you sneak out of the house at night.

Most likely set in the early '80s, *Monster House* seems more targeted toward young adults than to children. Those under seven years old might be too frightened when the house stalks its victims or when the character of D.J. trips and lands directly on top of an obese corpse. There is also some dialogue pertaining to a goth babysitter being a prude and a boy blaming his insecurities on puberty. But there is also much warmth and tenderness to this story, even in a hilarious moment where the character of Chowder affectionately whispers, "Don't be scared. That's not how I trained you. I love you vacuum cleaner dummy" as he pushes the bait closer to the house in an ill-conceived plan to drug the house.

The film also includes the voices of Kathleen Turner, Fred Willard, Catherine O'Hara, Kevin James, Jon Heder, and Nick Cannon (who scores big laughs as an overzealous rookie cop).

93

THE MONSTER SQUAD (1987)

Director: Fred Dekker
Cast: Andre Gower, Robby Kiger, Brent Chalem, Duncan Regehr, Stephen Macht, Tom Noonan
Length: 82 minutes
Rating: PG-13

Synopsis: Count Dracula arrives in a small town to gain possession of an amulet that will grant him world domination. For backup, he brings along Frankenstein's monster, the Mummy, the Creature from the Black Lagoon, and the Wolf Man. All goes well for them until a group of horror-loving kids called the Monster Squad discovers their evil scheme.

As summer was inevitably surrendering the limelight to autumn in 1987, I was filled to the brim with the excitement of seeing a scary movie in a theater for the first time. I stared at a promotional ad of a group of older kids propped against a car, with a backdrop consisting of Universal's most famous monsters like Dracula, Frankenstein, and The Mummy. They didn't totally resemble the monsters that I had seen from the black and white movies—they looked far more hideous and dangerous. In the theater, every deformity or fang would be so much larger than how it appeared on TV screens, the screams and scary music louder than any TV was capable of. But I knew I was ready for the big leagues, or at least one level beyond *Ghostbusters* and *Gremlins*, because I felt I had horror cinema in my blood, even at seven years old. My mom was less confident as she had to explain to me what a PG-13 rating meant. While at the theater, it was evident I wasn't quite ready to take the training wheels off, and I had to leave *The Monster Squad* after a mere 10 minutes because it was either too intense or just too loud. Fortunately, the same theater was showing an animated *Snow White* movie that alleviated all traces of trauma. While I am embarrassed to admit I couldn't sit through *The Monster Squad*, I feel so proud and privileged that it was my introduction to horror in a big scary movie theater because subsequent viewings taught me that this was a very special film.

Much like Fred Dekker's previous offering, *Night of the Creeps*, it revises classic eras of horror history and preserves the dynamics and mythology that made them so worthy of nostalgia. Dazzling effects courtesy of Stan Winston make the monsters look better than ever, but the movie still has the heart to lovingly bring back those clumsy bats that would circle around Bela Lugosi so many years ago. Also validating the film as perfect for Halloween is how it often ventures into pure '80s cheese—there is even your standard '80s montage as the kids (who moments earlier were hanging out in a tree house with a No Girls Allowed sign) prepare for battle.

One of the many great scenes takes place near the end, when Count Dracula is on a killing spree, throwing bodies around as he stalks in the vicinity of world domination. Then he spots a cute five-year-old girl, played by Ashley Bank, and slowly approaches. He gazes at her intently while reaching out to gently touch her cheek, making us wonder if Duncan Regehr's Dracula (easily one of the best Drac performances ever) is possibly as soft as Tom Noonan's Frankenstein's monster. He puts the kibosh on this odd moment of tenderness when he yells, "GIVE ME THE AMULET, YOU BITCH!!!!!" and reveals his red eyes and shark teeth. According to the DVD commentary track, the child actress asked Fred Dekker when exactly she was supposed to scream in the scene, and he said something to the effect of "Oh, you'll know."

Even though the Dustin Diamond scene was left on the cutting room floor, you still get to see plenty of Wayne from *The Wonder Years*, and he still plays a bully. Another familiar face is Jon Gries, whom many now refer to as Napoleon Dynamite's uncle, but if you're a little cooler, you'll also know him from *Fright Night Part 2*. And when the leader of the Monster Squad, who wears a t-shirt that says "Stephen King rules," receives a peculiar letter from a man named Mr. Alucard, those familiar with *Troll 2*'s goblin-filled town of Nilbog will see this "twist" coming immediately!

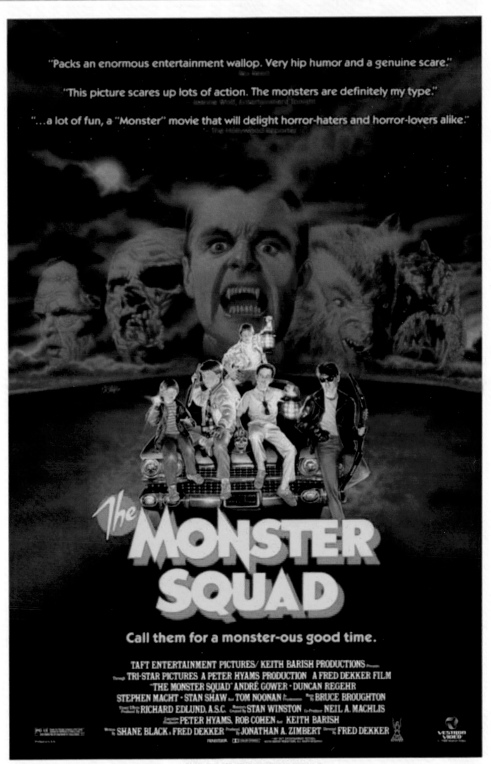

Poster for *The Monster Squad* (1987). TriStar Pictures.

NEAR DARK (1987)

Director: Kathryn Bigelow
Cast: Adrian Pasdar, Jenny Wright, Bill Paxton, Lance Henriksen, Jenette Goldstein, Tim Thomerson
Length: 93 minutes
Rating: R

Synopsis: A happy-go-lucky cowboy gives an attractive young woman a ride home, but when he asks for a kiss, he gets more than he bargained for. Once bitten, he is forced to join her gang and the insidious vampirism lifestyle as they travel through the vast Southwest deserts in search of fresh blood.

The other 1987 Hollywood vampire offering, *The Lost Boys*, made getting a lovebite from a fanged creature of the night seem like a glamorous party compared to the agony that our hero Caleb languishes in with this horror-western. On his first night as a member of the undead, he is hungry but has trouble eating a simple candy bar. He tries to go home, but he can't even sit still enough to ride the bus. He is also so sick he can barely walk. A few hours ago, he was a care-free kid with the world at his feet, but now he's stumbling through the desert, not knowing what he is or if he'll ever see his family or even another sunrise again.

Near Dark is definitely not your average vampire movie. In fact, the word "vampire" is not used once, and you won't see fangs, capes, coffins, or animal transformations. This takes the *Bonnie and Clyde* approach of enlarging your gang and traveling without a destination, stirring up trouble at every stop. Add this to lovely Southwest imagery and cold, futuristic music courtesy of Tangerine Dream and you have the kind of mood that is rare for an '80s horror flick. The material is very serious, but there are some hilarious lines like "I fought for the South—we lost" and "Those people back there, they wasn't normal. Normal folks, they don't spit out bullets when you shoot 'em, no sir."

The most emotional moments come when Caleb knows he has to kill a man who has been so friendly to him, and when Caleb's old family meets his new family after searching tirelessly for him. Now-famous director Kathryn Bigelow even manages to throw in some excessive gore, particularly during a run-in at a hick bar (where *Phantasm II* star James LeGros plays an innocent cowboy playing pool).

Harming the film are dawns that seem to come impossibly quickly and a lame ending that seems painfully inconsistent with what came before it. But overall it's an impressive reunion for Bill Paxton, Lance Henriksen, and Jenette Goldstein, who were all together one year prior in James Cameron's (who would later marry Bigelow) terrifying *Aliens*.

THE NIGHTMARE BEFORE CHRISTMAS (1993)

Director: Henry Selick
Cast: Chris Sarandon, Danny Elfman, Catherine O'Hara, William Hickey, Glenn Shadix, Ken Page
Length: 76 minutes
Rating: PG

Synopsis: Jack Skellington, the Pumpkin King of Halloweentown, is sick and tired of doing the same things every year. On a contemplative walk in the woods, he stumbles into Christmastown and experiences happiness and excitement for the first time in ages. He returns home with plans to celebrate Christmas, and even though his intentions are good, he cannot quite master the concept. Only his secret admirer, a sad girl with ominous premonitions, knows that mixing the holidays will lead to disaster.

People sometimes debate on whether this whimsical masterpiece is more suited for Halloween or Christmas, but Halloween should be the obvious choice, for the majority of the film takes place in Halloweentown, and even when the boils and ghouls of every age attempt to embrace the Christmas spirit, they fail miserably and still rely on their tendency to spook and scare.

Pushing originality and imagination to the next level, producer Tim Burton and director Henry Selick created something otherworldly, timeless, and iconic. Shot entirely with stop-motion animation over the

German lobby card for Buena Vista International's *The Nightmare Before Christmas* (1993). Singer Nina Hagen provided the voice of Sally in the German-dubbed version.

course of more than three years, *The Nightmare Before Christmas* is an orgiastic feast for the senses; your ears, eyes, and heart fall in love with every shot to the point where you might not notice you've been smiling for several minutes.

Every shot has a plethora of things going on; even on your tenth viewing, you will notice tiny things creeping their way into the corners of certain frames that you failed to detect before. What makes this such a warm, sentimental treat for all ages is how it handles Halloween and Christmas with equal reverence and internalizes what makes both holidays so magical. As far as movies for Halloween night go, it doesn't get much better than this. The residents of the surrealistic Halloweentown are all fairly grotesque-looking, but they have as much warmth and personality as the Muppets or the employees of *Monsters, Inc.*, especially when they sing songs written by Burton's partner-in-crime, Danny Elfman, who even provides Jack's singing voice (*Fright Night* star Sarandon does the speaking voice). The songs are all quirky and well-written, the best ones being

Jack's solo number, where Christmas festivities leave him baffled, and the opening anthem that you should blast with open windows in order to mix menace into the autumn air.

Jack Skellington, who made his first appearance in Burton's *Beetlejuice*, is one of the most bewitching heroes ever, and his romance with Sally moves even the most cynical among us. They are both melancholy dreamers and delicate creatures that yearn to fill the emptiness within them. It was only a matter of time before their faces were printed on t-shirts, posters, patches, and every other accessory imaginable, in addition to being tattooed on the pale skin of lots of The Cure fans. This film eventually became a cultural and marketing phenomenon to the point where even a Jack Skellington cotton candy maker could possibly exist.

Making this film was a painstaking project that required an insurmountable level of patience and passion from a talented crew. Everybody involved, from the animators to the caterers, should feel proud and privileged for being a part of something that gives 76 minutes of pure joy to people everywhere.

A NIGHTMARE ON ELM STREET (1984)

Director: Wes Craven
Cast: Heather Langenkamp, Robert Englund, Johnny Depp, Ronee Blakley, John Saxon, Jsu Garcia
Length: 91 minutes
Rating: R

Synopsis: A group of friends discover that they have been having nightmares about the same maniac, a horribly burned man who wears a glove with "finger knives" on his right hand and calls himself Freddy. When a girl is brutally murdered in her sleep, they know that once they fall asleep, they may never wake up.

The overabundance of sequels turned one of the scariest villains of all time into a cartoon character who was eventually reduced to battling Jason Vorhees in hell—Jason provides the thrills and Freddy provides the jokes. This causes people to lose sight of just how innovative, visceral, and utterly terrifying the original *A Nightmare on Elm Street* is, and there is no better night than Halloween to revisit Freddy Krueger in all of his glory.

Unlike Jason and Michael Myers, Freddy Krueger actually has a personality and he uses it to mock and taunt his victims, assuring they're having their worst night of sleep ever. One wonders how a child murderer who was burned to death by a mob of angry parents can have such a glorious sense of humor. He doesn't just walk up to teenagers and cut their heads off; he plays them like puppets, placing them alone and vulnerable in the scariest of dream worlds before making his presence known. Just to intimidate his victims and express what he is capable of, he's not afraid to slice off three of his own fingers, to drive his knifed glove into his stomach to reveal a mass of green goo and a family of maggots, or to propose the innocent, thought-provoking question of what is more hideous: a horribly burned face or no face at all.

Wes Craven takes advantage of the freedom of dreamland to create a series of atmospheric, bizarre action scenes where anything can happen and

Lobby card for *A Nightmare on Elm Street 3: Dream Warriors* (1987). New Line Cinema.

even mundane objects, like a staircase, serve as nearly insurmountable obstacles. In a genre where audiences yell at teenagers for doing the most idiotic things to convenience the plot, Craven allows his teenaged characters to act intelligently. There's not much they can do to protect themselves against Freddy other than to stay awake, and it's only a matter of time before their eyelids grow too heavy to keep lifted. Therefore, we can never really blame any of these characters for getting killed.

Only a sequel-hungry ending and too many religious undertones prevent this film from reaching perfection, but it comes awfully damn close. This is also the only film you will find with an opening credit that reads, "Introducing Johnny Depp." The sequels might have tainted its reputation, but *A Nightmare on Elm Street* proved that an '80s slasher could be both imaginative and popular.

A NIGHTMARE ON ELM STREET 3: DREAM WARRIORS (1987)

Director: Chuck Russell
Cast: Heather Langenkamp, Craig Wasson, Patricia Arquette, Robert Englund, Rodney Eastman
Length: 97 minutes
Rating: R

Synopsis: A group of troubled teenagers staying at a psychiatric institution share two common links: they are all being tormented in their sleep by a monster with burned skin and knives for fingers, and their parents were all responsible in some way for his death many years ago. Nancy, who has become a psychiatrist since battling Freddy, works with the kids and teaches them how to use their dreams to protect themselves and hopefully to defeat Freddy once and for all.

In the '80s, Freddy Krueger and Jason Vorhees clashed in a war to see who could spawn the most sequels, who could make the most money, and who could keep horror fans begging for more. What the second sequel to *A Nightmare on Elm Street* proves is that Jason Vorhees doesn't even deserve to be mentioned in the same sentence as Freddy "Bastard Son of 100 Maniacs" Krueger. The hockey-masked machete-man has never come close to being in a film this creative, stylish, scary, and entertaining.

It gets off to an impressive start because no composer is better than Angelo Badalamenti at making you feel a score rather than just hear it as the opening credits appear. Whether it's something

delicate and graceful like his score to the G-rated *The Straight Story* or something unsettling and dark like *Lost Highway*, his music leaves you so hypnotized that you're at the mercy of the film.

Here we have a gallery of spooky visuals, but the scariest moment comes right away when, in the first dream sequence, a little girl leads Patricia Arquette (who, in her film debut, really gets to show off her screaming talents) into Freddy's House of Horrors. Any teenager who can have a dream this terrifying has earned our sympathy instantly. With this movie, we actually care about the teenagers and we secretly want them to be OK, so every one of Freddy's unorthodox killing methods makes an impact on us. Mr. Krueger becomes more confident with his one-liners in this installment, and he also cleverly disguises himself so that each death is like no other. You will see him as a snake slurping up his screaming victim, a puppet master using somebody's veins as strings, a violent television set, and at one point he replaces his trademark glove for ten syringe fingertips as he stalks a former drug addict. There is also one of the most cringe-worthy gags of all time when a french kiss goes terribly wrong. Add to all of this a great sense of humor, a skeleton Freddy, and doses of '80s hard rock courtesy of Dokken and you have a film that's as good as the original.

NIGHT OF THE COMET (1984)

🎞 **Director:** Thom Eberhardt
⭐ **Cast:** Catherine Mary Stewart, Kelli Maroney, Robert Beltran, Sharon Farrell
🎞 **Length:** 95 minutes
👤 **Rating:** R

🗑 **Synopsis:** Two teenage sisters are among the only survivors in Los Angeles after a comet's rays turn people into piles of dust. They are resilient in making the most out of a bad situation, but they soon learn that the other survivors aren't as friendly.

Had this movie been displayed more prominently in video stores or given the theatrical release it deserved, then this fun, flashy sci-fi flick would have been an instant classic for children of the '80s. Maybe its cult status would be a bit larger had it kept its original title: *Teenage Mutant Horror Comet Zombies*. But since plenty of you are surely nostalgic for the '80s, and since this movie received an absolutely beautiful DVD transfer, it's better late than never that you two get acquainted, and what better time than an October night?

Right from the start this movie sets a peppy tone, with its totally awesome '80s soundtrack and colorful montage of people celebrating the arrival of the comet as if they're excitedly counting down on New Year's Eve. We then spend some time in a movie theater, as our gorgeous leading lady, Regina, is obsessing over an arcade game while the projectionist geeks out over obtaining a print of *It Came from Outer Space*. Eventually they turn their sights on each other and allow their teenage hormones to interfere with witnessing the celestial miracle plunging down on their planet.

Once we see the aftermath of the comet— which makes an unfavorable first impression by wiping out almost the entire population and reducing the partygoers to piles of dust—we learn that *Night of the Comet* is not only a fun and goofy time at the movies but also a truly beautiful-looking piece of art. A breathtaking series of shots shows deserted streets, a store's mechanical clown that continues to greet customers, and rubber duckies, all beneath an intensely red-tinted sky. While it only has a few decent scares (zombie with a wrench, little boy zombie attack, and a terrifying shopping mall thug who plays Russian Roulette with Regina and her cheerleader sister), it has enough weirdness and potential danger to keep viewers on edge. The majority of post-apocalyptic films are dreary and depressing, but the perky and confident characters in *Night of the Comet* refuse to let silly inconveniences like the end of the world break their spirits—they spend less time mourning their friends and family than they do indulging in trying on clothes and make-up at the mall (in a montage to "Girls Just Want To Have Fun" that's sure to bring a smile).

NIGHT OF THE CREEPS (1986)

🎞 **Director:** Fred Dekker
⭐ **Cast:** Jason Lively, Tom Atkins, Steve Marshall, Jill Whitlow, Allan Kayser, Bruce Solomon, Wally Taylor
🎞 **Length:** 88 minutes
👤 **Rating:** R

**"I've got good news and bad news, girls.
The good news is your dates are here."
"What's the bad news?"
"They're dead."**

Synopsis: Two plump aliens accidentally drop a parasite from their spaceship onto Planet Earth, where it infects a fraternity boy. His body is kept in a cryogenic state until two college dorks release it to pass a fraternity initiation. The body releases slugs all over campus that attack the students by laying eggs in their brains and turning them into zombies.

Fred Dekker's first film is a sincere gift to old-school horror fans. He obviously has an infinite amount of reverence for the horror genre, for in a running time of just 88 minutes, he pays homage to science-fiction b-films of the 1950s, Romero's brain-chewing walking dead, and even *Jaws*, while naming the majority of characters after influential horror directors. To blend so many genres and ideas could spell disaster for a first-time director, but Dekker is fearless and just wants to have fun as he opens his film with aliens that resemble cheap looking miniature Stay Puft marshmallow men. He then takes us on a nostalgic trip to 1959 and Anytown, USA, where in black-and-white scenes, teen romancers not only have to worry about the strange object that crashed from the sky, but also the ax-wielding maniac who has just escaped from the police. When we return to the present, things get even stranger, as evil slugs and zombie pets roam

the streets. The cast members are all competent and have faith in their director, so even the most ridiculous scenes are somewhat credible.

Tom Atkins is to-die-for as the cranky chain-smoking detective who stops to smell flowers as he makes his way toward crime scenes. He's bossy and condescending, but delivers quotable one-liners and contains enough depth to be the kind of hero we cheer for. At one point, he tells a student about his painful past and has the commanding storytelling qualities that Robert Shaw was praised for in *Jaws*, thus transforming a seemingly emotionless authoritative character into a real human being, full of vulnerability and remorse. This hypnotic scene even ends on a laugh as the bewildered student says, "Other than just kinda wanting to confess to a murder, is there a point to this story?"

Fans of '80s pop culture will grin at the synthesized soundtrack, a cameo from the scene-stealer Dick Miller, the very truthful words "Stryper rules!" scribbled on a bathroom stall, and Bubba from *Mama's Family* playing the villainous fraternity leader. Gore adorers will also have a lot to smile for as several heads split open and one even ends up in the blades of a lawnmower. The final ten minutes are so satisfying and explosive that no matter what time it is when the ending credits roll, the night will seem young. There are two different endings for this movie, and hopefully the version you watch ends with a graveyard, full moon, and spaceship—and not with that damn dog!

NIGHT OF THE DEMONS (1988)

Director: Kevin S. Tenney
Cast: Linnea Quigley, Amelia Kinkade, Cathy Podewell, Billy Gallo, Alvin Alexis, Hal Havins
Length: 89 minutes
Rating: R

Synopsis: On Halloween, teenagers go to their gothic classmate's party in Hull House, a former funeral parlor with a dark past. They dance, play party games, fornicate, and then fight for their lives when they discover the house is possessed and is turning the party-goers into hideous demons.

After a delightful animated title sequence that is as charming as classroom walls adorned in paper cut-out Halloween decorations, we are treated to your typical obnoxious, over-aged teenagers who drink and drive, torment an elderly man walking down the street, and

ominously discuss the history of the legendary haunted house that they're spending Halloween in, and that miraculously remains unlocked after all these years. *Night of the Demons* is formulaic, but it has slick photography, disgusting special effects, dozens of scary moments, and superb direction from Kevin Tenney to make it one wickedly good Halloween romp.

It takes a while for the mayhem to erupt, but when an exciting demon POV tracking shot ends with a close-up of Linnea Quigley's open mouth, the demonic infestation and brutality is relentless. Tenney infuses the film with energy and keeps his characters on the run, exploring every inch of Hull House. He even provides plenty of comic relief by having the demons use their hilarious death-metal growls to taunt and spew one-liners at the few remaining 20-something teens.

Amelia Kinkade has turned her hostess with the mostest, Angela, into possibly the only franchised female monster in horror history. She is positively bewitching in a lengthy dance scene accompanied by a strobe light, a Bauhaus tune, and well-placed jump cuts that further disorient the viewers. Her line,

"I was just warming my hands in the fire," is one of the film's most chilling moments.

Night of the Demons has much more to offer than the much talked about special effect involving an exposed nipple and a tube of lipstick.

NIGHT OF THE DEMONS 2 (1994)

Director: Brian Trenchard-Smith
Cast: Cristi Harris, Robert Jayne, Merle Kennedy, Jennifer Rhodes, Johnny Moran, Christine Taylor
Length: 96 minutes
Rating: R

Synopsis: Misfit students from a Catholic school attend a Halloween party at Hull House, where several students were mysteriously slaughtered several years ago. They leave with a special souvenir from the house, which allows the demonized Angela to follow them back to the campus.

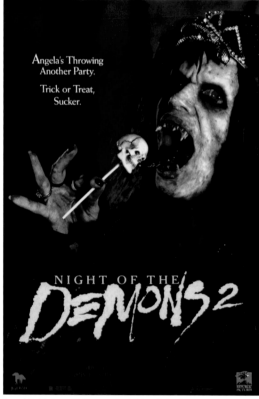

Republic Pictures VHS cover for *Night of the Demons 2* (1994).

This ghoulishly witty no-holds-barred sequel brings back the debauching hostess, Angela (confidently played by Amelia Kinkade), as she spreads her wicked ways onto another pack of Halloween party guests. The tube of lipstick that shared a memorable scene with Linnea Quigley in the original also returns with detrimental intentions.

Thanks to its sexy young cast members, excessive, cartoonish violence, quotable one-liners, lightning-fast pace, and frequent doses of nudity, the film seems to test how long it can keep that goofy grin on your face. Much of the humor comes from Jennifer Rhodes, who is a real hoot as Sister Gloria, a nun who carries a yardstick everywhere she goes. For the film's first half, she's the no-nonsense curmudgeon, punishing students who misbehave and placing her yardstick in between couples who are standing too close together, insisting that they "leave a little room for the Holy Ghost." But once her students start playing basketball with their severed heads and the religious statues start crying blood, she prepares for the inevitable battle between good and evil by practicing her kung fu moves and filling up water balloons with holy water.

You'll also cringe in devilish delight as characters get spiked baseball bats drilled into their craniums and victims of a Super Soaker filled with holy water fall to pieces, their torsos swimming in the gooey

mess of their insides. Its soundtrack is also conducive to the Halloween aura, offering plenty of organs and two tracks from the death metal group Morbid Angel.

While it uses every cliché in the book, from having the last remaining characters purposely split up in the haunted house just to save time to the old "I will be dying any second, but first let me tell you some final words of wisdom" routine, *Night of the Demons 2* does contain some very unexpected deaths. In fact, it might be fun to predict with your friends which characters will survive—the pair of Jehovah's Witnesses do not count; of course they will be sliced and diced! Pair this up with *Leprechaun 3* for an interesting and fun double feature; that 1995 film briefly reunited director Brian Trenchard-Smith with a few of his *Night of the Demons 2* stars.

NIGHT OF THE LIVING DEAD (1968)

Director: George A. Romero
Cast: Duane Jones, Judith O'Dea, Karl Hardman, Marilyn Eastman, Keith Wayne, Judith Ridley
Length: 96 minutes
Rating: Not Rated

Synopsis: Radiation from a Venus probe is causing corpses to rise from the grave, hungry for human flesh. A group of people are trapped inside a Pennsylvanian farmhouse while zombies are trying to find a way inside, and their failure to work together cohesively diminishes their chance of survival.

As a storm brews, a bickering brother and sister travel down lonely, winding roads that lead to a cemetery they visit once a year. After placing a wreath on their father's grave, they notice a tall stranger stumbling towards them, and the brother teases his frightened sister, insisting that, "They are coming to get you, Barbara." This scene ranks right up there with the Monster coming to life in *Frankenstein*, the opening scene of *Jaws*, the alien bursting from John Hurt's stomach in *Alien*, and the shower scene from *Psycho* as one of the proudest, most unforgettable moments in the history of horror cinema.

George Romero's classic, trend-setting debut is one that traumatized thousands of children during

UK poster that proudly displays the original X rating for *Night of the Living Dead* (1968). Continental Distributing.

its theatrical release. They were expecting the kind of silly, harmless horror film that was easy to find in the late 1960s. They might have thought they were getting it in the first half, but then a truck unexpectedly explodes and the zombies feast on the remains of the bodies inside. They chew severed limbs and play tug-of-war with intestines right in front of the unflinching camera. From this point on, Romero breaks all of the rules and gives us no indication of what in the hell is going to happen next.

The shoestring budget, hand-held cameras, unknown actors, and grainy black and white photography contribute to a quasi-documentary feel. When the characters hide inside the farmhouse, there is a real sense of dread and claustrophobia that escalates with every scene, hitting its peak with a stomach-churning stabbing scene. The message is of total cynicism as Ben and Harry abrasively compete over power of the farmhouse instead of working together to save their lives, touching on societal themes given the time period and the fact that Ben is African-American and Harry is white. You should have something fun planned immediately afterwards to cheer you up after an ending that is ironic, downbeat, abrupt, and soul-sucking.

NIGHT OF THE SCARECROW (1995)

Director: Jeff Burr
Cast: Elizabeth Barondes, John Mese, Stephen Root, Bruce Glover, John Hawkes
Length: 85 minutes
Rating: R

Synopsis: The spirit of a warlock is awakened in a cornfield, and after being crucified by the townspeople and then imprisoned inside of a scarecrow for hundreds of years, it has a bit of a temper.

Often overlooked for its mid-90s direct-to-video status and overshadowed by the well-respected and similarly titled *Dark Night of the Scarecrow*, this gruesome and hilariously perverted thriller deserves to find an audience as well as a higher Internet Movie Database rating. Already with sequels for *The Texas Chainsaw Massacre*, *The Stepfather*, *Pumpkinhead*, and *Puppetmaster* under his belt, Jeff Burr certainly knew the techniques in creating suspenseful chase scenes, violence that elicits both squirms and chuckles, and surroundings that are spooky even when there isn't a demented scarecrow on the loose.

In a creative back story, we learn that this small farming town was made prosperous thanks to a warlock who mysteriously showed up one day, gracing the crops with magic spells. It didn't take long for this man to rule over the town and turn a devoted Christian community into an orgy lustfully serving his will. Fearing that they may have made a deal with the devil himself, a group of priests poison the warlock and then drag him to the middle of a cornfield to be crucified. Learning from the magic book of spells, they bury his bones deep underground where they will forever keep the soil fruitful, and then display a scarecrow over the tomb to serve as constant reminder to keep the town free of sin.

With the scarecrow lurking through town and crippling the residents with paranoia, the mayor tries to convince his cop-brother to pin the murders on a local alcoholic, but the body count soon becomes too high to continue hiding their ancestors' dirty little secret. The most conventional death here is the old pitchfork and weedwhacker combo; most of the others just need to be seen to be believed. The sickest one comes when the scarecrow barges into a steamy strobe-lighted van to plant his peculiar seed inside a promiscuous teen, prompting a chest-bursting response much like John Hurt in *Alien* but going one step further. The local minister doesn't fare much better when, after kneeling before the Jesus statue, pleading forgiveness for being turned on by sexy lingerie catalogs, he looks up to notice that his savior has much more straw than before, and also some mighty impressive sewing abilities.

Scarecrows, ugly straw guardians of the crops, have been a symbol of Halloween dating all the way back to the harvest festivals in the ancient times. Farmers still depend on them to keep hungry birds away and scarecrow contests are still as prevalent as they were back in the late 1800s with Zuni children of the American Southwest. At first, it looks like the scarecrow in this film isn't doing its job because, when we first see it, a crow is pecking at it and dislocating one of its button eyeballs. But then the crow suddenly drops dead, becoming just one of its many, many victims.

THE OLD DARK HOUSE (1932)

📽 **Director:** James Whale
⭐ **Cast:** Gloria Stuart, Ernest Thesiger, Boris Karloff, Melvyn Douglas, Lilian Bond, Eva Moore
🎞 **Length:** 70 minutes
🎬 **Rating:** PG

🎞 **Synopsis:** A rainstorm of epic proportions traps travelers in the outskirts of Wales. Their only possibility for food and shelter comes in a gloomy house belonging to the bizarre Femm family.

When you have a film called *The Old Dark House*, directed by the man who gave us *Frankenstein*, *Bride of Frankenstein*, and *The Invisible Man*, that stars the ghoulish duo of Boris Karloff and Ernest Thesiger (who would be reunited in *Bride*), and that is only 70 minutes long, how on earth could it not be appropriate for Halloween? Although the last 5 minutes is a big, fat disappointment, this is an entertaining black-and-white horror-comedy that features a family so strange they would send the Addams and the Munsters running to the hills.

A pounding thunderstorm is an essential ingredient in black-and-white haunted house movies, but none have reached the threatening, cataclysmic nature of the one shown here; it becomes just as dangerous as what lurks inside the old, dark house, providing no safe options to the travelers. Lucky for them, they are a mordant, strong-willed bunch that doesn't scare easily. Even as they are knocking on the front door, they remark on the appropriateness of discovering evil creatures inside. First, they are "greeted" by the Femm Family butler, a colossal, severely-scarred alcoholic. Then they meet the owners, an effeminate elderly man who is too afraid to go upstairs in his own house, and his hateful, deaf, Jesus-preaching sister. The comfort of drinking brandy by the fireplace is too hard to resist, so the drenched travelers stay, even while the butler, who becomes aggressive when he drinks, is pouring liquor down his throat. Since this trio of oddballs is forced to keep their violent, pyromaniac brother locked upstairs, we foresee his inevitable presence to be on the scary-as-hell side. But *The Old Dark House* can't rise from its stagnant, uneasy atmosphere to elicit any shocking moments, and even the quiet tension is lost when the storm finally dissipates. Still, it was first-rate filmmaking all around until the lame climax and the corny ending, thus deserving of 70 minutes of your time during October.

THE OMEN (1976)

📽 **Director:** Richard Donner
⭐ **Cast:** Gregory Peck, Lee Remick, David Warner, Billie Whitelaw, Harvey Stephens, Patrick Troughton
🎞 **Length:** 111 minutes
🎬 **Rating:** R

🎞 **Synopsis:** An eccentric, seemingly insane priest tells the American Ambassador to Great Britain that the son he adopted five years ago is actually the spawn of Satan. Naturally, the family man doesn't believe this, but when the priest predicts deaths and horrible actions that come true, he must confront the evils that lay within his only child.

You can tell right from the start that this film means serious business because Jerry Goldsmith's intense, award-winning score just about knocks you over. After being nominated for an Academy Award eight times, it was nice this legendary composer finally got to walk away with the gold for this film; he would go on to receive another eight nominations before passing away in 2004. Following in the footsteps of previous Satanic-related psychological thrillers *Rosemary's Baby* and *The Exorcist*, *The Omen* shows how simply scaring an audience can be performed so artistically.

With all of the peculiar, hazardous events that befell the crew and cast of *The Omen* during production, anyone had the right to be a nervous wreck about simply walking across the street for a cup of coffee. But the filmmakers prevailed over speculations of a cursed movie and made an absolute classic. Because

The Omen is so classy and sophisticated, its moments of graphic violence really catch the viewers off guard. Its opening scenes don't suggest that you're going to see an unrelentingly brutal attack from a pack of devil dogs in a cemetery or such a sudden, explicit decapitation via a runaway pane of glass. And a young woman hanging herself during a child's birthday party is horrific in itself, but having the merry-go-round continue spinning while her body dangles on display is one of the many touches Richard Donner threw in to make this scene so unforgettable.

There is also a particularly Halloweenish moment when a neurotic priest finds himself caught in the kind of windstorm that only the evilest of forces could produce.

THE PEOPLE UNDER THE STAIRS (1991)

Director: Wes Craven
Cast: Brandon Adams, Everett McGill, Wendy Robie, A.J. Langer, Ving Rhames, Kelly Jo Minter
Length: 102 minutes
Rating: R

Synopsis: Desperately needing money to pay for his mother's operation and to avoid eviction, a young boy breaks into his landlords' house to steal their collection of gold coins. Inside, he discovers that his landlords are psychopaths and that he may never get out of the house alive.

The first 15 minutes certainly aren't Halloweenish, presenting a bleak and angry tone by focusing on racism, discrimination, and the corruption of the ghettos. But once our young hero and his criminal mentor enter the house they've been warned not to go near, Wes Craven delivers the chills in one suspenseful scene after another. This is the kind of house with so many booby-traps, secret passageways, and bloodthirsty residents that not even Ving Rhames can take it on. It remains a constant factor: just about anything in the world could jump out of nowhere and eat you alive. Within the walls, Craven has created a labyrinth of horrors with no clear exit. Say what you want about the film's plausibility, you can't deny its high level of excitement.

The grisliness mixes well with colorful, maddening performances from Everett McGill and Wendy Robie, who played a married couple in the unforgettable series *Twin Peaks*. They were kind-hearted and sweet on the show, but here he's adorned in black leather bondage suits and she constantly spits out religious zealot venom. And if they hear one blasphemous word, they will cut out your tongue and throw you in the dungeon with the others.

The People Under the Stairs also offers several opportunities for a good chuckle, like when the demented couple call for some "serious spring cleaning" or when they curse at the vicious family pet, Prince. Be sure to take a shot every time you hear the words "burn in Hell!"

Press photo for *The People Under the Stairs* (1991). Universal Pictures.

PHANTASM (1979)

Director: Don Coscarelli
Cast: A. Michael Baldwin, Angus Scrimm, Bill Thornbury, Reggie Bannister, Lynn Eastman
Length: 87 minutes
Rating: R

Synopsis: A teenaged boy begins to see strange things at Morningside Cemetery, and his curiosity leads him to the Tall Man, a sinister mortician who transforms corpses into vicious dwarves to serve his will before sending them to an alternate universe.

Usually when you watch a film, you are reminded of others, but that probably won't happen when you see the freaky world that Don Coscarelli has created in his beloved *Phantasm,* which he was inspired to make after he witnessed how audiences reacted to the scary scene in his previous film, *Kenny & Company.* Flowing between reality and dreamland, it takes us on a journey that starts out by exploiting our fear of death and undertakers, and then proceeds to take one left turn after another until we're speechless, confused, but ultimately satisfied. All we know for sure is that Reggie and Mike are two people we wish we could hang out with in real life.

After an unusual set-up involving creepy trolls that a character describes as "little and brown and low to the ground" and the most intimidating mortician we've ever seen, we know that something spectacular is going to happen when our barely-teenaged protagonist roams alone through the mortuary in the middle of the night. He had just broken in and used his lighter to guide his way out of the dark storage room. Then he had to resort to hiding in a coffin to avoid being caught. Once he's back on the marble floors, we are at the edge of our seats and prepared for just about anything, but certainly not for what mysteriously floats into the shot.

The Halloween gods shine immediately when this flick opens with a classic combo of spooky music and a couple making out in a graveyard, and for the next hour-and-a-half, we get to witness a fortune teller, menacing trolls, a chase scene with a hearse, a severed finger that drips yellow blood and morphs into a large insect, wind from a machine so forceful it nearly killed one of the crew members, and a "space room" obviously inspired by *2001: A Space Odyssey,* equipped with glowing walls and chrome poles. The only thing that would make this more Halloween friendly is if there was a scene where the Tall Man goes trick-or-treating and throws brainsuckers at the houses with the porch lights off.

PHANTASM II (1988)

Director: Don Coscarelli
Cast: James LeGros, Reggie Bannister, Angus Scrimm, Paula Irvine, Samantha Phillips, Kenneth Tigar
Length: 96 minutes
Rating: R

Synopsis: Mike, a survivor from the original, keeps sensing that the girl of his dreams is in trouble. Meanwhile, his buddy Reggie has another encounter with the Tall Man and his army of minions. This leads everybody to the mausoleum for another battle between good and evil.

One doesn't have to see the original first because this is more like a big-budgeted remake than a sequel. It tells the same complicated story, but the grisliness is multiplied by three because this time we get three brainsuckers, flying spheres that drill into humans and shoot their blood out like water through a hose. To see them work together is both hilarious and disgusting.

Phantasm II plays like a dream when you've had way too much caffeine the night before. Weird things

If this one doesn't scare you... You're Already Dead!

PHANTASM

"PHANTASM" Starring MICHAEL BALDWIN, BILL THORNBURY, REGGIE BANNISTER, KATHY LESTER and ANGUS SCRIMM as The Tall Man Written and Directed by DON COSCARELLI Produced by D.A. Coscarelli Co-Producer PAUL PEPPERMAN Music: FRED MYROW and MALCOLM SEAGRAVE Prints by CFI SOUNDTRACK AVAILABLE ON VARESE SARABANDE RECORDS AVCO EMBASSY PICTURES Release keep appearing and vanishing with no rhyme or reason, and before you can collect your thoughts, you find yourself in a brand new unsettling environment. Because of its surreal tone and insane visuals, you shouldn't find yourself feeling too frustrated when you can't follow the hectic, often incoherent plot. This is a film to be watched for its aesthetic elements and for having one of the most beloved horror icons in the Tall Man, the kind of villain that you want to give a big hug to despite his evilness.

In *Phantasm II*, you'll see a sympathetic grandmother transformed into an evil dwarf, a hilarious chainsaw duel in a mortuary cellar, a man chop off his arm with an axe, a silver sphere drill its way into the same man's stomach and then force its way out of his mouth, and a portal that sends our heroes into another dimension that has to be seen to be believed. Because of executives at Universal Pictures insisting that Don Coscarelli wouldn't be allowed to bring back both of his original stars, this is the only entry in the series that has somebody other than A. Michael Baldwin playing the role of Mike; James LeGros does an admirable job in his first starring role but had the casting director chosen a different young man who auditioned, we may have seen an "And Introducing Brad Pitt" credit. Give this under-appreciated sequel the respect it deserves, ghouls and BOOOOOOOOOOOOYYYYYYS!!!

POLTERGEIST (1982)

🎬 **Director:** Tobe Hooper
⭐ **Cast:** JoBeth Williams, Craig T. Nelson, Heather O'Rourke, Zelda Rubinstein, Oliver Robins, James Karen
🎞 **Length:** 114 minutes
🧍 **Rating:** PG

📖 **Synopsis:** A family suspects that their new suburban home may be haunted and are amused at first, but one stormy night they learn just how unfriendly the ghosts are when the son is attacked and the youngest daughter is taken to a parallel universe.

Lobby card for *Poltergeist* (1982). Metro-Goldwyn Mayer.

It's kinda cute how some of the scariest, psychologically scarring movies of all time have a PG rating—the best examples being *Jaws* and *Poltergeist*. But the PG rating was an entirely different beast back then and you could get away with showing a killer shark gobbling up a boy or showing a man peel off his face while looking into a mirror. Tobe Hooper was confident that he could even obtain a PG rating for *The Texas Chainsaw Massacre* by limiting the blood and violence, but instead it was given an R and was even banned in several countries. Hooper got his desired rating with the Steven Spielberg–produced *Poltergeist*, a very successful film that traumatized children and breathed new life into the haunted house theme. This time the house isn't a towering and decrepit mansion at the top of a hill, but the most normal-looking house in the most normal-looking neighborhood.

In only the first 20 minutes, you'll see so many sensational, bone-chilling visuals that you'll wonder how Hooper can possibly keep this kind of pace going. But he succeeds and proves that he's capable of making an unforgettable horror film with an $80,000 budget, like with *The Texas Chainsaw Massacre,* or a $10 million dollar budget, like with *Poltergeist.*

The movie seems to know all about the scariest nightmares a child can have. The boy in *Poltergeist* not only has to deal with his toy clown that comes to life, but also with a ghoulish-looking tree that stares at him through his bedroom window. These scenes, among many others (including one where the mother swims with several skeletons), are elevated by a powerful rainstorm with the type of lightning that resembles a strobe light. A little subtle humor is also thrown in, such as when the little girl's doll's head keeps falling off.

Because Craig T. Nelson and JoBeth Williams play such intelligent, loving, responsible parents, the film does lose a little credibility when only one day after they finally rescue their precious daughter from the clutches of evil, they let her sleep in the same bedroom where she was stolen, without even watching over her! Fool me once, shame on you, fool me twice, the clown deserves to take my child.

POOH'S HEFFALUMP HALLOWEEN MOVIE (2005)

Director: Saul Blinkoff, Elliot Bour
Cast: Jimmy Bennett, Kyle Stanger, Jim Cummings, John Fielder, Ken Samsom, Michael Gough
Length: 67 minutes
Rating: G

Synopsis: After Pooh eats everybody's Halloween candy, Roo and his best friend, Lumpy, attempt to conquer their fears by finding the dreaded Gobloon in order to save Halloween. If they catch him, then they will be granted one wish, and if the Gobloon catches them, they will be turned into "jackety lanterns."

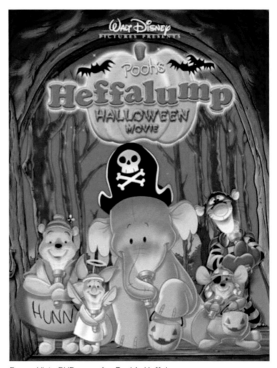

Buena Vista DVD cover for *Pooh's Heffalump Halloween Movie* (2005).

Wanting to cash in on the sudden popularity of the newest character of the Hundred Acre Wood group, the British Lumpy, Disney basically took the 1996 TV special *Boo to You Too, Winnie the Pooh* and added 20 minutes of new material. This profit scam obviously angered those expecting to see Winnie the Pooh and his friends engage in an all new Halloween adventure. Sneaky tactics aside, this is still a good way for children to spend 67 minutes during the Halloween season. The day scenes are filled with vibrant, warm colors, and once the sun falls, out comes appropriately spooky imagery of "terror trees" and plenty of things that go bump in the night, but nothing that would be too intense for the youngsters.

What really makes the film worth watching is Tigger, easily the most entertaining and spirited of the bunch. He leads his friends in a terrific Halloween number in the beginning portion and always tries to make the most of every moment—to waste one second on Halloween is practically blasphemous in his book. Unfortunately for him, his companions are not the best people with whom to spend Halloween. One of them eats all his candy and two others threaten to turn a Halloween into a "Hallo-wasn't."

When it looks like his friends are going to ruin yet another Halloween, he wisely departs and attempts to scare himself, relishing in the ghoulish holiday magic.

There is also something oddly endearing, wise, and inspirational about a line like "This is gonna be the best Halloween ever because it's our first Halloween together."

PUMPKINHEAD (1988)

Director: Stan Winston
Cast: Lance Henriksen, Jeff East, Cynthia Bain, John DiAquino, Kerry Remsen, Joel Hoffman
Length: 86 minutes
Rating: R

🎞 **Synopsis:** After his son is accidentally killed by a group of city youths, an avenging storekeeper visits a witch to conjure a folkloric demon. The summoned Pumpkinhead stalks and dispatches the youngsters, but refuses to go away.

Pumpkinhead is a mélange of Southern Gothic atmosphere, morality storytelling, and all of the necessary components for a one-of-a-kind creature feature. It is a great horror film on any night of the year, but on October 31st, it provides the desired ambience for a perfect Halloween experience, containing an equal balance of fright and fascination. While not directly associated with the holiday, its blue-tinted exterior scenes are filled with a veil of autumnal gloom, courtesy of heavy fog that radiates through cornstalks, wind so fierce it sounds like a cicada gathering, and dead leaves that swirl menacingly. These moments are made even more magical and threatening by the obvious contrast of the candlelight and warm colors that dominate the interior scenes. Makeup maestro Stan Winston is clearly aware that the buildup for the monster is even more important than the monster itself, and he makes the waiting worth it in his directorial debut because this is one impressive looking creature. It's so madly detailed that you cannot look away; if the Creature from the Black Lagoon ever mated with Alyda Winthrop from the *Unnamable* films, their wicked spawn might look a lot like Pumpkinhead. It is also not the kind of creature you want to anger; it disposes of its victims in excruciatingly slow methods, yet no two killings are the same. It's also proud of its predatory ways because it parades its half-dead victims around like a cat who is eager to show off his latest rodent-kill to his owners.

Genre star Lance Henriksen is in top form as a bumpkin who could easily answer most questions with "I reckon," but who is also a loving and supportive father. More surprising is the level of

Poster for *Pumpkinhead* (1988). United Artists.

professionalism from the group of young actors and actresses whose only real purpose is to get turned into chum. Most of their characters seem intelligent and sincere, but fortunately we don't learn enough about them to withhold a cheer when Pumpkinhead impales one of them with a rifle.

RACE WITH THE DEVIL (1975)

🎬 **Director:** Jack Starrett
⭐ **Cast:** Peter Fonda, Warren Oates, Loretta Swit, Lara Parker, R.G. Armstrong
🎞️ **Length:** 88 minutes
👤 **Rating:** PG

🎞️ **Synopsis:** While on vacation in an RV, two couples witness a Satanic ritual involving a human sacrifice and then attempt to flee the scene. "If you're going to race with the devil, you've got to be fast as hell!"

If the power of Lucifer compels you on Halloween night and you want a little detour from the usual exorcisms and omens, then how about a terrifying ride through what Sarah Palin refers to as "Real America," as a group of travelers are terrorized by a Satanic cult so large in numbers that they cover multiple Texan towns and frequent just about every possible gas station, bar, trailer campground, and police station?

The movie gets off to a suitable beginning by having a twisted, claw-shaped tree silhouetted against some of the angriest-looking clouds you've ever seen accompany the title sequence. Soon we are introduced to a quartet of refreshingly mature protagonists (including *M*A*S*H*'s Major Margaret Houlihan!) whose cross-country vacation hits a sour note once they unwittingly make their presence known right after a young blonde woman is impaled for Satan. So they have to put aside their plans of skiing and dirt-bike racing and instead drive as fast as they can in an RV while avoiding rings of fire and anyone who looks like an extra from *Deliverance*.

A popular '70s drive-in B-movie, *Race with the Devil* is an adrenaline-fueled hybrid of *Duel* and *Rosemary's Baby*, dishing out some incredible stunt work and car chases among effective horror clichés. Even if you don't suffer from ophidiophobia, you'll be gasping for air at the scene when Peter Fonda and Warren Oates (looking like a half-gruff, half-suave John Cougar Mellencamp in the film's best performance) battle a pair of rattlesnakes. Just as suspenseful is when a group of redneck Satanists runs after the RV that's going stubbornly slow—as they bash in the back windows, the brake lights illuminate their faces into devilish glows. According to director Jack Starrett, he hired actual Satanists, but this statement could have just been for publicity.

THE RAVEN (1963)

🎬 **Director:** Roger Corman
⭐ **Cast:** Vincent Price, Peter Lorre, Boris Karloff, Hazel Court, Jack Nicholson, Olive Sturgess
🎞️ **Length:** 85 minutes
👤 **Rating:** Not Rated

🎞️ **Synopsis:** Respected sorcerer Dr. Craven gets a surprise visit from a talking raven, who asks to be returned to human form. Once the process is complete, he admits to seeing the Dr. Craven's deceased wife wandering around in the castle of Dr. Scarabus, the most powerful sorcerer in England.

After making several morbid, solemn films together, Roger Corman and Vincent Price were probably in need of a good laugh. *The Raven* is a deliciously witty parody of their Poe adaptations, full of colorful characters and wacky visuals. To see a talking raven enter a man's house and criticize his cooking methods confirms that this film was made to make the viewers smile. It is quirky, bizarre, ridiculous, and one of the most entertaining Poe adaptations you'll ever see.

Vincent Price, Peter Lorre, and Boris Karloff all have a terrific time with their roles as sorcerers with contrasting personalities. Even though he's still tormented over the loss of his dear departed wife, this is one of Price's most uplifting characters. Lorre once again plays a drunk who can't say no to a bottle of wine, but this time he's clumsy and harmless. Made only six years before his death, the always professional Karloff proves that he was still a powerful presence and a terrific actor in the last stages of his career.

The best scene comes near the end, with a "duel to the death" between Price and Karloff. This battle of superiority includes just about everything imaginable, such as eggs dropping on Karloff's head, a cobra that Price turns into a scarf, a chair that floats to the ceiling and then sinks beneath the ground, baby birds that fly from Price's coat, fireballs, growling gargoyle statues, and plenty more.

Be sure to look for an extremely young Jack Nicholson as Lorre's son.

Lobby card for *The Raven* (1963). American International Pictures.

RE-ANIMATOR (1985)

🎬 **Director:** Stuart Gordon
⭐ **Cast:** Jeffrey Combs, Bruce Abbott, Barbara Crampton, David Gale, Robert Sampson
🎞 **Length:** 86 minutes
🧍 **Rating:** Not Rated

🪦 **Synopsis:** A nerdish, arrogant medical student discovers a green serum that can bring the dead back to life. Not only does he have to worry about a bullying professor who wants to steal his work, but also the experimented bodies who resurrect with a murderous rage.

Few films can be this sick, perverted, and disgusting without being offensive, and few films can be this hilarious, yet still manage to scare the living daylights out of you. This '80s gore-o-rama helped make actor Jeffrey Combs, director Stuart Gordon, and producer/director Brian Yuzna three of the most reliable and respected workers in the horror genre today. Very loosely based on an H.P. Lovecraft short story, *Re-Animator* shows us right away that we're in for a bloody good ride when, even before the opening credits, a man's eyeballs balloon and then explode, squirting blood over his screaming secretary. However, nothing could prepare us for some of the shocking events that transpire later in the film; this is one audacious movie that goes way beyond what people are used to seeing.

Stuart Gordon originally planned *Re-Animator* to be part of a PBS television series that would have been devoted to various works of H.P. Lovecraft, but when that obviously couldn't work, he re-shaped the script into a screenplay that would become his feature film debut. Teaming up with producer Brian Yuzna gave him the freedom to do just about anything he wanted, and his vision wouldn't even be compromised by the MPAA because Yuzna decided to release the film unrated. This move resulted in a very limited PR campaign, but had the MPAA gotten their slimy hands on it, who knows what our darling *Re-Animator* would look like today. It ended up earning a special critics prize at Cannes (and a slew of positive reviews would follow, even from some of the most respected critics, like Roger Ebert and Pauline Kael) as well as some of loudest and most enthusiastic theater audiences ever. If any movie was going to blatantly steal Bernard Herrmann's score from *Psycho*, I am glad it was this one.

One audience member who wasn't vocal or giddy was the wife of actor David Gale; she walked out in the middle of an initial screening, and it was probably around the time her husband's decapitated head was giving head to a young woman he had been lusting over when he was alive. I suppose one advantage of being re-animated is no longer giving a shit about societal restraints. Other gloriously sick sights include the professor splitting open a human head (peeling it like an orange) to pull out its brain, a college dean getting his fingers bitten off by a man strong enough to have been cast as Arnold Schwarzenegger's body double in *The Terminator*, a decapitation via shovel, a zombie kitty, and a near strangulation with intestines.

Considering the youth and inexperience of Gordon, it's an incredible feat that he was able to stick to a three-week shooting schedule and extract such strong performances from his cast, who were forced to take a tour of a morgue before filming commenced. Jeffrey Combs is indomitable in the Dr. Frankenstein-esque character of Herbert West, and Barbara Crampton succeeds in making her character so much stronger and smarter than the blonde beauties you're used to seeing in '80s gore-fests. In what had to be a ludicrous transition in her acting career, she went from lounging around Palm Springs in the teen comedy *Fraternity Vacation* to being strapped naked to a table and groped by a zombie whose severed head drools uncontrollably next to her.

This was followed by two sequels, spread several years apart: the decent *Bride of Re-Animator* and the godawful *Beyond Re-Animator*.

[REC] (2007)

Directors: Jaume Belagueró, Paco Plaza
Cast: Manuela Velasco, Ferran Terraza, Jorge-Yamam Serrano
Length: 78 minutes
Rating: R

Synopsis: A group of firefighters respond to an emergency call and along for the ride is a television host and a cameraman, who are documenting their experiences for an upcoming episode. They enter a dark apartment complex to a chaotic and nightmarish scene, and are then locked inside.

At the moment, the found-footage subgenre that often uses a single, hand-held camera for the entire duration is really wearing out its welcome, giving horror fans something else to complain about rather than remakes and sequels. But as you are squirming and shaking your head during the trailer for yet another *Paranormal Activity* movie, it's important to remember that found-footage has produced some real gems over the years: *The Blair Witch Project, Trollhunter, Cloverfield, The Last Exorcism*, and a low-budgeted offering from Spain with the unusual title *[Rec]* that gives me the willies just thinking about it. And much like Sweden's *Let the Right One In*, it was instantly hailed as a masterpiece and then immediately plagiarized by American producers fully aware that mainstream American audiences are either too dumb or uncultured to appreciate a film with subtitles; both *Let Me In* and *Quarantine*, the bastardization of *[Rec]*, were released less than two years after the original films.

Everything we see comes from the camera of a character named Pablo, and since he's an experienced cameraman, *[Rec]* avoids the overwhelmingly shaky, dizzying cinematography that similar films are known for. He is working on a late-night television program called "While You're Asleep," hosted by the perky and pretty Angela Vidal. They aren't feeling too good about this particular episode, which chronicles the lives of firefighters in Barcelona. What was supposed to be thrilling television documenting heroism in the face of unparalleled danger is turning out to be a crushing bore: monotonous and uneventful. The easy-going Angela doesn't want harm to come to anyone, but if this episode is going to be successful, they need an emergency call, and boy do they get one! It has nothing to do with fire, but even if it's just an elderly woman who fell down, at least it gives them some footage of sliding down the pole and riding in the truck. At around the 15-minute mark, this old woman bites a huge chunk off of a man's face. From this point on, the movie becomes an unrelenting chaotic nightmare (that uses a smart "real-time" approach and lengthy shots) and we are placed right in the middle of it. It's hard to imagine a more frightening Halloween scenario than being trapped in a building sealed off for security reasons by the Biological, Nuclear, or Chemical Protocol,

and given no explanation as to why some people inside are bleeding to death and others violently losing their minds. Never for a moment does it feel like we are watching a scripted movie. When Angela and Pablo aren't engaged in arguments with the officers over their desire to tape everything to show the world what's happened, they are showing us how entirely believable people react in the midst of a horrible crisis. Just like in real life, some people, like the medical intern, will do everything they can to help; some, like the elderly couple, will never stop bickering, and some will even be able to provide humor: in this case, it's the very suave Cesar who is concerned about the camera capturing his most flattering angle, and who isn't aware the camera is recording his racist comments about Asians. These few moments of comic relief are a blessing because your heart is given permission to beat at a normal rate again. Most of the movie feels like you're speeding down a seemingly never-ending rollercoaster hill: possibly hazardous to your health but so much fun!

In one of the most startling moments, a camera pokes through an opening in the ceiling and slowly pans around. I have a pretty high tolerance for suspense but my core was really tested here, and after I stubbornly refused to look away, I later wished I had.

THE RETURN OF THE LIVING DEAD (1985)

Director: Dan O'Bannon
Cast: Clu Gulager, James Karen, Don Calfa, Thom Mathews, Beverly Randolph, Linnea Quigley
Length: 90 minutes
Rating: R

Synopsis: Two workers at a medical supplies store accidentally release a toxic gas that spreads throughout the neighboring cemetery, causing the dead bodies to rise from the grave. This poses a problem for a group of teenaged punks on a graveyard rendezvous.

In a move that could have pissed off fans of Romero's brainmunching classic, *Alien* screenwriter Dan O'Bannon has a character in his semi-sequel spoof actually explain how *Night of the Living Dead* wasn't just a movie, but a fabrication based on a real-life event. The proof lies in the basement of a medical supplies store, where an air-tight canister containing a corpse was sent from the army. There is even a silly warning before the film begins, indicating that "the

events portrayed in this film are all true." But the late O'Bannon deserved the right to parody and reference any classic he wanted because *The Return of the Living Dead* was one hell of an exciting and fun directorial debut.

The characters are all pretty comedic, but unlike those in most movie spoofs, they actually react sensibly to the bizarre circumstances. When driving a pickaxe through a zombie doesn't work, they proceed to cut off its head. After all, these people have seen *Night of the Living Dead* and know that you can kill the ghoul by killing its brain. They obviously start to panic when they have to resort to chopping the ghoul into little pieces, and even that doesn't work—the pieces are moving around just as aggressively as the dead butterflies decorating the walls. They come to the logical conclusion to incinerate the pieces, but unbeknownst to them, they are only making matters worse. In another hysterical moment, two men affected by the toxic gas are pronounced "technically not alive" by paramedics, who are understandably baffled because dead people don't move around and talk. Because the protagonists are capable of showing intelligence and emotion, there is a real sense of dread and rising tension when the film explores more traditional horror territories in the second half. The zombies also display common sense this time around, making things even more hopeless for the humans trapped inside. They are able to devise tactics to ambush police officers (they even use equipment to request more cops like they are ordering pizza) and operate heavy machinery to remove locked doors. Some are even given moments of humanity, such as when one of most recent members of the living dead commits suicide, and when a captured zombified torso explains why they are after human brains: "Eating brains makes the pain of being dead go away," an angle that is explored further in part 3.

There are also several imaginative shots of corpses rising from the grave, good use of slow motion, an energizing goth-punk soundtrack, one of the most awesome nude scenes of all time, the unbelievable Tarman ghoul, disgusting and creative special effects, and an interesting cast. There is even a rainstorm so brutal, the hapless teens are forced to practically swim through the cemetery as they are being chased.

Also highly recommended is a 2011 documentary called *More Brains: A Return to the Living Dead*, in which the cast and crew share many outrageous and entertaining behind-the-scenes stories. This was made by the same creative team who gave us the award-winning *Never Sleep Again: The Elm Street Legacy*.

RETURN OF THE LIVING DEAD PART II (1988)

☲ **Director:** Ken Wiederhorn
★ **Cast:** Michael Kenworthy, James Karen, Dana Ashbrook, Marsha Dietlein, Philip Bruns
✪ **Length:** 89 minutes
👤 **Rating:** R

🎞 **Synopsis:** While examining a mysterious canister found near a cemetery, a couple of kids release trioxyn gas into the air. Moments later, dead bodies rise from their graves on a quest to find "brains, more brains."

While not as funny or scary as the original, Part II isn't as bad as some would have you believe. Filmed in deliberate comedy mode with actors mugging to the camera, it is more tongue-in-cheek than the original, and is just as much of a remake as it is a sequel. The always welcome duo of James Karen and Thom Mathews return to play the same characters, doing the same thing and meeting the same slow demise where a doctor pronounces them not alive just before they kick into full zombie mode. At one moment that probably looked wittier on paper, Matthews even addresses his déjà vu skepticism by saying, "It's like we've been here before." Karen is even whinier and more pathetic (but just as loveable) this time. In one scene, he groans in horror as he pulls a hungry severed zombie head from his backpack. He screams "Oh my God!!!" just before slowly and voluntarily inserting his fingers inside the zombie's mouth, and then acts surprised when it bites him! An even bigger laugh comes later in the scene when Dana Ashbrook (whom *Twin Peaks* fans will know as Bobby Briggs) stabs the head with a screwdriver, to which it replies in a cranky Southern drawl, "Get that damn screwdriver out of my head!" Another memorable line comes courtesy of youngster Kenworthy: "I'm not even out of grade school and I'm already gonna die!"

Much like its predecessor, this earns its R rating with plenty of gross brain chomping shots. There are also a couple of shots that point out the mess you're bound to make when you punch a zombie in the face—its face will implode and you'll pull out your hand in a way that resembles tugging at pumpkin innards. The gross-out gags are fun until an ill-conceived and needlessly disturbing scene in which zombies break into a pet store when their lust for extra servings of human brains goes unfulfilled.

A much more ambitious and extraordinary sequel arrived in 1993 with Brian Yuzna's *Part 3*, which presented a melancholy Romeo-and-Juliet-in-hell storyline that left viewers wondering what on earth it was doing in this silly series.

SATAN'S LITTLE HELPER (2004)

Director: Jeff Lieberman
Cast: Alexander Brickel, Katheryn Winnick, Amanda Plummer, Stephen Graham, Joshua Annex
Length: 96 minutes
Rating: R

Synopsis: On Halloween, a young boy with an obsession over a video game called Satan's Little Helper mistakes a serial killer for the fictional character of Satan, and enlists his services to get rid of his older sister's boyfriend.

There have been numerous movies set on Halloween, but *Satan's Little Helper* accomplishes what very few movies have: offerings of holiday flavor in just about every shot. When you are constantly gazing at seasonal motifs like neighborhood decorations, cider, and wickedly good costumes on a picturesque autumn day, it's easy to forgive some slow patches and gags that try too hard to be depraved and instead come off as desperate, from bludgeoning a cat against a wall and writing "Boo" with its dead carcass to killing an elderly woman with a walker.

Satan's Little Helper was Jeff Lieberman's (*Blue Sunshine, Squirm,* etc.) first film after a 16-year hiatus and fortunately the long absence didn't impair his creativity and cult appeal. It gives a dark comedic edge to the theory that video games can make it hard for troubled youths to separate reality from fantasy, and it's hard to think of a youth more troubled than Dougie; he wants to marry his older sister and he fends off the neighborhood kids by saying, "Just wait til I find Satan and he sends you all to Hell." While taking a stroll in his devil costume, he watches in awe as a hulking masked brute drags a dead body to his front-yard cemetery and proudly puts it on display. A partnership is then established as the boy brings his new friend home, whom the sister mistakes as her theater boyfriend faithfully staying in creepy character.

Most of the humor is provided by the serial killer, who proves that Halloween night is such an easy time to be a psychopath, since everyone will open their front door to you even if you are disguised and holding sharp weapons, and you don't even have to worry about getting blood on your clothes. Despite not having a single word of dialogue, Joshua Annex gives a charismatic performance with the kind of body language that makes you think he's probably smiling brightly behind that awesome mask. One of his funniest moments comes when he is asked to pose for a photo with a group of girls trick-or-treating.

SCARECROWS (1988)

Director: William Wesley
Cast: Victoria Christian, Michael Simms, Ted Vernon, Richard Vidan, Kristina Sanborn, B.J. Turner
Length: 83 minutes
Rating: R

Synopsis: After heisting millions of dollars from the government, thieves take a pilot and his teenaged daughter as hostages and demand to be flown across the border to Mexico. One of the men then betrays his partners and parachutes out of the plane with all of the money, safely landing in a condemned cemetery filled with scarecrows in need of fresh body parts.

Yet another great, obscure movie that recently got its much-deserved DVD release, this strikingly original creepfest is as compelling as it is terrifying. Taking place entirely at night, the circumstances which lead the criminals and a hostage to an abandoned house in the middle of nowhere demonstrate that William Wesley is not only a gifted filmmaker, but a remarkable writing talent as well. The script is so smart that when the characters unwisely split up while they are being chased, it is for believable reasons.

Gore-enthusiasts will be happy with the scarecrows' creative ways of killing. Though never gratuitously

Screen Media DVD cover for *Satan's Little Helper* (2004).

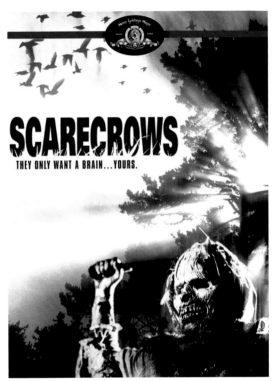

MGM DVD cover for *Scarecrows* (1988).

bloody, they saw off body parts, stab faces, and tear torsos open to fill them with straw. There is even a decapitation that, like in many intelligent horror films, doesn't necessarily mean the end of that character.

The character dynamics are refreshingly involving, though it was a silly mistake for the girl to be shown applying make-up and fixing her hair while she is being held hostage by people who could very well murder her and her father. With all of the conflicts and mistrust among the human characters—some who are trying to retain the money they have fought so hard for, and others who are simply fighting for their lives—and considering the bloodthirsty scarecrows on a killing spree, the film possesses an uncharted sense of danger and possibility.

It was wise for this story of demonic possession to take place in the rural South, where in the earliest Halloweens in America, African slaves spread folklore of demons and voodoo.

SLEEPY HOLLOW (1999)

📽 **Director:** Tim Burton
⭐ **Cast:** Johnny Depp, Christina Ricci, Miranda Richardson, Michael Gambon, Jeffrey Jones
🎞 **Length:** 105 minutes
🧍 **Rating:** R

🗑 **Synopsis:** A New York detective is sent to the town of Sleepy Hollow at the end of the 18th century to investigate the beheadings of several residents. The locals swear it is the work of the Headless Horseman, avenging his death from several years ago.

Tim Burton was the perfect choice to rejuvenate the classic Washington Irving novel. He brings his unmistakable flair to an already creepy tale and it ends up being one of his best films ever. It bears little resemblance to the novel and to the previous adaptations, mostly because Johnny Depp is like no other Ichabod Crane we've seen.

Sleepy Hollow gets off to a marvelous start as a man journeys into a field of cornstalks and showers the witnessing jack-o'-lanterns in blood as he gets decapitated. The film unflinchingly offers countless

beheadings, each one graphic and distinctive, but they aren't meant to simply gross out the viewers. Like everything else in the film, the decapitations are performed in an artistic style that scrutinizes even the smallest of details so that watching them in slow motion is like watching the scariest paintings come to life. The horseman is a diabolical killing machine, taking the heads of not only men, but also women and children, yet at no moment does this film make you feel uncomfortable; it contains just as much joy and magic as Burton's lighter efforts.

It's easily one of the best-looking horror films of recent memory. A veil of mist floats in nearly every exterior scene, the architecture is looming and threatening, piles of dead leaves whirl from the impact of running horses, and the cinematography is hauntingly beautiful. Burton also uses some very subtle movements to a great, ominous effect, like the wind manipulating a scarecrow or a scary face morphing in a fireplace.

Depp has created one of his most irresistible characters in the cocky New York detective whose sophisticated, progressive, scientific methods cry out for the end of barbaric forms of torture that are still common in 1799. His appearance suggests buoyancy and arrogance, but he's really innocent and childlike, shrieking at the mere sight of a spider. We learn a lot about this character from dream sequences that start out gracefully with flower petals falling on smiling faces, but then turn tragic, focusing on the murder of his mother and his hatred for his father.

Fans of Burton should be reminded of Large Marge (from *Pee Wee's Big Adventure*) at a particularly startling shot involving the local witch. Christopher Lee has an early cameo as the old-fashioned judge who disapproves of Crane's revolutionary tactics. And just wait until you see who plays the headless horseman (in the scenes when he has a head)!

SLITHER (2006)

Director: James Gunn
Cast: Nathan Fillion, Elizabeth Banks, Gregg Henry, Michael Rooker, Tania Saulnier, Don Thompson
Length: 95 minutes
Rating: R

> **Synopsis:** An alien entity lands in a small Southern town, interrupting the celebratory first day of deer hunting season when a parasitic worm infects one of the residents and transforms him into a squid-like monster with a constant craving for meat.

Old school horror fans sickened at the sight of PG-13 remakes and torture-geek shows hogging the theater screens were finally given a reason to rejoice when writer-director James Gunn, all warmed up from his dynamic *Dawn of the Dead* script, reminded us just how much fun watching a horror film can be. He understands the genre in and out and is a natural when it comes to making the audience squirm, laugh, and scream in rapid succession.

When a phallic tentacle excitedly bursts through the stomach of Grant Grant (yes, that's his name and not a typo), played with both ferocity and forlornness by Michael Rooker (*Henry: Portrait of a Serial Killer, The Walking Dead*), while watching his wife taking a shower, it's clear that their marriage is going to need more than a counselor. Their love for each other remains an abiding factor even when he grows to behemoth proportions and produces alien slugs that crawl into the mouths of citizens (turning them into zombies serving his will), giving a touch of compassion to even the most outrageous scenes.

Right from the very beginning, *Slither* is a generous film that nails every scene; to miss one moment would be a huge mistake (two of the biggest laughs occur in the opening scenes), so make sure your Halloween guests don't arrive late. Although its plot might make it seem like a *Night of the Creeps* clone, it actually has quite an imagination. For one, it is innovative how all the acid-vomiting zombies respond to a central host and inherit its mind, and therefore, are all hopelessly in love with Grant's wife (played by the Hitchcockian beauty Elizabeth Banks). It has its fair share of shock and suspense, but what makes it rank so high on the pumpkin meter is just how funny it is. The wittiest and most quotable lines come from the selfish, foul-mouthed mayor, who at one point goes on an epic temper tantrum when his secretary (played by *The Office*'s Jenna Fischer) forgets to pack his favorite soda. You and your friends should also get a kick out of the hilariously bad karaoke performance to "The Crying Game," the red-state shenanigans of the residents, two girls reading R.L. Stine's *Goosebumps* books in the most appropriate of nights, a pair of cops who are too occupied discussing how fast a particular bird can fly to notice the giant meteor crashing behind them, and the squirm-inducing, over-the-top deaths.

While *Slither* failed to make an impression at the box office, this flick has serious cult potential, so hopefully people will be discovering these awesome psycho slugs from hell for many years to come. Helping its chances is how its star, Nathan Fillion, has lately become the ultimate heartthrob for nerds and geeks everywhere.

SOMETHING WICKED THIS WAY COMES (1983)

Director: Jack Clayton
Cast: Jason Robards, Jonathan Pryce, Vidal Peterson, Shawn Carson, Diane Ladd, Pam Grier
Length: 95 minutes
Rating: PG

Synopsis: A small Illinois town is jeopardized by a carnival group, led by the sinister Mr. Dark. Wishes are granted and souls are taken, and only two young boys know the truth.

Walt Disney Studios Home Entertainment DVD cover for *Something Wicked This Way Comes* (1983).

To translate the poetic imagery of a classic Ray Bradbury novel into cinema is no easy task, but it helps when the man himself wrote the screenplay. The film opens with sensory shots of a crisp autumn day, with two children frolicking through foliage to a field of thousands of pumpkins, ready to be cut. Narrator Arthur Hill reads the words of Bradbury with the wistfulness of an adult who vividly remembers what it was like to be a boy in October.

Will Halloway and Jim Nightshade, born only a couple of minutes apart, are best friends and next door neighbors. They're at the kind of age that gives you so much energy, you feel the need to run everywhere, and nothing says Halloween more than two boys running through a graveyard in the middle of the windiest of October nights to catch a glimpse of a train that appears to be full of ghosts. The train is actually carrying a traveling carnival led by Mr. Dark, who looks like Satan himself when compared to the innocent and quaint citizens of Greentown, Illinois. He is able to see past their cheerful dispositions to uncover their regrets and yearnings, and then offers them something they never thought they could receive: a second chance. But much like the Monkey's Paw, these deepest wishes all come with a devastating price.

The movie works best when it focuses on the mysterious spell that a carnival casts on children and a sense of the macabre looms in the air, even amongst all the laughter and smiles. It's not surprising to learn that the story was inspired by an experience Bradbury had at a carnival as a child, when a magician told him to live forever. The scenes where the two boys react to the carnival come closest to matching the power of the novel, one of the greatest things you could possibly read during October. Also outstanding are the scenes where Mr. Dark clashes with Will's father, an almost-retired librarian unforgettably played by Jason Robards. Ideally, he would be easy pickings

for Mr. Dark since he laments youth on a daily basis, but he surprisingly puts up one hell of a good fight. And a warning to arachnophobes: *Something Wicked This Way Comes* contains one of the scariest tarantula scenes ever filmed, so proceed with caution.

The journey to celluloid was long for *Something Wicked*. Several years before Bradbury published the novel in 1962, the story existed as a film treatment that greatly excited his close friend, Gene Kelly, who hoped to direct. Despite all of his success with *Singin' in the Rain*, studio executives wouldn't back the project, so Bradbury decided to expand the story into book form. It would take another twenty years for Hollywood to finally come to its senses, and thankfully, at the time, Disney didn't shy away from scaring the hell out of youngsters.

SPACED INVADERS (1990)

Director: Patrick Read Johnson
Cast: Douglas Barr, Royal Dano, Ariana Richards, Gregg Berger
Length: 100 minutes
Rating: PG

Synopsis: Fifty years after Orson Welles caused mass hysteria with "War of the Worlds," a radio DJ re-airs the broadcast, and this time it's the aliens that are fooled.

A group of dimwitted Martians mistakes the show for a real invasion and are determined to relish in the glory, but when they land their spaceship to support their brethren, they find themselves all alone to battle country roads and earthling germs. And since they happened to land on Halloween night, the citizens of Big Bean, Illinois, assume they are just trick-or-treaters whose dire warnings need not be heeded. At one point, one of them is overwhelmed and defeated, realizing that there are five of them against four billion humans, John Wayne included. Just when things can't get any worse for the idiotic invaders, they suddenly remember a nifty device of theirs called the donut of destruction, capable of blowing up the earth while leaving the Martians completely unscathed.

There is a happy innocence to this sci-fi comedy that will work wonders with children, and for adults who are very young at heart, it will keep you very entertained for at least the first 45 minutes. Early on in the film, a trio of elderly people sits on the porch, listening to the radio and reflecting on what it was like hearing *War of the Worlds* for the first time. When the woman teases her husband for reacting by wearing a bucket on his head and going out to battle the aliens, the man replies with, "Ain't you dead yet?" Ten minutes later, all three are wearing buckets. Equally charming is when the aliens tag along with several trick-or-treaters as they are being driven house-to-house by the always entertaining character actress Patrika Darbo (who you will surely recognize from at least a couple of TV shows), and when the deputy, who couldn't be more excited about handing out his first speeding ticket ever, catches the lucky winner going 3,000 miles per hour in a 55 zone. But *Spaced Invaders* is probably a tad too infantile and repetitive to keep you fully engaged, so if you find yourself craving a goofy, no-brainer Halloween flick even with eyelids that are getting heavier by the minute, this is a great movie to fall asleep to.

If E.T. had gotten the opportunity to phone home more often, he probably would have mentioned at some point to his alien friends that Halloween is a great time to visit Planet Earth.

SPOOKIES (1986)

Directors: Eugenie Joseph, Thomas Doran, Brendan Faulkner
Cast: Felix Ward, Maria Pechukas, Peter Iasillo Jr., Peter Dain, Nick Gionta, Lisa Friede, Dan Scott
Length: 85 minutes
Rating: R

Synopsis: A group of late-night partiers stumbles into a mansion that belongs to a lovesick sorcerer named Kreon. He needs their life essence to bring his deceased wife back to life, so he unleashes a variety of monsters to do his dirty work. Not only do the partiers have to worry about the haunted mansion, but also about the swarms of zombies lurking outside.

Only the most awesome of video stores will have the obscure treasure that is *Spookies*, a celebration of silliness and imagination that calls out for not only b-movie fans, but also for those who simply want something different. Directors Thomas Doran and Brendan Faulkner had shot a film called *Twisted Souls* (which the world will sadly never get to see), but the studio hired Eugenie Joseph to blend some of the previously shot scenes with some new ones of her own. So the final product, *Spookies,* is essentially two separate films spliced together, and it's remarkable

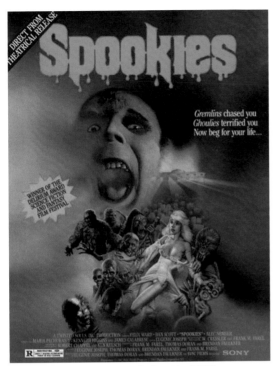

Sony/Columbia-Tristar VHS cover for *Spookies* (1986).

up into separate groups and explore the entire house, making them easy pickings for evil. However, it's not common for a low-budget '80s film to display such an excellent, versatile army of monsters. Members of this ultimate monster mash include a cat-like henchman with a hook for a hand, a she-demon conjuring evil with her beloved ouija board, wind-breaking muck-men who can be killed with wine, a combustible grim reaper, a slimy little lizard-gremlin thing, a grotesque witch with icy-cold breath, an Asian woman that can transform into a giant spider, peculiar strobe lights that instantly cause severe aging, an adolescent druid with fangs, a towering, fleshless creature whose intestines can strangle and electrocute you at the same time, and the never-ending swarm of zombies. It's also not common for such a goofy film to be graced with such serious, oddly beautiful music. You can either love or hate this film, but you can't deny its ambition and originality.

Watching *Spookies* is like walking through a commercialized haunted house during the Halloween season. Sometimes it's too dark to see anything and sometimes it's hard to understand what the monsters are saying behind their masks, but you're having such an amazing time because you know that any second, something will jump out and surprise you. And it is obvious that the workers have really put their hearts into trying to show you a good time.

Unfortunately, *Spookies* has yet to find a home on DVD in the States, but for now, definitely keep an eye open for VHS copies. It's also available on a certain popular video sharing website, and even though this movie deserves to be seen on a big screen, a computer screen is better than no screen at all.

how you wouldn't know that from watching it. For those interested in how this worked, pay close attention to when the lizard-creature attacks the British woman, Adrienne. Joseph's elegantly-lit shots of the voyeuristic cat-demon peering through the window are convincingly thrown into the *Twisted Souls* footage to create one of the film's most effective scenes.

It's common in horror films for a bunch of morons to wander into an old, dilapidated mansion just to escape boredom. Then, of course, they will all split

SPOOKY BUDDIES (2011)

Director: Robert Vince
Cast: Harland Williams, Rance Howard, Jake Johnson, Skyler Gisondo
Length: 88 minutes
Rating: G

Synopsis: After a puppy looks into a mirror and says the name three times, Warwick the Warlock is awoken after a 75-year-slumber. It's Halloween and he needs only three items so the evil spirits of the netherworld can remain on Earth forever: his magic staff, his spell book, and the souls of five young puppies.

Following in the paw prints of *Air Bud* (1997), *Air Bud: Golden Receiver* (1998), *Air Bud: World Pup* (2000), *Air Bud: Seventh Inning Fetch* (2002), *Air Bud: Spikes Back* (2003), *Air Buddies* (2006), *Snow Buddies* (2008), *Space Buddies* (2009), and *Santa Buddies* (2009) comes a Halloween adventure that will fill you with the kind of jubilance you receive when you open the front door expecting to see ordinary trick-or-treaters in lame superhero costumes, but instead before you is an adorable astronaut dog carrying a sack of treats in its mouth.

After a double dose of nihilistic brutality courtesy of *Frontier(s)* and *I Saw the Devil*, a movie featuring talking dogs was exactly what I needed. My exposure to the *Air Bud* movies never went beyond snickering and ridiculing them at video stores, and I fully expected to turn *Spooky Buddies* off after five minutes. But when a movie opens on a full-mooned Halloween night in a town with the motto "where anything is possible," inside a gothic manor where a warlock that seems to be channeling John Hodgman (both his appearance and personality are eerily similar *The Daily Show*'s deranged millionaire) is, with the help of his talking Eurasian eagle owl Mr. Hoot, summoning the one and only Halloween Hound, telling it, "I have the five puppy souls of the blood. I believe they are what you need to open the portal," and when the production designer is named Michael Bolton, how can I not be in this movie for the long haul?

Surprisingly, the film has a lot more to offer than just five adorable golden retriever puppies with minimal facial expressions following their trick-or-treating masters, visiting the local doggie psychic (appropriately named Zelda), running from a bullmastiff larger than all of them combined, and making obligatory puppy puns like "it's so great to have a new leash on life" and "Halloween is my favorite day of the year, paws down." For starters, this is a film that oozes Halloween adornment; a substantial portion of the budget clearly went to ransacking all of the Spirit stores near Vancouver, British Columbia, and once the thousands of yard inflatables, strings of holiday lights, jack-o'-lanterns, gravestones, and animatronics were emptied from U-Hauls, they were arranged with much precision and care. The special effects partnered with vibrant colors create numerous awe-inspiring moments of characters flying, spells cast, and fog creeping through trees of the dead.

As far as non-canine characters go, the kids are predictably the least interesting of the bunch but at least they are well-mannered and likeable. Supporting characters like the perky Mrs. Carroll (played by the loveable Jennifer Elise Cox), feisty mother Janice (Elisa Donovan, who starred with Lance Henriksen in *The Dog Who Saved Halloween*

the same year), and the clumsy Sheriff Dan (Michael Teigen, who plays the same role in *Super/Santa/Space/Snow Buddies*) are well equipped to hold your interest whenever the buddies aren't around. Best of all, Rance Howard (father of Ron and Clint) plays a gravedigger and church organist whose warmth and tenderness is a perfect contrast to the cartoonish, eeeeeevil buffoonery of his longtime foe, Warwick the Warlock. More time should have been spent on naming his character though because the line that serves as a final blow at the climax, "the name's Joseph! Joseph Johnson!" packs a puny punch.

It won't take long at all to recognize which film *Spooky Buddies* tries desperately to emulate, from the flashback prologue where townsfolk storm onto the property of an evil local who has captured a child to the climax where all it takes is the rising sun to drive away Satan's army for good, *Hocus Pocus* is all over this movie, but if you're going to steal from a Halloween movie, then you might as well choose a good one. The similarities start off as minor but there is a large section in the middle that is laughably faithful: desperate to find his book of spells, the warlock squirms through trick-or-treating streets, surprised and spooked by how the town has already been taken over by evil until he discovers that they are just children in disguise. Meanwhile, the children, unaware they are being pursued by the warlock's possessed zombie servant (well, technically he's a surfer Frankenstein), enter the Spooky Brew-Haha where the adults are partying to a costumed band performing "The Monster Mash." Of course, the parents don't believe their crazy stories so the kids interrupt the performers by jumping on stage to warn everybody of the warlock. Instead of heeding the warnings, they give the warlock a huge ovation for having the best costume of the night. By this time you already have Bette Midler's rendition of "I Put a Spell on You" stuck in your head.

Because *Spooky Buddies* turns the cuteness level up to 11 in the third act with its many close-ups, it's surprisingly easy to forgive all the Bible references and the ridiculously juvenile ending. I would have much rather seen Air Bud himself make an appearance to save the day; after all, puppies are cute, but sometimes a full grown dog can be cuter.

STAGEFRIGHT/DELIRIA (1987)

⬚ **Director:** Michele Soavi
★ **Cast:** David Brandon, Barbara Cupisti, John Morghen, Martin Philips, Lori Parrel
⊕ **Length:** 90 minutes
⚐ **Rating:** Not Rated

🎬 **Synopsis:** A psychopath escapes from a mental hospital and pays a surprise visit to a group of thespians rehearsing a horror musical called The Night Owl.

In the film medium, if you want to take a tired formula and give it a lavish makeover, then you probably should hire an Italian director. Michele Soavi, the former Dario Argento protégé who is mostly known for his audacious *Cemetery Man/Dellamorte Dellamore*, managed to conduct a formulaic slasher with a proclivity for lush colors, bizarre set designs, and spine-chilling sound effects. And much like his mentor does, he tops it off with outlandishly gory action scenes that we watch with morbid fascination, because the characters aren't the least bit identifiable, making their fates meaningless to us.

The film mostly takes place inside a theater, a great location for a game of hide-and-seek with a homicidal maniac. These players utilize every square inch and have to worry about trap doors and dangerously high catwalks in addition to the killer's assortment of power tools.

Even the killer has been given more depth and personality than the standard teenager-slaughterer. In a visually dazzling scene, hundreds of feathers flutter around the maniac, who is sitting still on the stage with the mutilated corpses of his latest victims. He's wearing an oversized owl mask, staring straight ahead and gently petting a cat (who is also a member of the hallucinatory musical's cast). Feline lovers will be nervous at this point, but *Stagefright* is too smart to resort to killing animals for shock value. However, it is not quite smart enough to know when to quit, or else we wouldn't be stuck with a tacky next-day resolution that gets just about everything wrong.

SUSPIRIA (1977)

⬚ **Director:** Dario Argento
★ **Cast:** Jessica Harper, Joan Bennett, Alida Valli, Udo Kier, Stefania Casini, Flavio Bucci, Miguel Bose
⊕ **Length:** 90 minutes
⚐ **Rating:** Not Rated

🎬 **Synopsis:** Soon after enrolling in a German ballet academy, a young American dancer not only has to deal with the strange noises that keep her up at night, but also with the mysterious deaths of her classmates. Plunged into a nightmarish world, she discovers that the famous dance academy is actually a secret coven for witches.

Drenched in saturated primary colors and pulsating with a harrowing score by the Italian progressive-rock band Goblin, Dario Argento's three-strip Technicolor-printed masterpiece is one of the best looking and best sounding horror movies of all time. It not only honors German expressionism, but also the wonderful work of Jean Cocteau. It also contains the kind of

chilly, mysterious atmosphere you wish you could experience in real life on Halloween, just as long as you can avoid sharp objects and maggots.

Argento's skilled direction takes us along a dark and twisted path that begins with a young woman arriving at her new school in the midst of a rainstorm, only to be greeted by a fleeing, delirious student and then by a voice on the intercom telling her to go away. The young woman is played by Jessica Harper, whose resemblance to Snow White adds to the film's fairy tale logic. Argento has stated that he even used *Snow White and the Seven Dwarfs* as inspiration for *Suspiria*'s color scheme.

As one would anticipate with an Argento film, the gore is plentiful and is to be looked at with perverse wonderment, especially during the methodical, drawn-out stabbing death of a female student in the beginning (which remains just as shocking on repeated viewings). He clearly has no inhibitions when it comes to how he treats his characters. Other victims include a blind pianist who gets chewed to death by his mercurial canine and another female student who leaps out a window and unfortunately lands in a dark pit full of barbed wire that slowly but surely swallows her whole. Considering that the academy includes a barbed wire pit, thousands of maggots that fall from the ceiling, and killer bats that make unexpected appearances, young Suzy obviously made a poor choice in schools, but at least it has interesting neoclassical architecture.

This movie definitely isn't for everyone, but if you're dying to impress artsy friends with a taste for the dark side while at the same time offending other friends who prefer their art sunny and simple, then this is the perfect choice. And be sure to get your hands on the soundtrack by Goblin because it will provide perfect background music for when you carve pumpkins, read scary stories, or put on your costume.

TALES OF TERROR (1962)

🎬 **Director:** Roger Corman
⭐ **Cast:** Vincent Price, Peter Lorre, Basil Rathbone, Joyce Jameson, Maggie Pierce
🎞 **Length:** 88 minutes
👤 **Rating:** Not Rated

🎃 **Synopsis:** In this adaptation of three Edgar Allen Poe stories, a tormented loner is visited by his daughter, who might be possessed by his deceased wife; an alcoholic man devises the ultimate revenge for his unfaithful wife and her lover; and a dying man is put under hypnosis, which results in his mind staying alive and active even after death.

This is one of the better films based on the work of Edgar Allen Poe, mostly because of its no-nonsense script, Gothic imagery, and three wickedly good performances from Vincent Price. In the first tale, "Morella," he plays a lifeless geezer who has spent half his life constantly mourning over the death of his wife. Roger Corman doesn't let you feel a second of ease because right away he shows unexpected close-ups of things like tarantulas and corpses to keep your heart beating rapidly. "Morella" also contains hauntingly gorgeous shots of an angry ocean pounding against Price's gloomy mansion, as well as a score that sounds like weeping ghosts.

Price has more fun with "The Black Cat," in which he plays a snobby, sophisticated, and overly proper professional wine-taster. This contrasts well with Peter Lorre's character, a selfish, abusive drunk who is so nasty, he deserves to be on the receiving end of one of Poe's torture chambers. In the film's best moment, the two characters compete in a hilarious wine-tasting contest, in which Price watches in horror at Lorre's "most unorthodox method of tasting."

The finale, "The Case of M. Valdemar," is truly twisted. Price plays an unfortunate man trapped in the tiny gap between life and death. Basil Rothbone is in great villain form as he manipulates Price and his loved ones, making sure that Mr. Valdemar remains in his tortured, frozen state. The extremely creepy ending assures you that these were 90 minutes well spent.

The second and third tales were remade by horror maestros George A. Romero and Dario Argento in 1990s *Two Evil Eyes*, which is also worth watching.

THEM! (1954)

⚑ **Director:** Gordon Douglas
★ **Cast:** James Whitmore, Edmund Gwenn, Joan Weldon, James Arness, Onslow Stevens, Sean McClory
⊗ **Length:** 92 minutes
🛡 **Rating:** Not Rated

🎞 **Synopsis:** As a result of the lingering radiation caused by an atomic bomb, mutant ants terrorize Southwest America. The fate of mankind is in jeopardy as they reproduce and destroy everything in their path.

There was an overabundance of cheapo big-bug thrillers in the 1950s that were entertaining but not much else. Directors would tackle these projects with a warped sense of humor, demanding their cast to overact while reciting horribly cheesy lines. Merely showing the humongous bugs trampling all over humans was seemingly all that mattered, and while *Them!* doesn't shy away from the trampling, it thankfully has much more to offer.

After the first 20 minutes of this Cold War-era film, you could swear you were watching a murder mystery. Two police officers find a little girl stumbling in the desert, clutching her broken doll. She's in shock and is unable to speak, and it is obvious she's been through a terrible ordeal. As the officers investigate, they come across houses that appear to have been torn apart by a tornado. Signs of struggles are evident, but the residents are all missing. The only available clues are sporadic footprints in the sand that baffle all the local the forensic experts. Because the set-up is so gripping and mysterious, when the ants show up, it doesn't matter so much what they look like. With *Them!*'s inferior companions, the bugs were the stars of the show. Even though the ants here look fantastic, Gordon Douglas places just as much emphasis on atmosphere, suspense, and interesting compositions.

The cast members are all on the same page as their director, all showing not a single error in tone and emotion. There are also plenty of opportunities for your skin to crawl, such as when government officials watch a film strip about ants, or when the mutated monsters have two children cornered in a dingy tunnel.

Them! also has a lot to say about the atomic age and the unspeakable dangers that could transpire from nuclear technology, but it never sacrifices fun for preachings.

TOURIST TRAP (1979)

⚑ **Director:** David Schmoeller
★ **Cast:** Chuck Connors, Tanya Roberts, Jocelyn Jones, Jon Van Ness, Robin Sherwood, Keith McDermott
⊗ **Length:** 90 minutes
🛡 **Rating:** PG

🎞 **Synopsis:** After their car breaks down, a likable group of twenty-somethings is assisted by kind, hospitable Mr. Slausen, the reclusive owner of an out-of-business museum. One by one, they disobey his warnings and venture off into the night, making them easy prey for a masked psychopath with telekinetic powers and hundreds of lifelike mannequins at his disposal.

As director David Schmoeller expertly peels away layer upon layer of logic and reasoning, lifting the boundaries between reality and fantasy, we feel as vulnerable and flabbergasted as our unfortunate protagonists do. What starts as a formulaic setup for a slasher picture (city slickers who venture into the middle of nowhere for a vacation and have car trouble at the absolute worst time and place, making the inconvenient delay only the beginning of a terrifying series of events) turns into a maddening world where absolutely no person or object can be trusted. It could have easily been a dazzling mess of a movie but *Tourist Trap* somehow ends up being a good contender for the most underrated horror movie of all time. Despite its intermittent incoherence, it's an amazing thriller with all the right pay-offs and heart-stopping jolts.

20th Anniversary Special Edition
TOURIST TRAP
EVERY YEAR YOUNG PEOPLE DISAPPEAR!..

WIDESCREEN

DVD

Cult Video DVD cover for *Tourist Trap* (1979). Compass International Pictures.

Chuck Connors is a sight to behold as the lonely but charming Southerner Mr. Slausen, inheriting the same sympathetic kookiness that made Norman Bates such a fascinating character. Who ever thought the former baseball player and *Rifleman* star could be so convincing as a sad lunatic who spends his retirement playing with dolls and caressing a wax statue of his dead wife?

Tourist Trap wastes no time and delivers one of the best opening scenes you'll ever see, when a man wanders into a run-down gas station and is confronted by a malevolent group of mannequins with mouths that drop, eyes that follow, and cackles that can easily drown out human screaming—it doesn't take long for him to realize he should have walked another hundred miles to the next gas station. But the most suspenseful scene takes place in the house next door to Slausen's museum, where a young woman is subjected to the kind of slow, agonizing, and terrifying death that will make you wonder what the MPAA board was smoking when they bestowed a PG rating. Schmoeller also shines during a first-class chase scene that is graced with comedic taunting from the villain and some superb music from Pino Donaggio.

This film also benefits from an assortment of really bizarre masks, shocking sight gags, a dreamlike feel, striking photography, and undoubtedly some of the prettiest music you'll ever hear in a horror film (especially during the closing credits). Don't let the fairly conventional synopsis fool you: this is one unforgettable film!

TRICK OR TREAT (1986)

Director: Charles Martin Smith
Cast: Marc Price, Tony Fields, Glen Morgan, Doug Savant, Lisa Orgolini
Length: 98 minutes
Rating: R

Synopsis: Eddie is an unpopular, heavy-metal loving teenage outcast whose rock hero, Sammi Curr, has recently died in a mysterious hotel fire. While playing Sammi's final record backwards, he unleashes demons that initially just want to destroy everyone who has bullied Eddie. But when a local DJ plays the record at midnight on Halloween night, the entire town is in danger.

It's this simple: If you were a metalhead in the 1980s and still have an innate tendency to bang your head,

then this movie would be a radical Halloween creature feature. Those with horror cinema and hard rock in their blood will surely identify with Eddie (played by the actor most commonly known as Skippy in *Family Ties*), whose "odd" tastes make him an outcast at school among the legions of preps and airheads. Because you see a lot of yourself in the character, it's discomforting in the opening scenes to see Eddie's torments but you'll get your Halloween buzz back in the form of catharsis when one of rock's chosen warriors returns in evil spirit form to avenge his number one fan.

In 1986, Tipper Gore's PMRC crusade was in full force, and *Trick or Treat* has a lot of fun at its expense.

Poster for *Trick or Treat* (1986). De Laurentiis Entertainment Group.

Ozzy Osbourne has an amusing cameo as a reverend who is outspoken about rock's evil nature and longs for the days of simple love songs with no hidden agenda. Gene Simmons has another cameo as a radio DJ who understands Eddie's devotion to the departed Sammi Curr, but warns him that his rock hero's angry Satanic roots led him down some questionable paths. Soon Eddie has to decide whether to betray his fallen idol in order to save everybody else that he cares for.

In addition to the glam metal music (courtesy of the band Fastway) and evil spirits sprouting from portal-to-hell stereo speakers, you also get an outrageous chase scene that utilizes the entire school (they even slow down considerably once they go through the library), a mesmerizingly sexy seduction via Walkman, a school Halloween dance where metal steals the show, a couple of jack-o'-lanterns that behave more like guard dogs, a possessed car running down a ghost trick-or-treater, and hilariously dated lines such as, "We just got call waiting. I feel like a total bigwig!" Two other '80s films that cater especially to metalheads are the highly entertaining *The Gate* and flawed-but-watchable *Black Roses.*

TRICK 'R TREAT (2007)

Director: Michael Dougherty
Cast: Dylan Baker, Brian Cox, Anna Paquin, Samm Todd, Quinn Lord, Leslie Bibb
Length: 82 minutes
Rating: R

Synopsis: Five tales of terror are interwoven on Halloween night in Warren Valley, Ohio, and the monstrosities include a pack of werewolves, a school principal/serial killer who hands out poisoned candy and demonstrates interesting pumpkin carving methods, mentally challenged adolescent zombies, and a pint-size pumpkin demon who makes sure that everyone follows the rules of Halloween.

October of 2007 was poised to be a very special day for horror fans, as Michael Dougherty's debut film, *Trick 'R Treat*, was scheduled to premiere nationwide. It had been many years since a horror anthology had been given a theatrical release and even longer for a horror movie with a Halloween theme (with the obvious exception of Michael Myers's endless offerings). Adding to the exciting buildup were a kick ass trailer and extremely enthusiastic reviews from its initial festival screenings. But in the late summer, Warner Brothers made a truly idiotic and cowardly decision by delaying its release until February because it didn't want to compete against LionsGate's *Saw* series, which had unfortunately dominated the box office for the previous three Halloween seasons. Another delay occurred; then suddenly Warner Brothers stopped talking about *Trick 'R Treat* altogether, keeping it on the shelves for two years, seeming incompetent on how to handle a horror movie that wasn't a sequel or a remake, and one that was just as funny as it was scary. It's a good thing *Creepshow* (an obvious inspiration) had the honor of being released in 1982, because in 2007, it would have been quietly released to video to fade into obscurity.

In the autumn of 2009, *Trick 'R Treat* on DVD was finally made available to the hungry fans, and we embraced it like a child embraces a full sack of trick-or-treating candy. The travesty of not being able to experience it on the big screen will forever sting, but at least now everyone can enjoy this marvelous movie anytime they want.

Trick 'R Treat unfolds like an EC comic violently blowing in the wind, interconnecting five stories and sporadically—and brilliantly—linking them all together. The essence and beauty of Halloween is captured here in exquisite detail: there seem to be more jack-o'-lanterns on display here than in Keene, New Hampshire's, annual pumpkin festival; autumn leaves dance with heavy fog; people of all ages parade in elaborate costumes; and of course a vicious little pumpkin demon, wearing orange pajamas and a burlap sack, walks around the whole town to make sure nobody is breaking the rules of his precious day. The film opens with a snippet from the kind of Halloween educational safety video you watched in elementary school, and everything that follows will make even the grouchiest Grinches feel sentimental and reflective on what Halloween has meant to them throughout their lives.

Dougherty was wise to include a wide variety of age groups in his tales, so we get to see how middle schoolers, twenty-something girls, and elderly men have their own holiday agendas. The standout section of the film plays like an episode of *Goosebumps*. It

Film still from *Trick 'R Treat* (2007). Warner Bros.

centers around teenagers exploring the myth of their hometown that a school bus driver purposefully drove his bus filled with mentally disabled children off a cliff, after being paid off by their ashamed parents—the flashback inspires the film's only daylight scene, and it's quite a sight to see the shackled kids in their horrifying vintage Halloween masks being bathed in harsh sunshine. The scenes of Dylan Baker poisoning and burying trick-or-treaters are also particularly effective, and it demonstrates how effortlessly *Trick 'R Treat* balances comedy and horror.

On October 28th, 2013, following a special *Trick 'R Treat* screening at the Egyptian Theater in Hollywood, a Q&A took place with Michael Dougherty and a few cast members. At one point, Sam himself came out on stage and handed Dougherty a note about making a sequel to *Trick 'R Treat*, but he claimed that it wasn't his call to make. However, sitting in the audience was Thomas Tull from Legendary Pictures, who stood up and said, "I can't say no to Sam. Let's make a sequel." Seconds later, a title card for *Trick 'R Treat 2* appeared on the screen and audience members who had been waiting years for this announcement appropriately went wild. Even though *Trick 'R Treat 2* hasn't even been written yet, I can already say with confidence that it will be one of the best movies to watch on Halloween.

TROLL 2 (1990)
Director: Claudio Fragasso
Cast: Michael Paul Stephenson, Connie McFarland, George Hardy, Margo Prey, Deborah Reed, Darren Ewing
Length: 95 minutes
Rating: PG-13

Synopsis: A young boy is warned by the spirit of his deceased grandpa that their family vacation to a small town called Nilbog could end in disaster. Young Joshua soon discovers that the residents of Nilbog are vegetarian goblins who transform humans into plants before devouring them.

If you take a vacation to a beatnik town whose name is "Goblin" spelled backwards, has only 26 residents (including a sheriff named Gene Freak), and whose general store owner says, "There's no coffee here in Nilbog. It's the devil's drink," then you really shouldn't be surprised when after eating the food, you start to bleed green chlorophyll and change into a plant.

The constantly hilarious and otherworldly *Troll 2* should be kept safely behind glass in every home to save Halloweens that aren't going so well. Drastic times call for drastic measures, and here is a film that fails on such a monumental scale that it will provoke enough unintentional laughter to perk up even the deadest of parties. If you are depressed by how few trick-or-treaters are knocking on your door or by how your cayenne-pepper heavy pumpkin seeds have given your friends stomachaches, then *Troll 2* will be there to cheer you up. *The Room*, *Manos: The Hands of Fate*, and *Plan 9 From Outer Space* have all achieved legendary status in the Heckle Cinema Hall of Fame, but there can be only one best worst movie and that is *Troll 2*.

Due to its unparalleled incompetence, *Troll 2* has earned both a legion of fans and a prestigious place on the Internet Movie Database's Bottom 100 List. Just to clarify, there is not a single troll in the whole film (Nilbog sounds better than Llort, anyway) and it has nothing to do with the original *Troll* (1986). The crew members were all Italians who spoke very little English and the cast were all Americans with little-to-no prior acting experience. Making matters worse was director Claudio Fragasso, who sternly insisted that the lines be read exactly how they appeared in the script, no matter how clumsy they sounded. The cast knew the script was ridiculous and nonsensical, but they were just so thrilled to be working in their first motion picture, they did what they were told. But nothing could have prepared them for just how embarrassing *Troll 2* ended up being, or how this small-budgeted horror cheapo shot in

Morgan, Utah, would become a cult hit many years later, celebrated in midnight screenings all over the world and inspiring events like the Troll 2 Olympics.

It's hard to fathom just how something like *Troll 2* can exist in this world, so allow your questions to be answered by the 2009 award-winning documentary, *Best Worst Movie*, directed by Michael Paul Stephenson, who starred in *Troll 2* when he was just ten years old. It catches up with just about everybody who was involved in the movie—from the director to the makers of those terrible goblin masks—and reunites them in festival screenings, and the result is one of the funniest, sincerest documentaries in recent years. The actors all seem like the sweetest, nicest people you could ever hope to meet, so you can't help but feel happy for their sudden, inexplicable fandom. Once you see it, you will immediately be adding George Hardy (who played the father in *Troll 2* and is now a dentist living in Alabama) to your Facebook friends—while he can't even make a line as simple as "Is breakfast ready, dear?" sound convincing, he is the kind of genuine and charismatic guy that makes everybody smile. Even his ex-wife absolutely adores him!

Troll 2 should be served with lots of green food as well as popcorn, lots of popcorn! Also have some corn on the cob handy because you never know when the irresistible queen of the goblins, Creedence Leonore Gielgud (played by Deborah Reed in one of the only good performances) might show up.

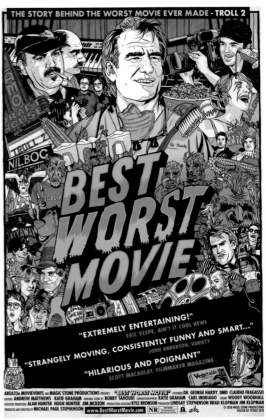

Poster for Magic Stone Productions' *Best Worst Movie* (2009), the documentary on *Troll 2*'s amazing journey.

V/H/S/2 (2013)

Director: Gareth Evans, Gregg Hale, Eduardo Sánchez, Jason Eisener, Adam Wingard, Simon Barrett
Cast: Adam Wingard, Lawrence Michael Levine, Kelsy Abbott, Jay Saunders
Length: 96 minutes
Rating: R

Synopsis: A student's disappearance prompts a couple of private investigators to search for clues inside his house. After finding a mountain of mysterious videotapes piled in front of a television, they watch footage of people who had the cameras rolling on the worst day of their lives.

The original *V/H/S* from 2012 merged together the horror anthology format with the found-footage presentation, and while I thought the concept was terrific, most of the stories simply weren't nearly interesting or frightening enough. Only the fifth and final tale, titled "10/31/98", is a must see. It's about a group of teens who enter a house they believe is hosting a traditional Halloween party, but there is a lot more to it than papier-mâché décor, cobwebs, and fog machines. Since we feel like we're placed directly into the action, it feels as if we're roaming around one of the mazes at Universal Horror Nights, and like the finest ones, it saves some of its most amazing tricks for the end.

Released less than nine months after the original, *V/H/S/2* is a gigantic step up in both storytelling and cinematography. The first segment is titled "Phase 1 Clinical Trials" and in just ten minutes, it frazzled more nerves than the entire original film did. It's about a man who goes through a bizarre procedure at a doctor's office after a car accident has robbed him of vision in one eye. Once again, he can see, but there is a catch: a camera has been implanted in his eye so that the doctor can monitor the progress anytime he pleases. To have your mind and vision manipulated the way this poor sap does is a fate worse than death—it's like constantly having one foot inside The Further from *Insidious* even while doing mundane chores around the house.

Next up is "A Ride in the Park" which mixes zombies and found footage so much more effectively than *Diary of the Dead* did. With a Go-pro strapped to his helmet, a young man on a bike ride stops to help an injured woman, but his good-Samaritan instincts are rewarded with a nasty zombie bite. The idea of a long, continuous zombie POV shot might not seem that entertaining, but it's truly fascinating to get a first-person perspective of someone undergoing the horrific metamorphosis from man to brain-munching living dead ghoul. It would be heartbreaking if it wasn't so damn fun!

Before you have time to catch your breath, you're plunged into "Safe Haven"—the best of all of the *V/H/S* tales—which contained the most shocking images in a trailer that was crammed with carnage and chaos. We know it shouldn't be difficult in making a religious cult look terrifying, but this tale clearly wanted to be much more than just another take on the Jonestown Massacre. A news crew manages to talk the elusive and distrusting leader of a controversial Indonesian cult into letting them enter the compound and conduct interviews, and once inside this haven that is anything but safe, the camerawork and delivery is so flawless that I couldn't help but be a nervous wreck the whole time. I was giggling with nervous anticipation when the camera was showing a classroom full of children or peeking inside a surgical room that the crew was supposed to stay out of. So much shit goes down in the final ten minutes that I felt the same kind of exhilaration as I did during the ultimate monster mash climax of *The Cabin in the Woods*.

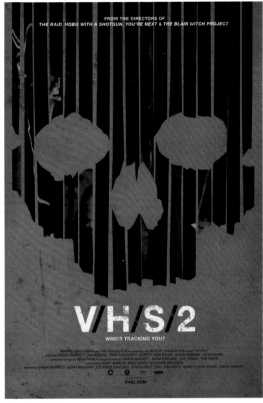

Poster for *V/H/S/ 2* (2013). Magnet Releasing.

The final tale, "Slumber Party Alien Invasion," is easily the weakest of the four but it still would have added some much needed fun and excitement to the first film. It gets off to a convincing and entertaining start as a group of youths take turns pranking each other—these days it's probably a common reaction to scream "Don't put this on Youtube!" the moment you realize your trickery has been immortalized on video. But sadly, once the aliens crashed the party, I started to lose interest because the extra-terrestrials didn't look anything special, and I was never able to accept the silly idea of a dog running around with a camera attached to its head.

THE UNNAMABLE (1988)

🎬 **Director:** Jean-Paul Ouellette
⭐ **Cast:** Charles King, Mark Kinsey Stephenson, Alexandra Durrell, Laura Albert, Eben Ham
🎞 **Length:** 87 minutes
👤 **Rating:** R

📖 **Synopsis:** A group of college students explore a mansion where gruesome murders took place a century ago, and soon meet the hideous creature which has hidden inside ever since.

The haunted house subgenre is intrinsically engaging on Halloween night, regardless of whether these movies are the artistic ones that gradually prey on your psychological weaknesses, or the ones that are packed to the brim with gore and nudity and not much else. This H.P. Lovecraft adaptation falls somewhere in between. It uses a clichéd but not necessarily tired formula: the house that has been an urban legend for many decades remains untouched and unlocked, so anybody can enter whenever they want. Four students enter and the door slams shut behind them and automatically locks, trapping them inside. Of course, they decide to split up (and occasionally take their clothes off) and one by one, they encounter the hideous creature lurking between these walls.

While this is a very loose interpretation of the Lovecraft short story, its sophistication and large vocabulary is preserved by the character of Randolph Carter, a loveable bookworm who is content to read by candlelight even when people are screaming and doors are slamming all around him. The way his eyes light up when he spots the sacred (and very dusty) *Necronomicon* is a thing of beauty.

The creature is Alyda Winthrop, a shockingly original-looking, hooved she-demon that hisses like a cat and rips out human hearts with ease. Up until the climax, there have been tiny glimpses of her, which arouses our curiosity and makes the game of hide and seek much more fun. We are treated to a violent scene involving her father in the film's first five minutes, so we know right off the bat that this chick can do serious damage, and she doesn't disappoint. One frat boy gets his throat torn open, veins splitting everywhere, causing so much blood to gush out that we start seeing bones. Another character gets pounded against the cement floor repeatedly until his head cracks open.

The Unnamable also benefits from appropriate low-key lighting and simple yet effective haunted house sound effects like heart beats and intermittent pounding. The ending is filled with a bunch of nonsense involving her father's journal that can awaken the trees to take her spirit away, or something like that. The spell couldn't have been that effective because a sequel followed four years later.

WACKO (1981)

🎬 **Director:** Greydon Clark
⭐ **Cast:** Joe Don Baker, Stella Stevens, George Kennedy, Andrew Dice Clay, Julia Duffy, Scott McGinnis
🎞 **Length:** 90 minutes
👤 **Rating:** R

📖 **Synopsis:** "It's October the 31st, 31 backwards is 13, it's Friday, it's Halloween, it's the 13th anniversary of the lawnmower killings, there's a crazy loose, it's prom night, I'm out of coffee."

This teen-slasher parody believes it is much funnier than it actually is, but it does have its moments (mostly found in the first 20 minutes). Joe Don Baker stars as a buffoonish cop who has become the town's laughing stock by tirelessly hunting a maniac who pulverized a few horny teenagers with a lawnmower 13 years ago. In one scene, he has to break the news to a married couple that their daughter has become the latest victim of a Halloween killing spree, but he is still wearing his clown costume, and proceeds to pacify them by offering a balloon animal. This scene is made even funnier by an accidental jump cut, one of many things that establish *Wacko*'s poor quality and amateurish execution.

This film tries really hard to be different by having the characters break out in song and dance for no reason, giving normal cars the ability to fly through the clouds, and displaying a warning to the viewers that an unnecessary dream sequence is coming up so it would be a good time to get refreshments—sadly, this is actually a wise piece of advice because the dream sequence is nothing special. Aimed at the *Porky's* crowd, this should please anybody who loves really bad '80s movies and low-brow humor. It spoofs (often lamely) *The Exorcist, Alien, Planet of the Apes, The Elephant Man*, but the only one that really works is when Mrs. Bates from *Psycho* shows

up at a dinner party. There are countless references to Sir Alfred Hitchcock, and the filmmakers decided for some reason that it would be hilarious to play the theme song to his legendary television program in just about every scene.

You would think that a film filled with moronic, sex-crazed teenagers in danger of being splattered by a lawnmower killer would have its fair share of gratuitous nudity and gore, but that is not the case here. At least the ending is so utterly ridiculous, it could come directly from a *Scooby Doo* episode. George Kennedy is a good sport as always, playing Mr. Doctor Graves, who works as a surgeon despite not having gone to medical school.

THE WATCHER IN THE WOODS (1980)

Director: John Hough
Cast: Bette Davis, Lynn-Holly Johnson, Kyle Richards, Carroll Baker, David McCallum, Richard Pasco
Length: 84 minutes
Rating: PG

Synopsis: An American family moves into an English mansion owned by an elderly woman whose teenaged girl disappeared many years ago during a solar eclipse. The two sisters start seeing and hearing paranormal activity that seems to be generating from a psychic force in the forest. Believing that the missing girl is trying to contact them, they try to solve the mystery of her strange disappearance.

Press photo for *Watcher in the Woods* (1980). Walt Disney Productions.

time to explain, but not nonsense involving a lunar eclipse that can arbitrarily transfer humans into a parallel dimension. This ending was added on after the original test screening produced unhappy results for being a little too scary—one of several ways Disney interfered with John Hough's vision.

People who saw this as children probably remember it being so flawless that they might be hesitant to watch it again. Now that they are older, they might not appreciate it like before, so why tarnish those great memories? But rest assured, because this Walt Disney chiller is still entertaining, scary, and thought-provoking after all these years. It will be much sillier than you remembered, but that just makes your reunion even more charming.

It opens with majestic shots of forests with sunlight trying to creep through, and with a score that sounds like a disoriented music box. The set-up is all-too familiar, but always welcome: American family moves into a creepy, old mansion that they wouldn't be able to afford in a million ears if it didn't carry a troubled past, and in no time at all, the children start seeing things that are invisible to the parents. Because we've seen this story many times, *The Watcher in the Woods* catches us off guard in the final moments when it decides that it wants to be science fiction. You tend to hear a lot of nonsense in haunted house movies when it comes

Bette Davis is marvelous as the ominous landlord that takes the art of grumpiness to a new level. Newcomer Lynn-Holly Johnson tries her best but is given too many clumsy lines like "I was yelling myself hoarse." The most unintentionally goofy moment comes when she meets Mr. Keller, played by Ian Bannen, at his front door; just pay attention to his line deliveries for a good chuckle.

There are a few good scares as well, most notably a cheap startle with a Halloween mask and a scene in a crypt that uses a blatant rip-off of John Williams's *Jaws* theme. As the film dishes out more and more nonsense, we end up with a list of questions that are never answered, such as why the ghost is able to give lots of small, vague clues, but never any helpful ones. All confusion aside, this would still be an appropriate Halloween companion. It even includes a creepy black cat and a spooky scene in a funhouse!

WAXWORK II: LOST IN TIME (1992)

🎬 **Director:** Anthony Hickox
⭐ **Cast:** Zach Galligan, Monika Schnarre, Martin Kemp, Bruce Campbell, Sophie Ward, Alexander Godunov
🎞 **Length:** 104 minutes
👤 **Rating:** R

🗑 **Synopsis:** The survivors of the first film go back in time to collect items that will prove their innocence. Throughout their journey they must battle aliens in outer space, monsters locked in dungeons, severed hands that won't stay dead, corruption in King Arthur's court, and an assortment of other demons.

Criminally overlooked, this dynamic rollercoaster is a special gift for horror experts everywhere. It is seriously all over the map and has a ferocious pace that tries to cover every horror setting and every horror cliché, yet the whole time it feels totally original. By faithfully and hilariously spoofing *Alien, Frankenstein, The Haunting, The Raven, Dawn of the Dead, Nosferatu,* and countless others, it's a film loaded with winking cleverness.

A severed hand chases the survivors of the original film home, chokes the girl's stepfather, and then gets a hammer to bash his head repeatedly. It then shifts its attention to the girl, where they engage in an outrageous brawl that includes the usage of mustard, hotdog buns, and a garbage disposal. The hand gets grinded to mush and the girl receives an even bigger bloodbath than at Carrie's prom. By showing this kind of action even before the opening credits, director Anthony Hickox has immediately laid all his cards on the table, assuring us he isn't interested in journeying down the same paths as the 1988 original.

In this time-travel saga, Hickox manages to re-create the look and feel of the films he spoofs, using the right kind of lighting, costumes, music, hairstyles, and cinematography. All goes well until an *Alien* parody drifts along aimlessly, and when it takes over 30 minutes for our protagonists to prevent an evil overtaking from Medieval times. Thankfully, our buzz is resurrected for the final act and we walk away wishing for a Part 3.

There is even a rather hypnotic, enchanting scene where the king gets drunk on wine while fire-breathers and belly-dancers with pythons draped around their necks twirl around him. It is an interesting contrast to scenes like The Monster squeezing Dr. Frankenstein's neck so hard that his teeth, tongue, and eyes pop out and smack against a grossed-out Zach Galligan (star of the *Gremlins* films). And just wait until you see Bruce Campbell having his insides chewed out by vultures as he fights back with hilarious one-liners. And what on earth are Drew Barrymore and David Carradine doing in this movie?

THE WICKER MAN (1973)

🎬 **Director:** Robin Hardy
⭐ **Cast:** Edward Woodward, Christopher Lee, Diane Cilento, Britt Ekland, Ingrid Pitt
🎞 **Length:** 88 minutes
👤 **Rating:** R

🗑 **Synopsis:** At the request from an anonymous letter, a police officer investigates a missing girl on an island dominated by Pagans. The clues he gathers make him believe that the girl is about to become a human sacrifice for their annual May Day celebration, to plead the gods for a plentiful autumn.

Lobby card for *The Wicker Man* (1973). British Lion Film Corporation.

the Pagan gods might be pleased enough to send delicious pumpkin seeds your way. A film about a devout Christian clashing with Pagans on an island off the west coast

It would behoove you to pay respect to *The Wicker Man* sometime in the 744 hours offered in October because of Scotland during an annual harvest festival is ripe for parallels with Halloween's early history. Sadly, the festival being celebrated is May Day and not Samhain, but rest assured that there are plenty of costumes and animal/human/ale sacrifices to go around.

Edward Woodward gives an exceptional performance as Sergeant Howie, who we first see landing his plane on the island of Summerisle to investigate a missing girl. He doesn't take kindly to the locals when they give mystifying answers to his reasonable questions and engage in drunken sing-a-longs and public copulation. His patience worsens when he witnesses a teacher's lecture on how the phallus symbolizes a force of nature in their religion to a room full of girls who worship old Celtic gods instead of Jesus Christ. When he complains about the children jumping naked over a bonfire, the friendly and suave Lord Summerisle insists that it would be much too dangerous with their clothes on. The leader of this heathen island is played by Christopher Lee, who still to this day says *The Wicker Man* is the greatest film he's ever been a part of. Watching it for the first time is one of the oddest cinematic experiences you'll ever have because it's like nothing you've seen before,

and you can't quite tell whether it's horror, murder mystery, dark comedy, or musical. I showed it to a group of friends recently who had never seen it, and I felt especially excited for them when the time came for Britt Ekland's seduction of the celibate Sergeant by singing the lovely "Willow's Song" nude in the next room, for the festival tradition of animal-headed men positioning their swords in the shape of the sun for a terrifying game of chance, and for one of the most unforgettable movie endings ever.

I'm not sure what's worse: the fact that one of the most respected and important horror films of all time could get so badly mistreated by its studio that several of its scenes were not just cut for the theatrical version, but are still lost to this day, or the fact when so many people hear the words "The Wicker Man," the first images that come to mind are a bear-suited Nicolas Cage punching women or screaming, "Oh no, not the bees!" thanks to the unintentionally hilarious Hollywood remake. There are probably multiple music groups out there fighting for the name "Not the Bees!"

THE WITCHES (1990)

Director: Nicolas Roeg
Cast: Anjelica Huston, Jasen Fisher, Mai Zetterling, Rowan Atkinson
Length: 91 minutes
Rating: PG

Synopsis: A little boy named Luke and his grandmother stay at a coastal hotel that is hosting a convention for the Royal Society for the Prevention of Cruelty to Children. Luke learns firsthand of their secret identity and what will happen to all of the children of England once they are given candy laced with the Grand High Witch's newest creation and greatest triumph: Formula 86.

The Witches works so well as a Halloween movie because in addition to showing off some of the ghastliest witches of all time, we also get other Halloween staples like candy, black cats, and overcast skies, as well as the ominous line, "You are in for a treat," which has been wisely included in countless Halloween sound effect collections. There's no telling just how many children this movie scared the living daylights out of, but unlike another "kids" movie that heavily used bald caps, the very disturbing *The Peanut Butter Solution*, which introduced youngins to the world of post-traumatic stress disorder, *The Witches* is remembered very fondly for showing people at a young age how much fun it can

be to be scared, and you'd have a hard time finding someone apathetic to it appearing in a Halloween movie marathon.

Based on Roald Dahl's 1983 children's fantasy book, *The Witches* feels very much like a Grimm Fairy Tale due to how face peeling and talking mice can appear together in the same scene. It was the final film that Jim Henson worked on before he passed away and you couldn't ask for a more appropriate swan song because it's full of the awe-inspiring puppetry and light-hearted whimsy that he was known for. It's a shame that he had to spend one of his final days writing an apologetic letter to Roald Dahl after the author hated the movie so much that he demanded all associations with his book be removed, including the title.

Even though *The Witches* does a good job in preparing us for the horrors to come, with a close-up of a cackling skeleton at the end of a Lego mouse track and a scene where a sketchy purple-eyed woman gives validity to the "never talk to strangers" rule as she tries to lure a child with a snake-candy combo, it's quite a shock when Angelica Huston tells her worshippers that they may remove their shoes and wigs, and then nonchalantly starts peeling her face off. I love the way the camera playfully roams around the faces of

Poster for *The Witches* (1990). Warner Bros.

the women during this transformation scene because these splendid prosthetics and make-up effects are worth showing off in as much detail as possible. It's no surprise that director Nicolas Roeg also has a ton of cinematography credits to his name because he also shows off a variety of tricks during the mouse transformation scenes; we could have easily laughed at these sequences but instead we learn that being turned into a mouse while an organization of witches all point and laugh at you is one of the cruelest fates imaginable. After what happens to Bruno when he only wanted to collect the "six whole bars of cream whip hazelnut milk chocolate" that was promised to him, it almost feels as if the movie is killing off its main character at the halfway point like Marion Crane when we get a point-of-view shot from Luke as he shakes and spins uncontrollably like he's having a seizure, and then shrinks down into his Fleece as the Grand High Witch mockingly waves goodbye. So it comes as a huge relief when Luke and Bruno discover together that being mice isn't so bad just as long as you're not being chased up a tree by a hungry cat. They are so mature and accepting of their new conditions even when their guardians react pretty much like real parents would.

I've seen my fair share of witch chase scenes, but this is the only one I can think of where a coven relentlessly pursues on foot a little boy at an appropriate gloomy British seaside—it's such a wickedly good image that I wish the filmmakers had given us a nighttime beach chase scene too. Making the Sanderson Sisters look even more like The Three Stooges in comparison, these PG-rated witches are so nasty, they take a break in the chase just to Battleship Potemkin a baby in a stroller, and even after they succeed in transforming Luke into a mouse, their work isn't over because then they compete over who can be the first to stomp him to death.

With the exception of a three-minute-short in which Mr. Bean watches a scary movie at a theater with his girlfriend, this is sadly Rowan Atkinson's sole contribution to cinema for pumpkinheads, and while he is far from Mr. Bean mode here, with his lusting over a staff member and shouting at another one, "Well, get your trousers off, you idiot!", he makes a great addition to the cast as the hotel manager who does his best to serve, but doesn't shy away from using an arsenal of snarky facial expressions when he encounters high-maintenance guests.

And because one of the film's most thrilling spectacles goes by in a flash, I recommend pressing pause many times during Angelica Huston's reprimanding of the woman who dare says that it wouldn't be possible to eliminate every single child in England.

WNUF HALLOWEEN SPECIAL (2013)

Director: Chris LaMartina
Cast: Paul Fahrenkopf, Leanna Chamish, Nicolette le Faye, Richard Cutting
Length: 83 minutes
Rating: Not Rated

Synopsis: A local TV station broadcasts live on Halloween night, 1987, at the notorious Webber House, the site of grisly murders and horrible memories, to hopefully find out once and for all if the place is indeed haunted.

Made for less than $1,500, WNUF Halloween Special is the ultimate product to surface from this sudden VHS revival in recent years. It will be especially charming to those of you who spent a lot of time in the '80s and '90s recording programs off the TV, and are unwilling to part with your VHS collection because of how many treasures you were able to capture. I still have about 50 videotapes, many of which go from professional wrestling to music videos to episodes of Mama's Family. I was also very militant in that I could always find the pause button at any given moment to avoid recording any of the commercial breaks, but now I wish I could revisit those hilariously cheesy local advertisements for the Bargain Barn or the local video arcade. I also wish I would have pressed record on those Halloween nights when I'd return from trick-or-treating to find various late-night Halloween specials on TV, but finding WNUF Halloween Special was like going through those videotapes that I never bothered to label and finding something unbelievably special that I never knew I captured from Halloween night decades ago.

What we have here is an actual WNUF TV 28 Halloween night broadcast from 1987, which begins with news anchor Gavin Gordon, dressed as Count Dracula, reminding viewers that they haven't mistakenly tuned into Transylvania's public access station. He and his co-anchor, the perky Deborah Merritt in a witch costume, go over the night's news stories, which include a Westboro Baptist Church–like group who prays for the end of Satan's holiday. They hold out signs like "Orange + Black = The Flames of Hell" and "Masks Won't Hide Your Sins" and warn viewers that the vortex of Hell opens on Halloween. Then we get local dentist Dr. Stanley Allen who is offering cash in exchange for every pound of candy you bring in the day after Halloween, and a recap covering the one-year anniversary of a little boy who was shot and killed by a shell-shocked war veteran who mistook him for a Vietnamese soldier. There are also Halloween safety tips (such as inspecting your candy so you don't accidently bite into a needle carrying the AIDS virus), footage of trick-or-treaters, and advertisements for pumpkin patches and pumpkin carving tips. An example of the obligatory corny banter that all news teams are forced to master is when Deborah is asked what her Halloween night plans are after the broadcast. "I think I'm gonna go home and play with my cats." "You know, I hope they're not…scaredy cats!" "Oh, Gavin!"

Following the evening news is sensationalist journalist Frank Stewart, who, along with two paranormal experts and a priest, enters the Webber House twenty years after the Spirit Board Murders in which Paul and Linda Webber were decapitated by their son Donald. Back in 1967, teenaged Donald began obsessing over the occult, and a spirit board he mysteriously discovered demanded that he perform ghastly depravity. Nobody has lived in the Webber House since the horrific murders shocked the residents of River Hill Township, and rumors of it being haunted continue to circulate, so Frank Stewart deems this an opportune time to channel Geraldo Rivera, who had opened Al Capone's vault one year ago. But what awaited Frank and his crew proved to be much more frightening than anti-climactic dirt and empty bottles.

If you didn't do any research on *WNUF Halloween Special* beforehand, you would be absolutely convinced that this grainy video equipped with tracking lines, desaturated colors, and periodic static snow was something that had been legitimately passed around from various video collectors for many years until it finally became available on DVD for the public to witness. Not for one moment does it feel anything less than 100% authentic. But instead, this is one of the most brilliant and creative uses of found-footage horror ever, as writer/director Chris LaMartina and his talented crew successfully transport us to pure '80s Halloween nostalgia in ways no other movie has.

About half of the running time is devoted to recreating local TV advertisements from the '80s, and it's truly remarkable how they manage to lovingly poke fun without ever losing credibility by swaying too far in tongue-in-cheek territory. Extra measures were made to ensure the authenticity of the ads, such as avoiding the use of any fonts that were not available in 1987. Using a mix of public domain stock footage, clips from old videos that his friends shot in the '80s and '90s, and new footage from S-VHS and DV cameras that was later run through a VCR a few times to achieve the right aged appearance, these commercials will bring back so many old memories of library reading clubs, hard rock compilation albums, demolition derby events, and the kind of failed teen sitcom or incomprehensible science-fiction show that could only exist in the late '80s or early '90s. Those who remember that Freddy Krueger once had his own phone hotline will smile at the commercial for 1-900 Monster: The Premiere Horror Hotline. Horror fans should also appreciate the creature feature host (speaking with a Bela Lugosi accent) who will be presenting *Monsters Invade the Wax Museum* (not a real movie) later that night, as well as how the candidates in the political attack ads for the upcoming Governor's race are named after two of the greatest vampires in '80s cinema, Dandridge and Barlow.

As funny as the commercials are, the biggest chuckles come when the snarky, sexist reporter Frank Stewart, terrifically played by Paul Fahrenkopf, interviews clueless and unruly locals (thankfully all draped in Halloween costumes), deals with prank callers during a live call-in séance, and engages in awkward and testy banter with the paranormal experts. The elderly husband-and-wife team of Claire and Louis Berger, clearly based on Ed and Lorraine Warren, take their work so seriously even when it involves placing a large set of headphones on their cat, Shadow—who they view as an essential member of their investigating team—so it's no wonder they don't respond well to Stewart's jokes that Claire should be nicknamed Claire the Clairvoyant.

As of early 2014, the unique and amazing *WNUF Halloween Special* is only available for purchase at Alternative Cinema's website.

THE WORST WITCH (1986)

🎬 **Director:** Robert Young
⭐ **Cast:** Fairuza Balk, Diana Rigg, Tim Curry, Charlotte Rae
🎞 **Length:** 70 minutes
👤 **Rating:** G

🎃 **Synopsis:** Mildred is an underperforming student who finds out that evil witches are planning on destroying her prestigious witch academy, which is preparing for its annual Halloween celebration.

Film still for *The Worst Witch* (1986). United Productions.

This is the kind of movie you figured was flawless as a child, but when revisiting as an adult, you're horrified to learn that it's actually a cinematic wreck. From the script to the songs, this is loaded with problems, but it still manages to be terrific entertainment.

It really makes one wonder if J.K Rowling was a big fan, as her *Harry Potter* series carries an alarming number of similarities. The setting for *The Worst Witch* is a pre-teen witchcraft school. The characters have names like Mildred Hubble, Constance Hardbroom, Agatha Cackle, Miss Spellbinder, Gloria Hobgoblin, and Misty Meadow. There is a stern and constantly grumpy headmaster, an elderly and kind principal, and a blonde-haired school bully. The kids have classes about flying with brooms and mixing potions. There is a scene where two of the girls make themselves invisible and another where a classmate gets turned into a hog. And Tim Curry's character seems to be an obvious inspiration for Gilderoy Lockhart. Also, the ending takes place at a big assembly that turns into a victory party for the heroic student (played here by a young Fairuza Balk) who saves the school from evil. But one thing *The Worst Witch* and the *Harry Potter* movies certainly don't have in common is the production budgets. And the super-lame game that the children play, a mixture of hide and seek and a scream-a-thon, is no Quidditch.

The special effects in *The Worst Witch* are laughably pedestrian, but they really add to the corny fun. You get a strong sense that the cast and crew had a blast making it and that just the idea of any kind of drama happening behind the scenes is implausible. Easily the greatest scene comes when Curry, playing the grand wizard with an unbelievably flamboyant cape, flies down during the school's Halloween party and breaks into a song about how anything can happen on Halloween. For four glorious, orgasmic minutes it's Tim Curry hamming it up as only he can, selling each awkward rhyme with charisma (he even breaks out a tambourine when he quickly runs out of things that rhyme with Halloween), while a chaotic green screen behind him displays every dated '80s video effect you can imagine. It's unclear whether the comedy is intentional or unintentional, but either way it's something that should be watched each and every Halloween. Another marvelous scene features the girls passing around a photo of Curry, each one swooning and kissing it before having to tragically pass it along; it eventually ends up in the hands of grouchy Professor Hardbroom, who immediately blushes and demonstrates that she doesn't always have to be such a hard broom. And if you pay close attention, you'll see that the girls also fancy David Bowie!

WRONG TURN (2003)

🎬 **Director:** Rob Schmidt
⭐ **Cast:** Desmond Harrington, Eliza Dushku, Emmanuelle Chriqui, Jeremy Sisto, Kevin Zegers, Lindy Booth
🎞 **Length:** 84 minutes
👤 **Rating:** R

🎃 **Synopsis:** A group of young people have car trouble in the backwoods of West Virginia, and eventually find a cabin in the middle of nowhere. Unbeknownst to them, this cabin belongs to a trio of cannibals, horribly disfigured from generations of in-breeding.

The year 2003 was a very profitable one for the horror industry, as several horror films made a killing at the box office, such as *Freddy vs. Jason*, *28 Days Later*, *Jeepers Creepers 2*, *Cabin Fever*, *House of 1,000 Corpses*, and a remake of *The Texas Chainsaw Massacre*. Yet somehow, *Wrong Turn*, an effectively creepy throwback to slashers from the '70s and '80s, got lost in the shuffle.

Wrong Turn really goes back to the basics, substituting character development for scary action scenes, one after the other. The story is simple. The editing isn't fancy. There are no twists at the ending. The characters do the dumbest things in order to convenience the plot. There is no irony or social commentary. Instead, the film's sole purpose is to scare you, and it succeeds thanks to the dread-soaked locations, horrifying make-up effects courtesy of Stan Winston, clever chase scenes, and three of the most intimidating inbred cannibals you'll ever see. It is basically just about a group of innocent youths (including the dreamy Jeremy Sisto, who gave two other excellent performances in 2003 with *May* and *Thirteen*) being stalked by mutant hillbillies until an inevitable showdown at the end where we find out if there will be any survivors. The film's most obvious inspirations are *The Hills Have Eyes* and *The Texas Chainsaw Massacre*, and even though it's not on their level of craftsmanship or importance, it's a much wiser choice for a movie on Halloween night.

One of the most suspenseful scenes in recent years comes when our unfortunate boys and girls try to sneak out of the blood-soaked cabin while the three cannibals are sleeping. Your heartbeat will become more rapid with each step they take, carefully inching their way to the door as quietly as possible. This is a slow and gripping scene, and gives us a good look at the three mutants with their make-up effects so professional and grotesque it was no surprise to learn that *Wrong Turn* was produced by the late, great Stan Winston.

WRONG TURN 2: DEAD END (2007)

Director: Joe Lynch
Cast: Erica Leerhsen, Henry Rollins, Texas Battle, Aleksa Palladino
Length: 96 minutes
Rating: R

Synopsis: A reality television program about wilderness survival gets unexpected participation from a family of deformed, inbred cannibals that hunts down the contestants one by one.

Joe Lynch's feature film debut reminded us that we shouldn't ignore flicks just because they were given the direct-to-video treatment. People shelled out $11 to have an absolutely miserable experience with another 2007 film, *The Hills Have Eyes II*, when for only a few bucks, they could have rented this far superior backwoods survival-revenge sequel. It's remarkable how a first-time director was able to find just the perfect, meaty area between camp and creepiness, where you're being scared shitless one moment and being grossed out the next, but always having an enjoyable time. It is a rare example of a sequel surpassing the original in just about every way—it takes the same "inbred mutants hunting teens in the woods" approach and has the same high suspense level, but it adds more gore, comedy, sex, and energy, serving as an unapologetic tribute to the early '80s slasher pictures.

Even if you hate reality television, like you rightfully should, you won't have a problem with the setup, which takes six contestants (all demonstrating certain stereotypes to appeal to large, dumb audiences) and places them in the post-apocalyptic Ultimate Survivor show, in which the winner walks away with a million dollars. Obviously, somebody didn't do the required research, because it's not long until they are stalked by the family of West Virginia cannibals, and instead of merely being eliminated for not completing a task like retrieving a key from a river, they are mercilessly dispatched in gory and hilariously over-the-top fashion. Fortunately, the show's host, an ex-marine sergeant played by Henry Rollins, is the ultimate badass, and is anything but an easy snack. The mutants here are nasty and despicable and even though the film does a good job of showing their family dynamics and loyalty, it's mighty exhilarating and rewarding to watch Henry's fists of fury (often followed with macho-heavy one liners) get some payback! The movie has a lot going for it, but Rollins's performance is what you will remember the most.

Wrong Turn 2 doesn't break any new ground and it contains one unbearably irritating character, but it's a bloody good time and you probably won't be able to predict which, if any, of the contestants ultimately survive. Kudos to the horror community for recognizing this as one of the best sequels in recent years, even if its success led to a string of much less admirable entries to the *Wrong Turn* series.

FUN-SIZED FILMS AND CREEPY, CRAWLY COMPILATIONS

BETTY BOOP'S HALLOWE'EN PARTY (1933)

⚰ **Director:** Dave Fleischer
★ **Cast:** Bonnie Poe
⊛ **Length:** 7 minutes

This Fleischer Studios short begins with an eerie farm scene, where a scarecrow violently thrashes in the wind while clouds pass a full moon and take on the silhouetted shapes of cats, witches, and bats. After the shivering scarecrow puts on a jacket, the wind carries an exciting invitation to him that reads "Halloween dinner party at Betty Boop's house. Right away! P.S. Bring your lunch." He shows up in time to help Betty—who's predictably dressed in a sexy French maid costume—with the decorations and to warm his highly flammable hands by the fire. The party consists of pumpkin carving, bobbing for apples, and watching Betty dance, but then an uninvited guest in the form of a womanizing gorilla shows up and is deservedly assaulted (even the jack-o'-lanterns get in on the action). No matter what your opinion of Betty Boop is, black and white animated Halloween shorts should work wonders for your holiday spirit.

BOOGEYMEN: THE KILLER COMPILATION (2001)

⊛ **Length:** 56 minutes

This compilation of horror movie villains includes scenes from *Hellraiser*, *A Nightmare on Elm Street*, *The Texas Chainsaw Massacre*, *Scream*, *Child's Play*, *Candyman*, *Leprechaun*, *The Ugly*, *Wishmaster*, *The Guardian*, *I Know What You Did Last Summer*, *The Dentist*, *Phantasm*, *Puppetmaster*, *Psycho*, *Jason Goes to Hell: The Final Friday*, and *Halloween*.

This is something you want to play during a Halloween party full of gore hounds when you only want the television to contribute to the mood instead of dictating it. The sound doesn't even have to be on and people don't need to watch attentively, because just having this mob of movie monsters slicing and dicing on the television screen achieves the kind of atmosphere you want for this occasion. For the most part, every scene is full of suspense and gore, giving each boogeyman a chance to shine. The lineup includes the most famous mainstream movie slashers, like Jason, Freddy, and Michael Myers, but also includes some lesser known entries, like Simon from *The Ugly* and Camilla from *The Guardian*.

With the exception of *Puppetmaster*, all of these films center on one villain who spends most of the movie stalking and killing people, so the criteria are a bit limiting. And since there is only one film made before 1974, Norman Bates seems conspicuously out of place. It makes us wonder where Frankenstein's monster, Dracula, and the other classic boogeymen are. I would much rather have seen them instead of dentists and puppetmasters. Also, they could have chosen a better clip from *The Texas Chainsaw Massacre*, such as when Leatherface emerges through the beam of Franklin's flashlight or when Jerry stumbles into the Sawyers' house of horrors.

Although it should have been much, much, much better, *Boogeymen* flows nicely and makes a worthy goody bag for horror buffs. Not only does it show fun pieces of trivia during the scenes, but it also includes the theatrical trailers for each of the films, which is a real treat. But if you can get your hands on the great 2004 Bravo Channel special "The Top 100 Scariest Movie Moments," watch that instead.

THE CANTERVILLE GHOST (1985)

Director: William F. Claxton
Cast: Richard Kiley, Jenny Beck, Shelley Fabares, Barry Van Dyke, Mary Wickes, Christian Jacobs
Length: 58 minutes

Oscar Wilde would have been proud of this made-for-PBS special, a classy production that finds grace and compassion in simplicity. It's a ghost story that really goes back to the basics, before special effects could make a haunted house do just about anything to shock an audience. This simply tells a story of a friendship between two loners from different worlds, without doing anything fancy.

The only moments of suspense come when the three Otis children deal with things that go bump in the night—in this case, the rattling chains, faint moans, and slamming doors courtesy of Sir Simon, a ghost that has haunted the Canterville halls for 500 years. Jenny Beck, who plays the youngest of the three children, might have been cast due to the success of *Poltergeist*, for she bears an uncanny resemblance to the late Heather O'Rourke. Nonetheless, she gives a splendid performance as a child with enough imagination, tenderness, and determination to put an end to a ghost's misery. It's no wonder she is so willing to help Sir Simon: her parents are too pompous, cocky, and condescending to really understand her; her big brothers won't include her in their games; and since the family just moved to England from Ohio, she is friendless. Her scenes with Richard Kiley, who plays the equally lonely Sir Simon, are sweet and heartwarming. Toward the end of the film, as a pleasing score is heard, he gives her and the viewers the important message that one should never be ashamed to be unique.

The days and nights go by at a rapid rate in this 58-minute film, and their consistency almost inspires unintentional laughs. Every single day in this English town looks like the most colorful and bright spring afternoon of your childhood, while every night provides the kind of possessed storm that could only be produced in autumn. You won't laugh, scream, or cry while watching it, but you will feel charmed.

CASPER THE FRIENDLY GHOST: "TO BOO OR NOT TO BOO" (1951)

Director: Izzy Sparber
Cast: Cecil H. Roy
Length: 6 minutes

If you need your heart warmed and you have only six minutes to spare, then this extremely satisfying Casper short will serve you well. While the other ghosts are laughing maniacally and flying over a graveyard under a full moon, Casper is leaning against his gravestone and reading a book about how to win friends. He gets the chance when two kids invite him to go trick-or-treating, and it all goes well until his damn transparency problem scares the hell out of everybody. He tries his luck again at a Halloween costume party in a barn, where he has a cute romance with a girl named Lou, bobs for apples, pins the tail on a real donkey, and swings his partner round and round in a dance-off.

DEAR DRACULA (2012)

Director: Chad Van De Keere
Cast: Ray Liotta, Nathan Gamble, Emilio Estevez, Ariel Winter, Marion Ross
Length: 46 minutes

Based on a children's book by Joshua Williamson, this animated short had its television premiere on the Cartoon Network in October 2012, right around the time it became available on DVD. This is not only excellent Halloween viewing material, but it's also the kind of uplifting project that gives you hope in the new generation because above all else it celebrates individualism and diversity. Hopefully it will teach youngsters to be proud of their unique qualities no matter what their classmates may say, and perhaps also turn several of them into classic horror aficionados like Sam.

Count Dracula is portrayed with as much reverence as Bela Lugosi received in Tim Burton's *Ed Wood*. Fully aware that he's no longer the most feared creature of the night, he has gracefully declined in his castle with his ever trusting assistant, unable to understand why the public has sided with chainsaw wielding madmen or pretty boy vampires. When a nervous delivery boy approaches the castle with a piece of mail, the Count feeds off his fear and it

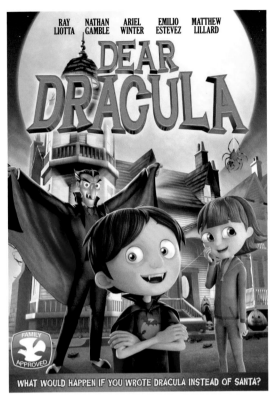

RAY LIOTTA   NATHAN GAMBLE   ARIEL WINTER   EMILIO ESTEVEZ   MATTHEW LILLARD

DEAR DRACULA

WHAT WOULD HAPPEN IF YOU WROTE DRACULA INSTEAD OF SANTA?

Cartoon Network promotional art for *Dear Dracula* (2012).

makes him feel young again. Raising his spirits even more is receiving his first piece of fan mail in years, which lures him out of his Transylvanian castle to the doorstep of an American house where an elderly woman lives with her grandson.

After hypnotizing Sam's grandmother so that she'll invite him inside, the Count is greeted with a huge hug from the adoring Sam, whose Halloween wish has miraculously come true. These two gothic misfits attempt to bond over a monster movie marathon on television but all this does is depress the Count, who is annoyed at the lack of suspense and wonder in these new horror films (most specifically attacking *Twilight* and *Saw*). Further alienating him is his inability to scare the young neighborhood girls, who chuckle as the angry Count reminds them that he used to terrify their great great great great great great great great great great great great great grandparents. Sam, meanwhile, has his own dilemma in the form of a girl who lives across the street. She clearly likes him but her popularity matched with his crippling shame of being an outcast causes him to refuse her invitation to a Halloween party.

Dracula obviously sees a lot of himself in his number one fan, and he does his best to raise Sam's self-esteem by pointing out that what makes him an outcast also makes him the most interesting boy

in the neighborhood. A deal is struck where if the Count trains and recaptures the magic to make the whole world quiver in fear, Sam has to accept the party invitation. The saccharine sweet ending gives Sam the girl, Dracula a Scariest Costume award, and us one of the most satisfying feelings we'll have all October.

DISNEY'S HALLOWEEN TREAT (1982)

⭐ **Cast:** Bobby Driscoll, Peggy Lee, Bing Crosby, Clarence Nash, Betty Lou Gerson
⊛ **Length:** 47 minutes

The greatest season of the year tragically flies by while the others drag on. We know the leaves won't be showering down for long so we feel pressure to take advantage of every fleeting October moment. As a result, the Halloween season tends to bring out our hyper sides because there is so much to do in such little time, and our attention spans suffer as a result. That's why it's great to have a movie like *Disney's Halloween Treat* around; whether we are children, suffer from ADD, or are just unwilling to concentrate on a storyline, this Halloween treat understands.

It feels like sitting down in front of the television with your favorite talking jack-o'-lantern as he wanders aimlessly around the dial. Starting things off is an original theme song set to the images of Disney's Halloween classic short, *The Skeleton Dance*, which has tragically undergone a horrible color conversion. Nevertheless, with lyrics like "Tricks and treats to try tonight, we'll be riding high tonight, the spirit's gonna fly tonight, Disney's Halloween Treat!" we are happily on board. Our pumpkin host explains that for a really good Halloween party, you need a few special ingredients: witches, villains, treats, tricks, and scares. He also believes that the greatest party guest is a real witch, and what better witch than Madam Mim from *The Sword in the Stone* (1963)? This fast-paced and very funny clip centers around a sorcery duel she has with Merlin, in which they transform themselves to various animals to attack each other, but she has a habit of breaking every rule she made, such as "No turning into a pink dragon."

Next up is one of the most Halloweenish moments, taken from *Fantastia* (1940), in which specters on horseback float in gothic nighttime gloom up to Bald Mountain where the winged devil rules. Anyone who was mesmerized with the illustrations in Alvin Schwartz's *Scary Stories to Tell in the Dark* trilogy should greatly appreciate this segment.

We invade classic cartoon violence at breakneck speed soon after with Donald Duck and his three nephews trying to out-scare each other when a monster gorilla happens to be on the loose, and with Pluto, who after terrorizing Figaro the Cat (who I was surprised to learn had a life outside of Pinocchio) gets sent to a Hell where felines are the judge, jury, and witnesses.

The pumpkin warns to "get your trick and treating finished up early because Halloween is a night when a lot of spooky folks come out to see what's happening," and then shows us the two clips that least belong in this mixtape, taken from *Peter Pan* (1953) and *One Hundred and One Dalmatians* (1961). Things pick up with a scene from *Snow White and the Seven Dwarfs* that sorta resembles a film that came out five years prior to it: Tod Browning's *Freaks* (1931). Come on, surely someone else thought of its ending when the Old Hag Witch is crawling in the lightning storm to get away from the dwarfs that are chasing her!

Disney's Halloween Treat concludes with the ultimate Halloween treat, courtesy of *The Adventures of Ichabod Crane and Mr. Toad* (1949). Ichabod finds himself in one of the spookiest forests Disney ever produced, as his whistles blend with the clip-clops of his nervous horse before an unexpected visitor arrives.

DVD Cover for *DreamWorks Halloween Double Pack* (2011).

patch in Modesto, California, and almost immediately the pumpkins learn to walk, talk (in jack-o'-lantern speech, that is), and create mayhem wherever they go. It's easy to think of *Gremlins* as these mutant pumpkins terrorize a wholesome community that is filled with holiday spirit—one house in particular has enough elaborate decorations to qualify for Griswold Family status—and also *Critters 2,* when the pumpkins use teamwork to become even more threatening. And just as *Gremlins* had a soundtrack filled with nostalgic Christmas carols, here we get the theme to *Halloween* as well as "The Monster Mash!"

That 27-minute short was a hard act to follow, but fortunately *Scared Shrekless* is up to the task, as it plays like a *Simpsons* "Treehouse of Horror" episode, brilliantly spoofing *Bride of Frankenstein*, *Psycho*, and *The Exorcist*. In the first story, a gingerbread man demands that a baker create a mate for him, but when too much sugar is added, a bride awakens with monstrous, overbearing qualities. Next, Puss and Donkey share a story that's set in the Bates Motel, but they can't agree on which one of them is the hero and which the victim. Lastly, Shrek tells the story that satisfies our lifelong curiosity about what Pinocchio the Puppet would be like if he were possessed by the devil!

DREAMWORKS HALLOWEEN DOUBLE PACK:

Monsters vs. Aliens:
Mutant Pumpkins from Outer Space
and *Scared Shrekless* (2011)

📺 **Director:** Peter Ramsey, Gary Trousdale, Raman Hui
⭐ **Cast:** Reese Witherspoon, Seth Rogan, Will Arnett, Hugh Laurie, Mike Myers, Cameron Diaz
🎞 **Length:** 48 minutes
🧍 **Rating:** PG

Kudos to Dreamworks for not only giving two of their popular franchises some Halloween love, but for making these two shorts as entertaining for adults as they are for children. Even if you are indifferent to the *Shrek* and *Monsters vs. Aliens* movies, you will thoroughly enjoy this mini double feature as long as you love Halloween.

In *Mutant Pumpkins from Outer Space,* a spaceship empties its septic tank on a pumpkin

FOLLOW THAT GOBLIN! (1993)

Producer: Jonathan Lubell
⭐ **Cast:** Daniel Diker, Chaya Golinkin, Daniel Rickin
🎞 **Length:** 28 minutes

After finding a VHS copy of *Follow That Goblin* at Goodwill, I took it as a sign because I had just revisited the potato-sacked vegetarian goblins in *Troll 2* the night before. I assumed it was going to be a tame and hurried rip-off of *Mad Monster Party*, but instead I got something reminiscent of the claymation spectacles in *Pee Wee's Playhouse*. People with huge imaginations clearly worked really hard on this children's special so it's disappointing that it has neither a *Wikipedia* page nor anything resembling a cult following. It's about a brother and sister who are at a carnival and get lost inside the haunted house that is scheduled to be demolished at the stroke of midnight. If only the funhouses at real carnivals these days could be half as interesting as the one found here. At one point, they lean against a revolving bookcase and after a few seconds of falling into complete darkness, land in a giant trick-or-treating bag where a rapping pumpkinhead dwells. Soon after, they encounter a giant piece of chewed bubble gum that also belts out a tune. As bizarre and trippy as it is, it's also really innocent and teaches important lessons about being yourself and being kind to people who are different from you.

GARFIELD'S HALLOWEEN ADVENTURE (1985)

Director: Phil Roman
Cast: Lorenzo Music, Thom Huge, Gregg Berger, C. Lindsay Workman, Lou Rawls
Length: 25 minutes

Garfield, the corpulent feline who embodies the art of laziness, is known for his sarcasm, egotism, and cynicism, but in this essential TV special, he learns about sharing and generosity. He even shows spurts of enthusiasm and excitement, for Halloween is his favorite night of the year. After all, this is the night when he can get his greedy paws on lots of candy, candy, candy, candy, candy, candy! If you find yourself in a moment of desperation and need to get excited about Halloween but only have 25 minutes to spare, then either *Garfield's Halloween Adventure* or *It's the Great Pumpkin, Charlie Brown* is probably your best bet.

There are many adults who still watch this animated TV special, originally titled *Garfield in Disguise*, every year because it's not only very entertaining, but it gives them a warm and fuzzy feeling like looking through a photo album of their earliest Halloweens. It's pure joy to get to tag along with Garfield and Odie on their trick-or-treating adventure that eventually sends them down the river to a scary house far away from Jon Arbuckle's. The

part when the old man inside the house tells his terror tale, portending the arrival of pirate ghosts at the stroke of midnight probably inspired some of my earliest childhood chills.

Plenty of songs are spread throughout, with the best one being "What Should I Be?," in which a contemplative Garfield rummages through the attic in search of a great Halloween costume.

Garfield's Halloween Adventure sadly isn't shown on TV anymore, but it's available on DVD, sharing the disc with the Thanksgiving and Christmas specials.

THE HALLOWEEN THAT ALMOST WASN'T (1979)

Director: Bruce Bilson
Cast: Judd Hirsch, Mariette Hartley, Henry Gibson, Jack Riley
Length: 30 minutes

Shown annually on TV during the Halloween season for many years until Disney started tossing toothbrushes

Oct. 26–Nov.1 1985 *TV Guide* ad for *Garfield's Halloween Adventure* (1985).

into our trick-or-treat bags, this excellent Monster Mash imagines a world without Halloween and its glorious traditions. After Count Dracula summons his army of monsters that includes Frankenstein, the Wolfman, the Mummy, and others to his castle, he berates them for their increasingly comical demeanors and demands that they return to their terrifying roots, for monsters are supposed to be feared and not laughed at. He also demands the identify of whoever is leaking the suspicious reports of Halloween's demise to the media, unaware that the witch is harboring deep resentment at being called ugly and mean. She refuses to participate in one more festivity, but without her annual ride across the moon, Halloween cannot officially begin.

A clash of thunder and the organs of "Toccata and Fugue in D Minor" open this made-for-television movie, and for its brief running time, the sole message is that Halloween is an incredible holiday and we absolutely need it; each scene is graced with reverence and holiday spirit. Whether we're seeing parents explaining to their costumed kids Halloween's origins or watching a goofy-looking bat converse with the witch in mid-air, we take in every moment knowing that even though we're sitting still looking at a screen, we are experiencing what this time of year is all about.

The ending has all of the sentiment of a Hallmark Christmas movie but it's hard to imagine a more satisfying conclusion. When a couple of forlorn trick-or-treaters plead to the witch, "Please change your mind. If you don't, there'll be no more Halloween, no more jack-o'-lanterns and pumpkin pies. Worst of all, no more trick-or-treats, no more fun dressing up in costumes to make believe you are someone else." Moments later, a party breaks out where the monsters succumb to disco fever (after all, this was 1979), and you know you have struck Halloween gold.

THE HAUNTED HISTORY OF HALLOWEEN (2005)

Length: 50 minutes

If you're in a funk and can't see the point of carving a pumpkin or wearing a costume this year, or if you want to finally contemplate just why you've had such deep connections to this holiday since childhood, then you should take a journey back in time courtesy of the History Channel and follow the fascinating and crazy saga of Halloween. The odyssey begins with

1980 *TV Guide* ad for *The Halloween That Almost Wasn't* (1979).

the Celtic warrior tribes in Ireland 3,000 years ago, who were at the mercy of nature and viewed winter with fear and trepidation, as this was the time they were reminded of their mortality. Samhain was the last day of the harvest and their most important time to pray because the transition of summer to winter meant the possibility of mysterious and strange things. This was the time where the dividing line between the living and the dead was so weak that everyone who had died within the past year had one final chance to roam the earth, and not all of them had good intentions. The Pagan Celts believed that you had to pacify these evil spirits or they would refuse to leave, so food and treats were left for them. Their most sacred of holidays was in serious danger once the ancient Romans conquered most of Northern Europe, and this would surely not be the first time Halloween was faced with considerable opposition.

In a brief 50-minute running time, this documentary teaches you about the origins of bobbing for apples, ghost stories, pumpkin carving, Halloween parties, and the name Halloween itself. It also points out how the customs of the holiday resonate within human nature because, how else could Halloween have withstood so many bans and persecutions over the centuries, to go away only to resurface later, sometimes in another continent? Halloween has been passed around by so many groups, religions, and countries, each putting their mark on it and merging their traditions with the old ones. The spirits of Halloween have overcome Pope Henry III's turning the most sacred Pagan holiday into the official day of the Church, the witch hunting in Europe and America, Martin Luther's Protestant Reformation, the Puritans in New England, World War II, the out-of-control youth leaving paths of vandalism and destruction, and the false stories of strangers handing out poisoned candy and razorblade apples to trick-or-treaters. This is the one holiday that allows us to escape, to fantasize, to make believe, and to revel in things that are off limits to us every other day of the year, and whether it's celebrated in Mexico as Day of the Dead or England as Guy Fawkes Day, these traditions are too popular and important to go away.

Even those already schooled in the history of Halloween would be wise to seek out this special because the impressive variety of footage includes a celebrity children's Halloween party featuring Judy Garland's daughter, the small town of Anoka, Minnesota hosting the very first Halloween parade, original newspaper clippings of events like the Devil's Night in Detroit, and modern Pagans bringing back the type of ceremonies from 3,000 years ago (though fortunately sparing us the animal sacrifices). Any documentary that starts with footage of trick-or-treaters and haunted houses set to the tune of "The Monster Mash" and ends with a mesmerizing scene from 1936's *Pennies from Heaven,* which has Louis Armstrong performing "Skeleton in the Closet," has given us one tasty Halloween treat.

Oct. 26–Nov.1 1985 *TV Guide* ad for *It's the Great Pumpkin, Charlie Brown* (1966).

IT'S THE GREAT PUMPKIN, CHARLIE BROWN (1966)

✂ **Director:** Bill Melendez
★ **Cast:** Peter Robbins, Christopher Shea, Sally Dryer, Kathy Steinberg, Gail DeFaria, Lisa DeFaria
⊛ **Length:** 25 minutes

No October can possibly be complete without watching this immortal TV special, still fresh and entertaining after 40 years. It manages to remind you of your earliest Halloweens without causing lamentation—instead, after a mere 25 minutes of staring at the television, you'll have the immediate urge to dive into a pile of dead leaves like Linus (just don't have

a wet sucker with you!) or visit a pumpkin patch to find the "perfect" pumpkin. It has the kind of spirit that could awaken all of the Halloween Grinches and inspire them to rejoice with the rest of us. It's also extremely uplifting and joyous (even in subtle moments, like when Linus grins and intuitively kicks a pile of leaves), as opposed to the severely melancholy Christmas special.

Sure, this is a wholesome and charming film, but some people might forget just how funny it still is. There is the famous football gag between the often-misunderstood Lucy and always-miserable Charlie Brown with a hilarious twist, Linus wanting to sing pumpkin carols, Charlie Brown's head being used as a pre-pumpkin carving sketch board, Snoopy's innovative way of helping his master rake dead leaves, and Lucy's psychotic behavior as she lustfully carves her pumpkin. For another good laugh, look closely at who is on the cover of Lucy's *TV Guide*! And only the coldest cynic will be able to keep a straight face during the scene in which Snoopy reacts to Schroeder's party music. As many people have probably noticed, Snoopy's antics as a red baron seem out of place, but these scenes are graced with marvelous animation and contain constant energy without relying on a single word of dialogue.

Charlie Brown's name might be in the title, but this is really Linus's story. In his mind, The Great Pumpkin is superior to Santa Claus, so he gets frustrated when the jolly fat man hogs all of the attention. It is sweet how his devotion remains steadfast even when his friends and sister relentlessly taunt him. Only Charlie Brown's sister believes him, and as a result, she suffers one of the worst occurrences ever: a wasted Halloween. Sally's justifiable rant about being cheated out of "tricks or treats" by sitting in a pumpkin patch with a blockhead demonstrates just how important it is to make the most of every second of Halloween night—as she eloquently reminds us, it comes only once a year.

If, after 25 minutes, you have saved room for some great pumpkin dessert, then allow me to present you with additional material. You can say what you want about Linus, but you can't deny he was faithful to his principles, and he stuck to his word that he wasn't giving up on his Halloween savior. It even cost him the chance to be school president in *You're Not Elected, Charlie Brown*, because he was going to win by a landslide before making a gaffe at the debate as damming as Romney's 47%: he professed his loyalty to the Great Pumpkin. *The Charlie Brown and Snoopy Show* ran from 1983–1986 as part of CBS's Saturday morning cartoon lineup. One of the episodes featured a cute, 6-minute short simply called "Great Pumpkin," which spends half of the time in a most-sincere pumpkin patch with Linus, Snoopy, and Sally (who still loves the pathetic, delusional blockhead), and half the time in a bowling alley with Peppermint Patty, Marcie, and good ole' Chuck. These two storylines literally collide in the end for a big laugh. Linus returns to the pumpkin patch again in *Snoopy! The Musical*, a made-for-TV movie from 1988, but his song is incredibly annoying so I can't quite recommend that. There have been multiple parodies of *It's the Great Pumpkin, Charlie Brown*, most notably a fantastic *Simpsons* "Treehouse of Horror" segment called "It's the Grand Pumpkin, Milhouse," but more on that one in the TV section. *Robot Chicken* included a twisted take in the episode "Vegetable Funfest" from season 1, which has Linus summoning the Great Pumpkin in a fiery pentagram, Charlie getting violent revenge on Lucy for years of humiliation, Linus (or whatever was left of him) being buried in his security blanket, Peppermint Patty and Marcie making out, The Great Pumpkin taking over Lucy's psychiatric booth, and an adorable dance-off in the pits of hell. Having a positive attitude with strong Christian overtones didn't help the Peanuts

gang this time around, but this 3-minute skit gives them the funniest material they have seen in years.

THE LEGEND OF SLEEPY HOLLOW (1972, 1949)

1972
Director: Sam Weiss
Cast: John Carradine
Length: 13 minutes

1949
Directors: Clyde Geronimi and Jack Kinney
Cast: Bing Crosby, Pinto Colvig
Length: 34 minutes

Out of all the adaptations of Washington Irving's short story, the 13-minute short from 1972 might be the strangest. Legendary actor John Carradine's narration perfectly sets the scene, and then we're equally startled and amused by an audacious color scheme and a most peculiar-looking Ichabod Crane, sharing the lanky stature of Jack Skellington and the face of the wicked witch from *The Wizard of Oz*. The prior adaptations gave Ichabod some questionable morale, but here he is a real bastard: he hits children in class, only to follow them home and impose himself on a dinner so big, he needs to sprout additional arms to operate all the silverware efficiently. He's also not madly in love with Katrina this time—instead, he's mad for her inheritance. Combine those qualities with his cowardice and the goofiest gait ever and you have a real piece of work, and it's a lot of fun to root for his rival Brom Bones and the headless horseman this time. Like the other adaptations, this one really comes alive once the old Dutch wives' tales of ghosts and goblins properly spook Ichabob right before he has to journey home on a dark, teeth-chattering night, full of visions of bats, ghosts, scary trees, and a strange horse that suddenly appears beside him with an even stranger rider. The music is also terrific here, ranging from twangy acoustic guitars that put you in a pumpkin-patch, harvest-festival kind of mood to eerie avant-garde reminiscent of King Crimson's strangest material.

If after 13 minutes you're still itching for some headless horseman/lanky doofus confrontations, then you should seek out the version that you probably adored as a child: the classic Disney short from 1949 that features narration from Bing Crosby and animation that looks more amazing every year. The exhilarating sensations of watching the final ten minutes has made me wish for years that some place like Universal Studios would create a Sleepy Hollow motion-simulation ride where you felt like you were Ichabod in that same exact forest. But until that time comes, I'll happily continue to watch the 1949 special every October.

LUMPKIN THE PUMPKIN (1991)

Director: Dan Peeler
Cast: Bobby Goldsboro, Christie Westmoreland
Length: 22 minutes

Singer-songwriter Bobby Goldsboro narrates and sings in this obscure 22-minute video targeted to very young children. It's Halloween and as part of a yearly competition, the witches see which one of them has chosen the scariest pumpkin, but the stakes are higher this time because whoever wins will be crowned the new head witch. A little witch named Tara has chosen a cute and pathetic little pumpkin named Lumpkin, which is laughed at and mocked from the start like Rudolph, but Tara doesn't mind because she had no intentions of scaring the trick-or-treaters anyway; she doesn't see why Halloween has to be frightening, so she chooses to spread goodwill and important lessons instead. After talking to a group of trick-or-treaters who are about to vandalize a mean old lady's house, Tara decides to actually ring her bell and talk to her—she's rewarded with lots of candy and fruit for being such a sweet and thoughtful girl. Later, she finds a little girl who is upset because her costume isn't scary and nobody wants to go trick-or-treating with her. So naturally Tara decapitates her with a chainsaw and feeds the brain to a ravenous Lumpkin. Nah, what really happens is Tara gives her some kind advice that saves her Halloween, and then, with the help of her puny, pathetic pumpkin with a hick accent, ensures the safety of trick-or-treaters everywhere by making them more visible to cars. While *Lumpkin the Pumpkin* suffers from cheap animation and a couple of grating voices, it has a big heart and great musical numbers. The theme song, which explains why tonight is such a frightful night for Halloween, is a playful amalgamation of a sea shanty, *Alfred Hitchcock Presents'* theme song, and "You're a Mean One, Mr. Grinch" that's easy to imagine being sung by Jack Skellington himself.

MICKEY MOUSE–HAUNTED HOUSE (1929)

Director: Walt Disney
Length: 7 minutes

You will see a lot of fierce storms in your pumpkin cinema, but there aren't many that are strong enough to literally tilt a house and make it shiver. After Mickey's umbrella is sacrificed to the gods, the mouse approaches the creepy house and is forced inside by some aggressive tree limbs. The front door locks itself and signals the bats and giant spider to come out and play, so Mickey decides to run upstairs so he can instead be terrorized by pitch black, scary shadows, and a grim reaper that forces him to play the organ so he and his many skeleton friends can dance. Animated shorts like this and the *Scary Stories to Tell in the Dark* trilogy should serve as training wheels for all up-and-coming horror fans.

PUMPKIN MOON (2009)

Producer: Catherine Robins
Length: 25 minutes

Based on the children's picture book by Raymond Briggs, the 1982 Oscar-nominated animated film *The Snowman* is a triumph of movie magic and is one of the most mesmerizing and enchanting things you could watch during the Christmas season. It took a very long time but now Halloween finally has its own *The Snowman* and it's called *Pumpkin Moon*. This time, instead of a little boy and his living snowman flying through the aurora on their way to the North Pole, it's now a cute cat flying on its living jack-o'-lantern. Based on a children's book from England, *Pumpkin Moon* gets off to a surprisingly somber start as a feline plants a pumpkin seed in the ground and lovingly protects it as it grows—frequently taking naps on it, rubbing its face against it, and giving it kisses—but then has to say goodbye when a bastard rat chews a hole through the gourd. The cat cheers up a little as it goes trick-or-treating, but later that night, while its owners are asleep, all of the Halloween decorations come to life and an evil witch declares a war on pumpkins. The chewed up jack-o'-lantern repairs itself and then takes the happy kitty on a Halloween night flight, but the witch and her minions are closely behind—in one of the only lines of dialogue, the witch says, "No more happy pumpkin rides! Cat, take the witch's side!" And like *The Snowman*, the soundtrack here is unforgettable. Music as playful as a frolicking feline is interspersed with eerie, cold soundscapes reminiscent of John Carpenter's scores, and it all builds up to the cat's musical number at the end, which is a legitimately wonderful song that you need to add to your Halloween playlist. If you like cats, Halloween, and are curious to see a swarm of jack-o'-lanterns flying through outer space, then I can't imagine a better way to spend 25 minutes of your time.

SCARY GODMOTHER'S HALLOWEEN SPOOKTACULAR

(2003)

⌛ **Directors:** Ezekiel Norton, Michael Donovan
⭐ **Cast:** Garry Chalk, Britt McKillip, Scott McNeil, Tabitha St. Germain
⊛ **Length:** 47 minutes

Based on the *Scary Godmother* children's books and comics by Jill Thompson, this made-for-TV movie reiterates the message that the masterpiece *Monsters Inc.* sent to children two years prior: not all monsters are scary and mean. In fact, the one hiding in your closet could end up being one of the best friends you'll ever have!

You can taste the apple crisp scents as you lose yourself in the opening shot, which starts with a full moon in a starry sky and then reveals a colorful CGI world of trick-or-treat sensory overload. We travel down a busy street occupied by costumed kids, adults, cars, and pumpkins until we catch up with a girl in a cat costume waiting impatiently at the cemetery gates. Her friends arrive but one of them has brought his younger cousin, a pitiful little thing named Hannah who wants desperately to fit in with the older kids but whose legs are so small they will surely cause a slower trick-or-treating pace than desired. So they do what any rational big kids would do in this situation: construct a scheme that forces her inside the scariest house on the street to toss a couple pieces of candy down the stairs as a sort of sacrifice to the evil spirits, and then trapping her inside the house.

Once the frightened girl starts bawling her eyes out, our scary godmother introduces herself and then comforts her by taking her to The Fright Side via an ultimate broomstick ride through prisms of clouds and ghosts. Hannah learns right away that the scary godmother throws an excellent Halloween party even if the invited guests make her frightened all over again. There is Harry the Werewolf, Skully Pettibone (the godmother's "broommate," the self-described skeleton in the closet, and easily the gayest skeleton you'll ever meet), a family of vampires, and worst of all, Bug-a-Boo, who scares Hannah the most with his intimidating size and many eyeballs. But once Hannah gets acquainted with this monster mash, she cheers up and has the kind of Halloween we would all wish for.

Much of the humor comes in the form of vampire puns and some of them work, such as when Ruby the "Queen of the Night" mentions that her preferred pizza is half O-Positive, half AB-negative. This is right after Count Maxwell, who is going through a midlife crisis, tries desperately to sound hip by saying pizza would be a groovy idea—his son then replies to an amused Hannah, "I know, they're so embarrassing, I could just live." This boy also thinks that Hannah's school, Sacred Heart, sounds very tasty!

Back in the real world, the big kids are learning that their scheme backfired when a jack-o'-lantern flickers out and the lights from neighborhood windows start falling like dominoes, signaling the end of Halloween—a tragically wasted night spent waiting for a traumatized girl who doesn't emerge, trading what little candy they have, and engaging in a game of rock-paper-scissors that resembles the *Seinfeld* scene when Kramer and Mickie assumed that nothing beats rock.

THE SKELETON DANCE (1929)

⌛ **Director:** Ub Iwerks
⊛ **Length:** 6 minutes

This Walt Disney Production opens with an owl staring at us during a lightning storm, not even blinking as the wind tries to force it off its branch. Nearby, vampire bats fly down from a watchtower, a hound howls at the full moon, and two black cats duel atop gravestones and awaken a friendly visitor who has mastered the bone xylophone. This black and white celebration of the macabre is the first of many in Disney's *Silly Symphonies* series and shows the ultimate Halloween dance off as four skeletons have some late-night cemetery fun while the living are asleep.

SPOOKY BATS AND SCAREDY CATS: A HALLOWEEN TALE (2008)

Directors: Nathan Smith, Christopher Robin Miller
Cast: Ruby Chase, Brock Holman, Ken Sansom
Length: 28 minutes

This 28-minute stop-motion animation special begins with a camera zooming in on a candle flame surrounded in darkness and then, in an impressive juxtaposition, zooms out to reveal a candle inside of a pumpkin that serves as a scarecrow's head, and right from the start, we know we're in for a real treat. Not for one second does *Spooky Bats and Scaredy Cats* cease to impress, mesmerize, and entertain us, and by the end you'll wonder how in the hell something like this could be so damn obscure. While trick-or-treating, a timid, vampire-clad boy named Makean and his older, cat-costumed sister Katie encounter The Candleman (just one glance at him and you'll understand why he's called that), an elderly and charming man who the kids like despite the fact that he dares to hand out vegetables on Halloween. He asks the kids if they wouldn't mind passing out a few party invitations, assuring them that taking on the task will give them treats beyond their wildest expectations. It turns out there are over thirty invitations, and to reach the invitees, Makean and Katie have to ride a horse and carriage through Spooky Hollow, walk through graveyards to the sounds of thunder, row a boat in a swamp while practically being swallowed by fog, fly on broomsticks through clouds and swarms of bats, and navigate through crypts, and like true trick-or-treating champions, never once drop their jack-o pails. After their odyssey takes them to a mummy, a swamp creature, a wolfman, the grim reaper, a scarecrow, a trio of laughing plants, ghosts, a witch, and a Frankenstein monster, a huge surprise awaits them inside the haunted castle. I think this is one video that Jack Skellington would enjoy watching in his downtime to find inspiration; in fact, there's a song in the middle that sounds eerily similar to Danny Elfman in both music and voice. This is one Halloween special I will probably revisit every October for the rest of my life—it's that damn good!

TERROR IN THE AISLES (1984)

Director: Andrew J. Kuehn
Length: 84 minutes
Rating: R

Donald Pleasence and Nancy Allen host this compilation of scenes from horror, science fiction, and crime films.

The flapping of a projector accompanies a particularly startling moment of *When a Stranger Calls*. Then Donald Pleasance himself takes us out of Carol Kane's babysitting nightmare and explains to us what the cinema is capable of doing, and how it caters to our desire to be scared. This is followed by a collage of clips from horror classics such as *Halloween*, *Jaws*, *Poltergeist*, *Psycho*, and *Carrie*. At this point, watching the clips in *Terror in the Aisles* has been like flipping through an old photo album. They have evoked sentiment but have offered no surprises.

Pleasence then gives special attention to *The Texas Chainsaw Massacre*, even informing/reminding us that it was loosely based on the notorious serial killer Ed Gein, from Plainfield, Wisconsin. Once we are treated to great clips from *Chainsaw* and *An American Werewolf in London*, it looks like this compilation was made primarily for Halloween parties. Just like the *Boogeymen* compilation, this is the kind of movie you want playing so people can take a short break from the socializing and the chaos by sitting in front of the television and watching scary clips before getting a second wind to rejoin the party— it contributes to the mood instead of dictating it. Unfortunately, the second half of *Terror in the Aisles* isn't so concerned with horror fans, as all traces of criteria vanish and crime pictures take center stage. The clips are still suspenseful and the editing still pulsating, but when you have a measly 84 minutes of movie clips of *The Exorcist*, *Rosemary's Baby*, *Jaws 2*, *The Thing*, *The Fog*, *Videodrome*, and *Halloween 2* mingling with *Ms. 45*, *Vice Squad*, *Marathon Man*, *Play Misty for Me*, *Klute*, *The Silent Partner*, and *Nighthawks*, what began as a concentrated, thoughtful reward for horror lovers ends up being convoluted and disjointed. On the other hand, I have to give it credit for reminding viewers that terror encompasses other genres besides horror, and for including one of the most horrifying and suspenseful films ever, *Midnight Express*.

Redemption is found later with its delightful montage of b-movies that might ignite a game of "Name That Movie," and with its perfectly chosen final clip: Leatherface fragging a convulsing body into the kitchen and then forcefully slamming the steel door. In 2011, *Terror in the Aisles* finally became available to watch in good quality, but in a peculiar fashion, existing as a bonus feature on the *Halloween II* Blu-ray.

WITCH'S NIGHT OUT (1978)

☗ **Director:** John Leach
⭐ **Cast:** Gilda Radner, Naomi Leach, Tony Molesworth
⊛ **Length:** 28 minutes

Considered a sequel to 1974's *The Gift of Winter*, this Canadian animated special aired on the Disney channel every October for many years. *Witch's Night Out* starts out with the adorable Casio-synthed tune of "Witch Magic Halloween" and then we're introduced to two kids named Small and Tender, who have big plans and big expectations for Halloween, and can't wait to scare everybody in town. Unfortunately their trick-or-treating adventure proves to be a disappointment because their costumes fail to frighten a single person, they are immediately called by their own names, and they get lousy treats like sardine meringue. Before going to bed, they wish they had a fairy godmother with the ability to transform them into a real wolf man and a real ghost, and soon they are visited by a wicked witch who does just that. The witch started her day feeling like a washed up, faded flower without a single plan for her favorite day of the year, but immediately cheered up when she found out that all the grownups in town are planning a Halloween party in her believed-to-be-deserted house. Harmless party pranks like turning hors d'oeuvres into horror-d'oeuvres eventually lead to the type of magical mischief that turns the town into a frenzied mob, but it all works out in the end when the witch and the kids remind the jaded adults of the true meaning of Halloween, and how it's the one night where you can pretend and let your fancies run wild. The cast includes Gilda Radner, who provides numerous character voices, as well as Catherine O'Hara as the character of Malicious.

HALLOWEEN ON THE SMALL SCREEN: THE BEST TV EPISODES

As popular as Halloween is and given how, in 2012, a record 170 million Americans spent close to $8 billion (according to the National Retail Federation) on costumes, pumpkins, decorations, and candy, you would think thank Hollywood would give a little more love to our favorite holiday. The first Halloween-themed film in years to receive a theatrical release, Nickelodeon's *Fun Size*, opened at #10 at the box office with a pitiful $4.1 million and currently holds only a 25% on Rotten Tomatoes, so it could be quite awhile until Halloween graces the silver screen again. If you want to watch fictional characters enjoy, discuss, and embrace All Hallows' Eve, the small screen is usually where you should go.

What I thought would be a fun little chapter in which I would recommend my favorite Halloween episodes of shows like *Roseanne* and *The Simpsons* proved to be the most daunting task in writing this book, as I decided to explore all the Halloween episodes I could find within the history of television—little did I know how painstakingly long that list would be. It seemed like nearly every show that ever existed generated at least one Halloween episode (even *Walker, Texas Ranger*!) so to narrow down the choices, I considered only the ones that were available on DVD or Youtube. Many series were only on for a single season, never to be released on video or DVD, and not accessible online, so what's the point in recommending something that's impossible to find, like *Drexel's Class*?

My criteria were just as strict as in the movie section so I would say that for every Halloween episode that made the cut, five did not. Here are the episodes that tested positive to produce quick bursts of Halloween cheer.

THE ADDAMS FAMILY
SECOND HALLOWE'EN EPISODE
📺 **Airdate:** October 29, 1965; Season 2

C'mon, what other family is going to bob for apples with the use of a see-saw, and prepare porcupine taffy, walrus tusks, and guillotine-sliced salamander sandwiches for the trick-or-treaters?

THE ADVENTURES OF PETE AND PETE
HALLOWEENIE
📺 **Airdate:** October 31, 1991; Season 1

This critically acclaimed '90s Nickelodeon program gave us one of the smartest, best-written Halloween episodes ever, in which a 15-year old helps his determined younger brother achieve his dream of breaking the all-time trick-or-treat record, but standing in their way is the notorious Pumpkin Eaters gang. Poetic and nostalgic, like *The Wonder Years,* and with a quirky execution similar to *Malcolm in the*

Middle, this will be equally adored by grownups, especially since kids aren't likely to appreciate a reference like Iggy Pop's character calling a teenage punk a stooge.

ALF
SOME ENCHANTED EVENING
🖥 **Airdate:** October 26, 1987; Season 2

While this isn't one of the stronger *Alf* episodes, you shouldn't pass any opportunity to watch our beloved Tanner family and their alien from the planet Melmac. When Kate and Willie forbid Alf to go trick-or-treating in danger of him being caught, he crashes their Halloween party wearing a big zipper to give the impression he's wearing a costume. As usual, the chemistry between Willie and Alf provides the funniest moments, such as when Willie, unable to completely mask his anger in front of his guests, asks Alf at the Halloween party, "Say, what….are…you…DOING HERE?!?!" If you'd like a double dose of Alf for Halloween, then check out the season 1 episode "La Cuckaracha," where a Melmacian cockroach escapes from Alf's spaceship and enters the Tanner house, where simple household products cause it to grow rapidly.

AMAZING STORIES
GO TO THE HEAD OF THE CLASS
🖥 **Airdate:** November 21, 1986; Season 2

While not specifically associated with the holiday, this special one-hour episode of the Steven Spielberg–produced anthology series is so perfect that it has to be considered required viewing during the month of October. It premiered in November but NBC commercials still called it a one-hour Halloween special. The show had invaded horror territory in previous episodes but never quite like this. Directed by Robert Zemeckis, it's about two high school students (Mary Stuart Masterson and Scott Coffey) who are determined to get even with their draconian English teacher, played by Christopher Lloyd in a performance that will both creep you out and leave you in stitches. By playing a heavy metal record backwards, they uncover a spell that will leave their unfortunate victim with a terrible case of the hiccups. All they need to do is go to a cemetery and gather items like dirt from a freshly dug grave and the fingertips of a deceased relative before the stroke of midnight, but man oh man do things go terribly wrong!

This magnificent hour will show you the foggiest graveyard known to man, a fierce lightning storm, a hilarious skull telephone, a drunk gravedigger, a bubbling cauldron, a classic scene from *House on Haunted Hill*, and the potential dangers that come with sexual attraction. If you have children around the age of 10, show them this episode and they'll be horror lovers for life—it might also give them a slight fear of high school teachers though. "PREPARE TO MEET THE MISTERS, MISTER BRAAAAAAAA-AAAAAAND!!!"

THE ANDY GRIFFITH SHOW
THE HAUNTED HOUSE
🖥 **Airdate:** October 7, 1963

Anyone who has seen *The Ghost and Mr. Chicken* knows that when Don Knotts stumbles around a creepy, cobwebbed house, trying his best to conceal his cowardice but failing miserably, it's as adorable and funny as a cat in a shark-costume chasing a duckling while riding a Roomba™ (the video exists, people!). That classic film could be considered an expanded version of this episode, which begins with Opie and Arnold accidentally breaking a window and then realizing they're too scared to retrieve their baseball from the old Rimshaw house with all of its strange noises. Barney, convinced that the wind was the sole culprit for these sounds, lectures the boys that they can't go through life being afraid of their own shadows; however, he can't seem to follow his own advice once Andy sends him and Gomer to the house, where eyes from paintings follow you and axes float in midair.

ARE YOU AFRAID OF THE DARK
THE TALE OF THE TWISTED CLAW
🖥 **Airdate:** October 9, 1994; Season 2

In this early episode of the popular Nickelodeon series, two teenaged boys play a prank on an elderly woman on Mischief Night. They visit her again on Halloween, disguised in their costumes, and she gives them a very special treat: a claw that will grant them each three wishes. This is an enjoyable take on the classic W.W. Jacobs' tale, "The Monkey's Paw," that teaches you to choose your words extremely carefully when declaring your wish.

BEWITCHED
THE WITCHES ARE OUT
Airdate: October 29, 1964; Season 1

Halloween is coming up and Samantha is fed up with how witches are constantly portrayed. This poses problems when Darrin is told to design a witch for the promotion of a new Halloween candy, and his boss insists on the ugliest warts and the pointiest of noses. When Darrin is fired for wanting to go into a more respectful direction, Samantha and her witch friends decide to pay the boss a visit. Can someone tell me why Aunt Clara was determined to steal all of his doorknobs?

CHEERS
BAR WARS V: THE FINAL JUDGMENT
Airdate: October 31, 1991; Season 10

Once again, it's the Cheers gang versus Gary's Olde Town Tavern in a duel of practical jokes on Halloween night, but early on Gary offers a truce after learning about his high blood pressure. Not believing him for a second, they frighten him later that night with the use of a ghost hologram. After discovering his lifeless body on the floor with the hologram hovering over him, guilt consumes the Cheers gang—all except for Sam, who is convinced that Gary is just pretending, even as the coroner pronounces him deceased, even as he is chosen to be a pallbearer during the funeral, and even as his casket is lowered into the ground and buried. If this really is all a prank, it's much more intricate than Woody's severed thumb gag!

COMMUNITY
EPIDERMIOLOGY
Airdate: October 28, 2010; Season 2

This recently cancelled prime-time comedy took its annual Halloween episodes very seriously, and the best one is found in Season 2. Students attending a Greendale Community College Halloween party become ill when they eat food that was unwisely purchased at an army surplus store, and when a sick Chevy Chase randomly grabs somebody's arm and bites down hard enough to draw blood, we see the workings of a zombie epidemic. The students are then locked inside with the zombies and an ABBA playlist that never stops. We've seen it all before, but zombie attacks accompanied by "S.O.S.," "Fernando," and

"Waterloo" pack a pretty powerful and humorous punch.

THE COSBY SHOW
CLIFF'S MISTAKE
Airdate: October 15, 1987; Season 4

While Halloween festivities only take up half of this season 4 episode, the other half features the always wonderful presence of Wallace Shawn, playing Cliff's friend who has a bit of a meltdown when his precious power drill goes missing. Meanwhile, the Huxtable children prepare for Halloween by turning the basement into a haunted house. There is another Halloween-themed *Cosby Show* episode, which even shows Claire in a simply dazzling Tina Turner costume, but this one will make you laugh more.

THE DICK VAN DYKE SHOW
GHOST OF A. CHANTZ
Airdate: September 30, 1964

Rob and the gang arrive at a fishing lodge only to find out that their reservations had not been secured like they thought, and that there are no vacancies. Mel tries to bribe the front desk clerk, who tells them that they can spend the weekend at a nearby cabin, just as long as they're OK with the fact that the cabin might be haunted. They become the cabin's first guests since a wealthy fisherman was supposedly murdered there, and it doesn't take long until everyone starts shivering and cowering like a bunch of Lou Costellos when things start going bump in the night. This was my introduction to *The Dick Van Dyke Show* and it managed to get me excited about the witching season in early February.

DIFF'RENT STROKES
A HAUNTING WE WILL GO
Airdate: September 29, 1984; Season 7

Although it's not directly tied to Halloween, this special effects–laden episode has Arnold and Sam exploring a haunted house to see if the urban legends are true. There they encounter an organ that plays itself, paintings with moving eyes, trap doors, mountains of cobwebs, candles that float across the room, a knight statue holding a sword with butter fingers, and John Astin, who probably felt right at home given the many years he played Gomez Addams. Taking advantage of premiering only a few months after the theatrical release of *Ghostbusters*, the boys here are donned in special ghost-fighting uniforms and even get slimed on one occasion.

DINOSAURS
LITTLE BOY BOO
Airdate: October 30, 1992; Season 3

While babysitting the Baby, Robbie Sinclair tells a scary story, supposedly true, about him being bitten by a rabid caveman in a graveyard and going through a bizarre metamorphosis. There is only one way to stop turning into a Were-Man, and that is the consumption of baby toes! The scary story is too much for The Baby and the only way Robbie can quell the cries is the promise of candy, so they go door to door and become the first trick-or-treaters ever. This show is every bit as charming and adorable as we remember, and with this episode you'll also get to revisit that music video starring the Baby.

DR. QUINN, MEDICINE WOMAN
HALLOWEEN
Airdate: October 30, 1993; Season 2

Every now and then veering into levels of corniness reminiscent of *Walker, Texas Ranger*, this show must be commended for showing us good old fashioned Halloweens in the Wild West. This episode starts out with three people sharing scary stories and summoning spirits as choruses of wolves, dogs, and crickets claim the nighttime. The next day the children are excited for a Halloween festival that involves a costume contest and bobbing for apples, as well as a couple of old traditions that supposedly predicted who girls would end up marrying: peel tossing and walnut roasting. The storylines include a man in town repeatedly dying in public places but then suddenly vanishing before Dr. Quinn shows up; a boy believing the local red-haired woman is a witch when all she really wants to do is make him the kind of scary costume his mother used to make; and Dr. Quinn being haunted by her lover's deceased wife, who demands that she stay away from her house and her family.

EVERYBODY HATES CHRIS
EVERYBODY HATES HALLOWEEN
Airdate: October 27, 2005; Season 1

All Chris wants to do is go to his first real Halloween party, but unfortunately it seems the older girl he admires is going out of her way not to invite him. Also making his Halloween difficult is his mostly white school turning into a warzone of eggs, toilet paper, and mischief, and the neighborhood butcher turning into Sweet Tooth the Pimp and stealing his candy. His mom attempts to cheer him up by making him a studly Prince costume (as opposed to the George Jefferson costume he donned the previous year), while his penny-pinching dad prepares the cheapest candy he can find for the trick-or-treaters: Nickers and Two Musketeers. Narrated by Chris Rock and based on his childhood, if the other episodes are as sweet, funny, and creative as this one, I can see why it was so critically acclaimed.

THE FACTS OF LIFE
THE HALLOWEEN SHOW
Airdate: October 26, 1983; Season 5

The girls have an awful lot to deal with on this Halloween! They discover that their restaurant used to be the home of the infamous Halloween massacre where three women were gutted with a butcher knife. Subsequent tenants allegedly went insane, so it becomes disconcerting when Mrs. Garrett starts behaving very strangely, and is quite possibly killing her customers and turning them into bratwurst! This leads up to a climax that has Mrs. Garrett luring two trick-or-treaters dressed as Hansel and Gretel into her kitchen. Implausible ending aside, this was a good introduction to *The Facts of Life*, and it's a shame they never attempted another Halloween episode.

FAMILY GUY
HALLOWEEN ON SPOONER STREET
Airdate: November 7, 2010; Season 9

While for some reason it took nine whole seasons to get our first Griffin Family Halloween, it was worth the wait because this episode has many laugh-out-loud moments. Although I would have liked Stewie's first trick-or-treating adventure to be more original than to involve your standard candy-stealing bullies, it's kind of sweet how Brian and Lois both try to come to his rescue. Meanwhile, Meg and her friends go to a Halloween party in hopes of hooking up with some boys, believing their costumes will surely cover up their geek status. Let's hope that it won't be another nine seasons until the next Halloween episode from this fantastic show.

THE FAT ALBERT HALLOWEEN SPECIAL

⬜ **Airdate:** October 24, 1977

Awww, the pumpkin has "Hey hey hey" carved into it, how cute. After getting kicked out of a costume store because old people are mean, Fat Albert and his friends get into some home-made costumes and head to the cemetery, where a spooky surprise awaits them. Then they catch a scary movie in a theater, play some pranks on the elderly, and visit the spookiest house in town. If only my Halloweens were this eventful!

FRASIER

TALES FROM THE CRYPT
⬜ **Airdate:** October 29, 2002; Season 10

Yep, yet another '90s sitcom with a Halloween episode that revolves around pranks, but few have made a more amusing victim than the sourpuss Frasier Crane, falling for tricks repeatedly and despite his superior intellect, not being able to come up with a suitable revenge—although there was something psychologically diabolical about his plans with a red balloon!

FREAKS AND GEEKS

TRICKS AND TREATS
⬜ **Airdate:** October 30, 1999; Season 1

If *The Wonder Years* had ever given us a Halloween episode, it might have looked something like this. Quirky and maudlin, this one takes us back to the time when you accept that you might just be too old for trick or treating, but aren't sure of how else to spend the holiday. Loveable characters try desperately to find the magic of Halloweens past but the universe throws them one cruel blow after another. The day starts out so promising for the Weir Family but then suddenly Sam is left alone on the streets (after his

friends have blamed him for their Halloween misfortunes), candy-less and pelted with eggs that his own sister threw, while their mother is heartbroken that the trick-or-treaters aren't accepting her homemade Halloween cookies, one of the many reasons her favorite day of the year has crumbled to pieces. Even though it will remind you of the worst Halloweens you've ever had, as well as the times you accidentally scared away the trick-or-treaters by getting too into character or got your shoe stuck while committing pumpkincide, it has so many funny moments that the episode is far more pleasure than pain. The geeks' creative Halloween costumes include Gort from *When the Earth Stood Still*, The Bionic Woman, and Groucho Marx, although the moustache goes from Chaplin to Hitler to Tom Selleck.

GOOSEBUMPS

ATTACK OF THE JACK-O'-LANTERNS
⬜ **Airdate:** October 26, 1996; Season 2

In this episode, four trick-or-treaters take a walk through the woods and end up in a neighborhood they didn't know existed—it's almost like a Halloween Shangri-La, where it only takes going a couple of blocks to fill up your pillowcase. But these trick-or-treaters are also being stalked by mysterious pumpkin demons who demand they go to "MORE HOUSES!!!" If you are the type that likes walking around outside during October just to admire the decorations, then this episode will surely win you over. The ending is so bizarre and random that one wonders if a child came up with it, since adults sadly tend to let logic get in the way of an utterly wacky imagination.

GOOSEBUMPS

THE HAUNTED MASK
⬜ **Airdate:** October 27, 1995; Season 1

This was the pilot episode of the popular *Goosebumps* series and showed that R.L. Stine's playfully spooky novels—which attracted younger audiences to the horror genre—could translate well to the TV screen. Even those outside of the *Goosebumps* target audience should at least be spooked out by the grotesque mask that Carly Beth buys for Halloween—its ghoulish details are made even more horrific when covered in the girl's sweat. Believing it to be the one night where she gets to have fun since she doesn't have to be herself, Carly Beth has a rather orgasmic reaction to masquerading in a new identity: a monster carrying around a head on a stick. When, at a cemetery late on Halloween night, she finally gets revenge on the classmates that have tormented her over the years, her victory is spoiled when she feels herself undergoing psychological changes while under the mask. The material gets surprisingly intense when she struggles to remove the hideous mask and notices in a mirror that the eyes looking back at her are not her own. There is also a surprisingly subtle and well-executed moment involving a talking severed head.

HAPPY DAYS
HAUNTED
☐ **Airdate:** October 29, 1974; Season 2

Ralph hosts a Halloween party in a supposedly haunted house that despite its grisly past (which involve beheadings), mysteriously remains open to the public. Halloween decorations are featured in just about every shot of this enjoyable episode, and there is never a dull moment. It makes you really want to jump in a time machine to experience Halloweens from decades before you were born, even if you constantly have to dodge water balloons. It also makes you wonder if it was customary for a grown man to ask a trick-or-treater for a little kiss!

HOME IMPROVEMENT
THE HAUNTING OF TAYLOR HOUSE
☐ **Airdate:** October 28, 1992; Season 2

Following in *Roseanne*'s footsteps, *Home Improvement* was also known for its high-energy annual Halloween episodes in which the characters play morbid pranks on each other. Each one has its moments and is filled to the brim with decorations, creative costumes, and most importantly, holiday cheer. This episode has The Taylors going to great lengths to make sure Brad's Halloween party is a spooky success and all goes well until his girlfriend shows up with another boy, leaving Brad heartbroken and miserable in his Raggedy Andy costume. This is probably the best *Home Improvement* Halloween episode and not just because it shows what pumpkin carving with "more power" is like.

HOME IMPROVEMENT
A NIGHT TO DISMEMBER
☐ **Airdate:** October 28, 1997; Season 7

Tim and Jill worry about their youngest son, Mark, who after spending several weeks withdrawn and moody, decides to make a short film about a misunderstood boy who turns his entire family into freaks and then murders them. While it's not as Halloween-centered as other episodes, it has a lot of fun with Mark's morbid movie and the hilarious ways his parents react to it. It also has a couple of standout lines that you wouldn't expect to hear in a *Home Improvement* episode: "We're going as the scariest people we could think of: Republicans" and "You really want to help? Let me chop off your heads."

IT'S ALWAYS SUNNY IN PHILADELPHIA
WHO GOT DEE PREGNANT?
☐ **Airdate:** October 28, 2010; Season 6

When Dee announces to the gang that one of them got her pregnant at the Halloween party, they gather and share their hazy recollections in a series of flashbacks where the details are hilariously altered based on the storyteller; for example, in the first couple of interpretations, Frank is dressed as Spiderman, but when it's his turn, he clarifies that he was in fact a Man Spider. As the stories unfold, they learn that a couple spontaneous costume changes resulted in some pretty twisted results, which is just the kind of debauchery you'd expect at Paddy's Pub on Halloween. Keep this consistently hilarious and unapologetically subversive show in mind a couple of months down the road, because it delivered one of the absolute greatest Christmas specials in recent memory.

KATE & ALLIE
HALLOWEEN II
☐ **Airdate:** October 27, 1986

Everybody is in the holiday spirit except for Allie, but she's a good sport and wears a white sheet to attend the local Halloween carnival. Kate mistakes her for another ghost and ends up bringing home a complete stranger, a strange man who talks to his invisible deceased wife. The man leaves but his wife won't, and she proceeds to haunt the house, prompting everyone to hold a séance. Having never heard of this show before, I was happy to hear it had a long, successful run because this episode impressed the hell out of me, due to the well-written, independent female characters, good costumes (especially Bride of Frankenstein), and fun paranormal special effects.

LATE NIGHT WITH CONAN O'BRIEN
SKELEVISION
🖵 **Airdate:** October 31, 2006

One of the many reasons why Conan is the king of late night television is his fearless attitude to try new things, no matter how silly or unusual. No other late night host would have gone through the painstaking process of re-shooting an entire episode and replacing every single person with skeletons, each with identifiable features and clearly visible wires for the puppeteers. Maybe this is what television will be like in the land of the dead: Conan, the Max Weinberg 7, Fabio, Larry King (of course wearing his trademark suspenders), Will Arnett...ALL SKELETONS! Premiering three years after an innovative claymation episode, this Halloween special opens with a spooktacular parody of his intro, where a hearse drives through a foggy cemetery as cheesy Halloween sound effects blend with an announcer who sounds like a cross between Igor and Vincent Price. Perhaps the funniest moment of the episode is when Conan gets a visit from Hannigan the Traveling Salesman, one of the best reccurring characters from the Late Night days.

LITTLE HOUSE ON THE PRAIRIE
THE MONSTER OF WALNUT GROVE
🖵 **Airdate:** November 1, 1976; Season 3

This one managed to put me in the Halloween spirit in March, so I can't wait to watch it again in eight months! It's Halloween Eve, a.k.a. Mischief Night, and Laura and Mary are out soaping windows when Laura observes something rather peculiar inside the Oleson house: Mr. Oleson cutting off his wife's head with a sword! Frustrated that nobody believes her outrageous claims, she takes her best friend to the scene of the crime to look for evidence, and it doesn't take long at all to convince him that what she saw wasn't simply her imagination. This episode starts with spooky music and a close-up of a flickering

jack-o'-lantern, and then the camera pans down to reveal Laura reading "The Legend of Sleepy Hollow" to her younger sister as she's tucked in bed. Right away we are taken back to our earliest Halloween memories and for 45 glorious minutes we remain there, remembering why our hearts have always bled for this holiday. Highlights include the youngest sister believing there is a monster under her covers, Laura walking through the woods at night to the sounds of crickets, owls, and things that howl, and best friends sitting in a cemetery and being thankful for the full moon light, but when it becomes covered by the clouds, they shiver and agree that the graveyard doesn't feel like this in the daytime. The most genuinely creepy moment—with the exception of the two intensely psychedelic nightmare sequences— comes when Laura and Carl are hiding in a closet, so frightened that they agree to hold hands. Laura asks, "Why aren't you holding my hand?" and Carl replies, "I am." Of course it wouldn't be a perfect Halloween episode if there weren't laugh-out-loud moments and this one has a real doozy: Mr. Oleson confronts Laura after the sword incident and explains that grownups sometimes lose their tempers. "It certainly took her by surprise, but she won't be saying anything about this sword from now on."

MARRIED WITH CHILDREN
TAKE MY WIFE, PLEASE
🖵 **Airdate:** October 24, 1993; Season 8

The Grim Reaper decides to finally answer Al's pleas with a visit on Halloween night. When Al has second thoughts, a deal is struck where if his family, at any time in the night, say they need him, then his life will be spared. This is a great episode all around, with Al in a dinosaur costume, Peg as the grim reaper, and a hilarious appearance from The Village People. What is just as upsetting is Fox not even telling the cast and crew that "How to Marry a Moron" was going to be *Married with Children*'s final episode is how this was The Bundy Family's sole Halloween adventure in all its 11 seasons.

MALCOLM IN THE MIDDLE
HALLOWEEN
🖵 **Airdate:** October 28, 2005; Season 7

When a haunted hearse tour makes a stop outside of the family's house, Hal is shocked to learn that nobody told him about the murder-suicide that took place before they moved in. On Halloween night, he starts hearing strange noises and wanders if ghosts are after him. Reese and Dewey spend the evening trick-or-treating, but problems arise when they anger an elderly man and mistake their costumed younger sibling for somebody else. It's great to see Hal hand out candy from his car (while listening to the Bee Gees' song "Too Much Heaven") because he's too afraid to go back inside. Considering how quirky and consistently funny this long-running comedy was, it's a shame they didn't do a Halloween show every year. One of the best lines has to be, "Hal, it's always something with you. You passed on that one house because you thought the doorbell sounded gay."

MARTIN
THE NIGHT HE CAME HOME
💻 **Airdate:** October 29, 1992; Season 1

On Halloween night, Martin and his friends light candles and tell scary stories, the shortest one being "It was a dark and stormy November. Bush got re-elected." Martin—the only one not sporting a costume—lacks the Halloween spirit and doesn't scare easily, so when it's discovered that his apartment has a murderous past, his friends decide to hold a séance to contact the ghost of Old Man Ackerman, who is anything but friendly. This episode is nearly flawless and delivers many solid laughs thanks to a smart script, an outstanding cast, and some devilish special effects.

MEEGO
HALLOWEEN
💻 **Airdate:** October 24, 1997; Season 1

On my eighth straight hour of a '90s Halloween TV binge on Youtube, I came across a series that only ran for a measly six episodes. It starts out like your typical TGIF sitcom, but then suddenly the living room couch morphs into a fanged demon that swallows the oldest sibling whole. Bronson Pinchot (who you definitely know as Balki from *Perfect Strangers* and hopefully also as the magazine-tearing, loony prick Craig Toomey in the zany *The Langoliers*) plays a shape-shifting alien who for some reason is working as a nanny in a Suburban home. Jonathan Lipnicki goes trick-or-treating with Ed Begley Jr. and their dog, Count Barkula. Was I really seeing this or was I just suffering from a Halloween overdose? Either way, it was one of the more entertaining episodes I watched all night.

MODERN FAMILY
HALLOWEEN
💻 **Airdate:** October 27, 2010; Season 2

This was my introduction to the show and I can see why it has so many fans and awards. Halloween is Claire's favorite holiday and she has turned her living room into a haunted house for the trick-or-treaters to walk through. She has the sound effects, the props, and the script, but her relatives/actors don't share the same passion or enthusiasm because they have all had a pretty rotten day. For example, Mitchell was misled into thinking that everyone dresses up for work on Halloween, so he spends the whole day dealing with a squeaky Spiderman costume, and whenever Phil wasn't scaring himself with the lawn decorations, he was having sudden insecurities about his marriage. This was the first Halloween episode I've seen that shows the work that goes into planning a neighborhood haunt and the devastation it can bring when the kids aren't impressed. Poignant but hilarious!

MY SO-CALLED LIFE
HALLOWEEN
💻 **Airdate:** October 27, 1994; Season 1

This Halloween episode swings for the fences and never misses, realistically portraying the highs and lows of teenage life and exposing all the possibilities that come with Halloween night. When the vampire-fanged Rayanne howls after making her Halloween plans, her spirit is so contagious that Angela and Brian go along even though the plans are quite absurd. They break into their high school at night in hopes of summoning the spirit of a boy whose death was as tragic as this much-beloved cult show lasting only a single season. In a sequence that is sorrowful and surreal, Angela wanders down the hallways alone and then finds herself transported back to 1963, where she engages with the classmates at a Halloween party before running into the handsome greaser boy who will lose his life in the gymnasium that night. Beautiful episode, just beautiful.

MYSTERY MAGICAL SPECIAL
💻 **Airdate:** October 31, 1986

For years an integral piece of Nickelodeon's annual "Nick or Treat" lineup was this Halloween special hosted by Marc Summers, whose *Double Dare* had just achieved immediate success. It begins with our genial game show host driving with three kids in his car (one of which is Jonathan Brandis) as they discuss the great movie they just saw, which involved a man turning into a skeleton. After being forced to take a detour, they get a flat tire and are stranded in front of a house that is looking awfully spooky thanks to the lightning storm and a nervous-looking John Astin (making a cameo) standing in front. Once inside, they are greeted with fireplaces that light themselves, paintings with moving eyeballs, revolving bookcases, and a front door that refuses to let them leave. As they explore the house, they occasionally take a break to watch magicians Lance Burton and Tina Lenert perform absolutely stunning routines that will surely give your Halloween a strong dose of wonder. The house continues to play tricks on Marc and the kids, but it's always in good, whimsical fun and they never seem to be in immediate danger. "Mystery Magical Special" is so wholesome, entertaining, and well-intended, I really wish I had known about it when I was growing up.

MY THREE SONS
THE GHOST NEXT DOOR
🖵 **Airdate:** October 25, 1962; Season 3

Entertaining Halloween episodes from '60s sitcoms were depressingly tough to come by, and even though this one has one of the least convincing laugh tracks in history and wastes plenty of time on an unfunny recurring joke about an elderly neighbor's rambling stories, there is enough here to recommend. Chip and Sudsy go trick-or-treating and are frightened when they see a moving candle illuminated from the creepy old house that's been abandoned for years, but after Fred MacMurray (who you absolutely must see in *Double Indemnity* if you haven't already) listens to their widely-embellished recollections, he assures that it's just their imaginations. The next day, feeling more confident, they dare each other to go inside the house, and they are of course greeted with a front door that creaks opens with the slight touch of a fingertip. This episode does a good job in showing the range of emotions that a kid goes through on Halloween: one moment, giddy and powerful behind a scary plastic mask, waiting for just the right moment to pounce on unsuspecting victims, and the next, devastated and embarrassed when the girls from school aren't the least bit scared; one moment, bored when your parents repeat the safety rules of trick-or-treating, the next, snatching candy from their bowl

and running into the night. Oh yeah, and you'll also get to see a creepy skeleton and clown trick-or-treating duo and the man himself, William Frawley (Fred from *I Love Lucy*)!

NIGHT GALLERY
A QUESTION OF FEAR
🖵 **Airdate:** October 27, 1971

While *Night Gallery* didn't produce any Halloween-themed episodes in its three seasons, the producers wisely chose this episode to air just a few nights before the spookiest day of the year. Fritz Weaver plays wealthy Dr. Mazi, who has never fully recovered from a night many years ago when a house terrified him so much that his jet-black hair instantly turned white. After meeting cocky war veteran Dennis Malloy, played by fellow future *Creepshow* star Leslie Nielsen, who claims that he's incapable of being afraid, a $15,000 bet is proposed that the eye-patched Malloy won't be able to spend an entire night in that house without being scared to death. From the very moment its visitor steps through the front door, the house unleashes manifestations at a ferocious pace while disallowing any form of escape with its windows that only reveal brick walls and a bed that comes equipped with its own guillotine. Episodes of *Night Gallery* were an hour long, split between two segments, and the far-superior "A Question of Fear" was paired with "The Devil is Not Mocked," in which a group of SS soldiers stumble into a castle owned by Count Dracula.

THE PAUL LYNDE HALLOWEEN SPECIAL
🖵 **Airdate:** October 29, 1976

Paul Lynde was a popular character actor who appeared in *Bye Bye Birdie*, *Betwitched*, and, for many years, was the center square in *Hollywood Squares*. Because of the times he was living in, he had to stay in the closet to sustain his career, but his sexuality was well known in Hollywood. Halloween was his favorite holiday (because as he said, when you're shaped like a pumpkin, it's easy to love Halloween) and his 1976 Halloween special, a variety show with musical numbers, stand up comedy, and sketches, is a real treat. Where else are you going to see a Halloween version of *Bye Bye Birdie*'s "Kids," Betty White as Miss Halloween 1976, and Florence Henderson singing at a haunted discothèque? Also appearing are Donnie and Marie Osmond, the band Kiss (who perform three songs), and Margaret Robinson who reprises her role from *The Wizard of Oz*.

PSYCHOVILLE
HALLOWEEN SPECIAL
⬜ **Airdate:** October 31, 2010

While you are patiently awaiting *Trick 'R Treat 2,* allow this hour-long episode of the award-winning British series to fill the Halloween anthology void. On a Halloween night that includes both a full moon and tons of lightning, a boy draws the short straw and has to sneak into a mental institution, where his strange encounters inspire four separate stories, all demented and hilarious. A grouchy, Halloween-hating clown meets two trick-or-treaters who proceed to haunt him throughout the night, even making cameos in a *Wiggles* DVD that the video store mistakenly had inside a case for *The Exorcist*. A man is furious at his wife for always messing up the kitchen and for obsessively nurturing a doll that she believes is a real baby—she even has it bob for apples and watch a puppet show starring Dracula and Frankenstein. An antique toy collector undergoes an eye transplant that later gives him an unfortunate side effect. And lastly, a mother and son dressed as Frankenstein and his bride have car trouble and are given a ride by a man who very well might be the serial killer who has been terrorizing the town.

PUNKY BREWSTER
LOVE THY NEIGHBOR
⬜ **Airdate:** November 17, 1985; Season 2

I felt strange about revisiting *Punky Brewster* after nearly 25 years but once this episode started I fell under its spell just like I did as a five-year-old. Punky, Cherie, and Allen, dressed as a '50s Gidget, a tiger, and Rambo, respectively, are trick-or-treating in their pumpkin-filled apartment complex (a neat contrast to your typical suburban Halloween TV kids) when their night is spoiled because of a mean old woman who is believed to be a witch. Punky seeks revenge in the form of a "flying foamie" trick but is caught in the act along with her partner in crime, her adorable dog Brandon. They are forced in the woman's apartment and when Punky suspects she is going to be thrown into the oven, she escapes, but is brought to tears when she realizes who she forgot to take with her. The show has so much heart and its characters are

so compassionate and engaging that I hope it won't be another 25 years until we meet again. After all, this was the program that taught me the important lesson that hiding in a refrigerator is not a good idea!

QUANTUM LEAP
THE BOOGIEMAN
⬜ **Airdate:** October 6, 1990; Season 3

Sam Beckett leaps into the body of a "Second rate H.P. Lovecraft" on Halloween of 1964, in Coventry, Maine. While he and his fiancée Mary are planning for their Coventry Presbyterian Halloween Spookhouse, a local handyman and an elderly neighbor die in circumstances so bizarre that Sam begins to wonder if Mary is possibly a witch. This is a slow-moving murder mystery that allows us all to leap to the crispest of New England autumn afternoons, where we are greeted by a flying skull, a terrifying Black Mamba snake, a young man excited to peel grapes for his bowl of eyeballs, lots of pumpkins, a heavily decorated house with the address 966 Salem Ave. (and you know just what those strong gusts of winds are going to do to that first digit), and one of the neatest looking scarecrows ever.

RAGGEDY ANN AND ANDY
THE PUMPKIN WHO COULDN'T SMILE
⬜ **Airdate:** October 31, 1979

In yet another Halloween gem that Disney used to air annually, Raggedy Ann and Andy can't help but notice how miserable the little boy down the street is, probably because his grumpy Aunt Agatha forbids him to go out on Halloween or do anything remotely festive. They hope to cheer him up by giving him a pumpkin, which leads them to a farm where one sole pumpkin remains: a glum jack-o'-lantern that mopes about being an unloved orphan and that cries pumpkin seeds because it will soon feel like a Christmas tree on December 26th. Will these two glum souls be able to cheer each other up, and will Agatha remember what it was like to be nine years old on Halloween night, long before she believed that trick-or-treating was just pure bribery? This Chuck Jones animated special will warm the hearts of anyone who has ever hugged their pumpkins or felt an emotional sting when the time came to toss them in the dumpster. One of the greatest scenes comes when the kids are trying to transport the pumpkin; after a few missteps and acts of clumsiness, we see a terrified-looking pumpkin riding downhill on a skateboard, giving a piggy-back ride to an even-more terrified black cat, with three ghosts chasing after them on bicycles. A very merry hallo and a happy new ween indeed!

THE REAL GHOSTBUSTERS
WHEN HALLOWEEN WAS FOREVER
🖥 **Airdate:** November 1, 1986; Season 1

Relics from 7th century Ireland signal the return of Samhain, the spirit of Halloween who after being imprisoned for centuries, is determined to make this Halloween last forever—he demands "eternal night, eternal Halloween, eternal me." He conjures up a midnight army of beasties so odd they resemble the Midians in Clive Barker's *Nightbreed*, and also kidnaps the Ghostbusters' sugar-addicted pet, Slimer. But are they any match for a blonde Flock of Seagulls–looking Egon, an Arsenio Hall Winston, or Peter Venkman with the actual voice of Garfield (Bill Murray would return Lorenzo Music's favor years later for the *Garfield* movies)? This episode is full of vibrant colors, excellent music, and enough Halloween spirit to give you the energy of an '80s child in the midst of a Saturday morning cartoon marathon.

THE REAL GHOSTBUSTERS
THE HALLOWEEN DOOR
🖥 **Airdate:** October 29, 1989; Season 4

Crowley, the total prick in charge of Citizens United Against Halloween and Lots of Other Stuff We Don't Like, steals a piece of Ghostbusting equipment that enables him to make Halloween and all of its customs disappear. He's ecstatic when the children can no longer dress as ghosts and goblins or allow their imaginations to run rampant, but he didn't consider how ridding the world of Halloween also breaks the agreement that the ancient Celtic priests made with the evil spirits 2,000 years ago, thus opening the door for them to pay us all a visit. This episode repeatedly stresses the importance of Halloween and even gives us a fun musical number where the Ghostbusters appear at an elementary school Halloween assembly.

REGULAR SHOW
TERROR TALES IN THE PARK
🖥 **Airdate:** October 10, 2011; Season 3

One day I watched several hours of children's television shows for this chapter and barely cracked a smile, but it was all worth it once I was introduced to this Cartoon Network show. It makes me wonder if the youngsters who watch this are going to develop issues because it seems much more targeted to Adult Swim stoners. In my favorite portion of this hilariously twisted episode, which borrows elements of *Drag Me to Hell* and *A Nightmare on Elm Street*, a fox named Mordecai is trick-or-treating and decides to egg a house after being denied candy. It turns out to be a big mistake because the house is owned by a vengeful wizard who retaliates by placing a most peculiar curse on him and also going after his friends—one character loses all his skin, another his head!

ROSEANNE

It's believed that the reason the Conners struggled with finances before winning the lottery and jumping the shark is because they spent most of their income on Halloween decorations and costumes; however, it was money well spent because for years they were the undisputed kings and queens of Halloween. Unlike the stingy Simpsons, who for some insane reason have yet to release a decent "Treehouse of Horrors" collection on DVD, the *Roseanne: Tricks & Treats* DVD offers all eight episodes in their original format. Here is how I would rank these episodes, from best to worst.

BOO
🖥 **Airdate:** October 31, 1989; Season 2
It was basically a coin toss between two episodes for the number one slot, but I think this one deserves to be at the top—had the very first Halloween episode not been a huge success, then the others might not have even followed. Some would say the Connors never made the holiday Halloween look more fun than they did here, and they didn't even have to leave the house once. Dan and Roseanne are embroiled in a war over who's the master of Halloween, with the momentum shifting back and forth as the tactics become increasingly diabolical. One thing's for sure: you won't find anyone with more Halloween spirit than the Conners, and their house—converted into the Tunnel of Terror—is where trick-or-treaters go to

have the highlight of their night and where young-at-heart businessmen go to be served some dead man's stew.

HALLOWEEN IV
⌨ **Airdate:** October 27, 1992; Season 5

Roseanne was such a successful series because it was equally funny and heartfelt, and nowhere is that perfect balance of comedy and tragedy more noticeable than in season 5. This Halloween episode starts differently than the others because Roseanne doesn't feel like playing pranks or even cracking a smile. Her family is hoping that her favorite day of the year will be what cures her depression, but when everybody is outside celebrating, she is nearly catatonic on the couch, alone and under heaps of candy wrappers. In an affectionate spoof of *A Christmas Carol*, she is visited by the Ghosts of Halloween Past, Present, and Future, who take her on an odyssey to remind her why she loves the holiday so much, and to show her how horrible her fate will be if she continues along this spiritless path. My personal favorite scene is when the Ghost of Halloween Present, a giant and jovial piece of Candy Corn, takes Roseanne to the Lobo Lounge to see how her friends are missing her and her pumpkin cookies.

TRICK ME UP, TRICK ME DOWN
⌨ **Airdate:** October 29, 1991; Season 4

When Roseanne's persnickety neighbor nervously enters the Conner house to find a gutted Dan lying on the kitchen table, the fun is just beginning. After this bloody good prank, Roseanne becomes paranoid of retaliation but Kathy Bowman won't even give her the time of day. This episode, mostly set in the impressively-decorated Lobo Lounge, features many of the familiar Lanford locals in amusing costumes. Even George Clooney returns for the first time since season 1; while he unfortunately spends most of the time under a moose costume, at least his final farewell was in one of the most satisfying *Roseanne* episodes ever.

HALLOWEEN V
⌨ **Airdate:** October 26, 1993; Season 6

Regaining all the spirit she lacked in the previous installment, here she is back in fine form and she's even prepared a list of pranks, dirty tricks, and flat-out mean stuff to do to her loved ones. While this episode doesn't have as much Halloween atmosphere as the previous four, it's still loaded with funny material. Dan is probably the most entertaining

character here, thanks to a classic prank which creatively uses a mugger and a rat, and a terrific subplot where he confesses what he really thinks about Nancy. Another storyline has David, making his first appearance in a Halloween episode, becoming infatuated with another girl while Darlene is away at college. Another strong supporting cast member also makes his Halloween episode debut: Leon, played by Martin Mull, who's a marvelous victim of Roseanne's macabre mischief.

TRICK OR TREAT
⌨ **Airdate:** October 30, 1990; Season 3

Considering how perfect the first Halloween episode was, it was hard not to be let down a little by this one. The main problem is that nobody seems to be having any fun. The bar is absent of any Halloween decorations or costumes, Crystal is devastated after a date ends horribly, DJ is upset that his dad won't let him dress as a witch, Dan is questioning his parental skills, and Roseanne's plans are ruined due to car trouble. On the bright side, there are really good scenes inside a foggy haunted house that people could walk through alone instead of in a ridiculously crowded conga-line fashion like we have to do today. And even though nobody even bothered to put up any decorations in the Conner house for some reason, at least they all sport awesome costumes—it's comedic gold to see how Roseanne handles hers while at a bar.

SKELETON IN THE CLOSET
⌨ **Airdate:** October 26, 1994; Season 7

This episode is a bit of a mixed bag of treats, where half of the candy is so tempting you want to eat it right away and the other half will still be unopened by Christmas. The scenes with Leon and Bev (two of the most consistently entertaining supporting characters) are great, as they are planning to knock Roseanne off her Queen of Halloween throne. Leon, who believes that Halloween belongs to the gays, throws a party at the Lunch Box where he dresses up as Hillary Clinton, and Roseanne is either a Barnie or a California Raisin. I know Roseanne was always a very progressive and gay-friendly show but this one is loaded with stereotypes that were dated even for the mid '90s. Also killing the momentum is a lengthy, boring scene where DJ asks David what it means to be gay. Still, "Skeleton in the Closet" provides several laugh-out-loud moments and should be considered the last of the good *Roseanne* Halloween episodes.

HALLOWEEN: THE FINAL CHAPTER
Airdate: October 31, 1995; Season 8

This episode never really takes off thanks to a double dose of lame, meandering scenes in the beginning, like when Roseanne's Queen of the Gypsies has a make-believe kitchen battle against Jackie's Wicked Witch of the Midwest (ugh, how dare she steal one of Roseanne's classic costumes and put such little effort into it!). It's not until the halfway point until we get anything that resembles a storyline: a Ouija board informs a pregnant Roseanne that she is about to give birth, so she is rushed to a hospital filled with costumed nurses, tie-dyed hippies dancing in psychedelic lighting, and the ghost of Jerry Garcia. There's one sweet moment when Roseanne is attempting to relax by mentally locating her happy place, which happens to be Halloween. Then we are treated to cherished memories of Halloweens past which just remind us how terrible this Halloween episode is compared to the previous ones.

SATAN, DARLING
Airdate: October 29, 1996; Season 9

Just one minute of this train wreck will remind you what a chore it was to sit through episodes of the final season of *Roseanne*, where the once identifiable, hard-working Midwestern family became bizarre cartoon characters whose relentlessly over-the-top histrionics would always signal the most rambunctious laugh track ever, causing viewers to constantly wonder what in the hell was supposed to be funny about what they were seeing. This episode is a hybrid of *Roseanne, Absolutely Fabulous,* and *Rosemary's Baby,* as Roseanne and Jackie meet Edina and Patsy at a ritzy party in New York City's Upper West Side. After a dreadful scene where the four sloshed women scream over each other's lines in the bathroom, Roseanne gets drunk and passes out to dream about Darlene giving birth to the son of Satan. Dan, Becky, DJ, David, and Mark are conspicuously absent, but instead we get fantastic guest stars like Jim J. Bullock, Kathleen Freeman, and Ariana Huffington, who are sadly given nothing interesting or funny to say.

RUGRATS
CURSE OF THE WERE-WULF
Airdate: October 20, 2002; Season 8

Even those entirely unfamiliar with this kids show will be immediately charmed by this fun-filled Halloween episode, in which an eccentric father delights in scaring his family, a group of newborns learn all about the customs of Halloween, and a manipulative little girl tortures her younger siblings by telling them that whatever they're dressed as for Halloween, they will transform into for all eternity. The grownups and the children all gather at a haunted amusement park equipped with haunted houses and trap floors that send you spiraling down massive slides: a better place to spend Halloween I cannot imagine.

THE SCOOBY-DOO SHOW
THE HEADLESS HORSEMAN OF HALLOWEEN
Airdate: October 9, 1976; Season 2

If you fancy a ride in the Mystery Machine this Halloween, then this is probably the wisest choice. But if you can't accept Scooby-Doo being equipped with a laugh track, then check out the *New Scooby-Doo Mysteries* episode "A Halloween Hassle at Dracula's Castle, which premiered on October 27th, 1984.

THE SIMPSONS: TREEHOUSE OF HORROR

Thanks to a tradition that is reaching a quarter century, it just wouldn't be Halloween without a dose of *The Simpsons*. Even people who pretty much gave up on the iconic Springfield family ten seasons ago still stick around for the mini slices of horror, dark comedy, and satire in the "Treehouse of Horror" episodes. This is when the writers get to use their most absurd and depraved ideas that would be inappropriate for any other time, like Homer being chopped into pieces by a demon in Hell or having Mr. Burns's severed head grafted onto his body. Too often in recent years they have satirized movies that have nothing to do with horror or Halloween, like *Avatar* or *Mr. & Mrs Smith*, but the recent "The Greatest Story Ever Holed" segment proved that they are still capable of delivering new 7-minute masterpieces that can compete with the early ones. This book gave me an excellent excuse to revisit every single "Treehouse of Horror" and find the ten greatest, which are listed below in chronological order.

I
Airdate: October 25, 1990; Season 2
Had the original "Treehouse of Horror" been a flop, we might not have been awarded any more, so we can thank our lucky stars it was as good as it was.

The frame story features Bart and Lisa telling scary stories in a treehouse after a night of trick-or-treating, the first one being a parody of *The Amityville Horror*. It proved that this was an animated prime time show unafraid to portray their loveable characters as bloodthirsty, ax-wielding maniacs for a few minutes. The second story would introduce us to two loveable aliens named Kang and Kodos who were so well-received they would return for each and every Halloween *Simpsons* episode, sometimes given lines and sometimes only mere Alfred Hitchcock-esque cameos. Here they get an entire segment, in which they teach us how to cook for forty humans. The final tale is a moody retelling of Edgar Allen Poe's poem "The Raven," narrated with eloquent dread by James Earl Jones.

II

🖵 **Airdate:** October 31, 1991; Season 3
Only two "Treehouse of Horror" episodes actually premiered on Halloween night, and one of them belongs to my favorite of them all. It uses a frame story that involves Bart, Lisa, and Homer gobbling down candy earned from trick-or-treating and then heading to their respective beds to introduce a nightmare from each. "Lisa's Nightmare" was inspired by the W.W. Jacobs short story "The Monkey's Paw" in which three wishes are granted but each one carries an enormous price. Highlights include the banter between Homer and the Moroccan vendor, a spoof of Alan Parker's 1978 film *Midnight Express*, and Kang and Kudos returning to enslave the human race after Lisa's wish for world peace eliminates all weaponry. "Bart's Nightmare" parodies a *Twilight Zone* episode about a boy who has all those "gnarly powers" that enable him to read minds, and if he doesn't like your thoughts, he'll turn you into a football or a jack-in-the-box. "Homer's Nightmare," one of the funniest segments in Simpsons Halloween history, has Mr. Burns play the Dr. Frankenstein role as he picks perhaps the worst brain possible to place into his robot. It also becomes one of the most ghoulish segments when Mr. Burns feels like a kid in a candy store while bodysnatching in a cemetery and when he uses an ice cream scoop to pull out Homer's brain, which he then places on his head and says, "Look at me, I'm Davy Crockett" with an evil laugh.

IV

🖵 **Airdate:** October 28, 1993; Season 5
This is the one that pays tribute to both of Rod Serling's anthology series, by using a *Night Gallery*-inspired wraparound (written by Conan O'Brien) that

connects three stories, one of which is a direct spoof of *The Twilight Zone* episode "Nightmare at 20,000 Feet," only this time it's a school bus instead of a plane. The biggest laughs in the episode come with Homer selling his soul to the devil (Ned Flanders) for a donut, and having to endure a day in Hell as he awaits trial. Based on the previous year's *Dracula* film, the finale has The Simpsons driving to Mr. Burns's castle after washing their necks as requested. They discover that Pennsylvania is every bit as frightening as Transylvania.

V

🖵 **Airdate:** October 30, 1994; Season 6
It's probably safe to say that this is the most popular "Treehouse of Horror" episode, both in terms of the fan base and critical reception. To give the three segments a tad more airtime, the idea of the frame story was dismissed and would never return. You know it's a strong episode when a disturbing segment involving teachers cannibalizing their students and a strange fog turning people inside out is clearly the weakest of the three. The other two are "The Shinning" and "Time and Punishment," spoofing the Stephen King novel/Stanley Kubrick film *The Shining* and the Ray Bradbury time travel short story "A Sound of Thunder" respectively. Much bloodier than previous years, this is the one with the running gag of Groundskeeper Willie getting bludgeoned with an ax in all three stories.

VI

🖵 **Airdate:** October 29, 1995; Season 7
In "Attack of the 50-Foot Eyesores," advertising statues come to life to obliterate the town of Springfield to avenge the kidnapping of the Colossal Doughnut by Homer. Then we get an amusing take on *A Nightmare on Elm Street* that has Groundskeeper Willie terrorizing the children in some really surreal and silly dream sequences. But the episode will mostly be remembered for the bizarre and beautiful Homer[3], which has Homer hiding from Patty and Selma only to unwittingly escape into another world, presented in striking 3D computer animation. After a rescue attempt similar to the one in *Poltergeist* is unsuccessful, Homer sinks into a black hole and falls right onto Ventura Blvd., where he finds a world even more terrifying than the previous one.

VIII

🖵 **Airdate:** October 26, 1997; Season 9
This episode starts with a TV-G rating but then a man

gets stabbed repeatedly with a sword, each time affecting the rating until a final stab leaves it at TV-666. Then it pays homage to *The Omega Man*, which leaves Homer the last man in Springfield after France launches a bomb to retaliate for a tasteless joke by Mayor Quimby. He can finally do all the things he's dreamed of, like dancing naked in a church, but his freedom is interrupted by the mutants. The Simpsons then succeed in making one of the most depressing horror movies ever, *The Fly*, an easy target by having Bart enter Professor Frink's new teleporter. Things get ever funnier with the final segment, set in Salem during the witch trials. When Marge is forced to jump off a cliff to either die a good Christian death or be found guilty of witchcraft, she flies away on her broomstick to reunite with her sisters. They decide to go door to door to eat all the children in Springfield but Maude Flanders gives them a gingerbread man instead, which they like even more. As a result, trick-or-treating becomes the new holiday tradition. But old habits die hard when Homer calls Lisa a witch after she points out that he has just egged his own house.

XI

📺 **Airdate:** November 1, 2000; Season 12

Laughter comes immediately with this solid episode as The Simpsons portray *The Munsters*, with Lisa carrying a book about copyright law. In the first tale, a horoscope warns Homer of his impending death, and while he narrowly escapes catastrophe several times throughout his workday, he becomes the victim of yet another broccoli death (as Dr. Hibbert says, broccoli even tries to warn you of its deadliness with its terrible taste). The next segment spoofs the *Grimm's Fairy Tales* stories "Goldielocks," "Rapunzel," and "Hansel and Gretel" as Homer abandons Bart and Lisa in the forest to make his disease-ridden peasant life a tad less stressful. The best is saved for last when Lisa pities a mistreated dolphin and sets it free, only to have it lead all the other dolphins in a war against the humans. The first vicious dolphin attack is against poor Lennie, who is boasting what a winning combination alcohol and night-swimming is.

XVI

📺 **Airdate:** November 6, 2005; Season 17

The funny-as-always opening presents Kang and Kodos using an accelerator beam to speed up the boring baseball game that is forcing *The Simpsons* Halloween episode to air in November, but ends up destroying the universe instead. The spoof of *A.I.*

keeps the energy level high due to its many bizarre sight gags and witty lines. The next story stars my favorite Simpsons character, Mr. Burns, who invites many characters to his house so that he can hunt them down one by one in a sensational live television show. It's such a delight when these newer Treehouse episodes—often veering further and further away from its horror roots—feature segments set on Halloween, and "I've Grown a Costume on Your Face" starts off at a Springfield Halloween parade, with a costume contest underway. The top prize is given to a witch, but is later revoked with the revelation that she's a real witch. She gets even by casting a spell that turns everybody into their Halloween costumes. A decapitated Homer, skeleton Marge, Dr. Hibbert Dracula (don't you dare call him Blacula!), and werewolf Bart are just a few examples of the daffy transformations of our beloved Simpsons characters.

XIX

📺 **Airdate:** November 2, 2008; Season 20

With nine episodes already chosen, I had a single slot left, and as much as I adored seeing Kang and Kodos appear on the *Jerry Springer Show* in TOH IX, I had to give the edge to this one, mostly due to the brilliant opening where Homer attempts to vote in the 2008 Presidential Election and the even more brilliant "It's the Grand Pumpkin, Milhouse," an adorable and affectionate tribute to a holiday classic. Milhouse is every bit as deluded and pathetic as Linus as he too waits in the pumpkin patch for the Grand Pumpkin, who finally sprouts thanks to Milhouse's tears and childlike belief. Except when presented with pumpkin bread, the Grand Pumpkin is outraged and goes on a killing spree—seeing pumpkin atrocities everywhere he looks—and eventually crashing the Springfield Elementary School dance. This is easily one of the funniest "Treehouse of Horror" tales of all time and will leave you feeling warm and fuzzy.

XX

📺 **Airdate:** October 18, 2009; Season 21

This one had just about everything going for it, including being the first Treehouse in nearly a decade to air before Halloween! Being one of the most horror-centered entries, it's only fitting that the opening would feature the Universal monsters wandering around Springfield in hilariously modern costumes like Harry Potter and Spongebob Squarepants. The black and white "Dial M for Murder or Press # To Return to Main Menu," has Bart and Lisa swapping the murders of their respective teachers in a spoof of Alfred Hitchcock's *Strangers on a Train*. Next comes an equally funny and clever spoof of *28 Days Later* in which Krusty's new burger (made from cattle that have eaten other cattle) turns the entire town into zombies. Even if the last segment were dull, this still would have been one of the wittiest Halloween episodes ever, but instead the *Sweeney Todd* spoof is perhaps the best of the bunch. In "There's No Business Like Moe Business," the perpetual lonely and lovesick Moe uses the blood from a recently-impaled Homer to brew a successful new beer.

SPONGEBOB SQUAREPANTS
SCAREDY PANTS
Airdate: October 28, 1999; Season 1

The lovable, flamboyant Spongebob Scaredypants is sick and tired of being the laughing stock of Bikini Bottom every Halloween, and he'll do whatever it takes to turn the tables, even if it involves hacking off large portions of his head and exposing his brain to the Flying Dutchman. If you don't smile when Spongebob carves from inside the pumpkin and then freaks out when he sees its scary face from the outside, then you have no soul. Also guaranteed to provide ten minutes of pure devilish joy is the episode "Late Shift" in which Spongebob and Mr. Krabs believe they have accidentally murdered a health inspector, so they gather their trusted shovels and head to the rain-soaked cemetery.

THE THREE STOOGES

My stooge phase hit me during the middle school years, and there was something really special about staying awake all Saturday night with Moe, Larry, Curly, Shemp, and Curly Joe—it was a great reward for loyal creatures of the night. I remember a few times when during the last hour of the weekly Stooge marathon, between the hours of 3 and 4 a.m., a short would come on that would legitimately give me the willies. Whether it was seriously creepy or just a side effect from three straight hours of Stooges and junk food, I wasn't sure, but I would never forget about those crazy monster chase scenes or the wind sound effects that seemed to come from Neptune. If any of you also went through a nocturnal Stooge phase, then you'll be happy to know that some of these shorts will fit right in during your all-night Halloween TV marathon. In "If a Body Meets a Body," (1945) the boys go to Curly's deceased uncle's mansion for

a reading of the will only to learn that the uncle was murdered and the killer is probably still loose in the house. There are some witty lines like, "The morbid the merrier," and "Blow it [the candle] out or I'll blow out your brains, or a reasonable facsimile thereof," but this episode is probably remembered more for its shots of horseshoe soup, a flying skull, a corpse suddenly emerging from his hiding place, and amusing physical gags with rain-soaked clothes. Also from 1945, the hilarious "Three Pests in a Mess" has Curly accidentally shoot a mannequin, which the stooges mistake for a real body. They decide to bury the body at a pet cemetery, but are interrupted not by Church and Gage, but by three threatening men in masquerade costumes. But the one that I am most excited to show off at my next October movie night is "Dopey Dicks" (1950). Moe, Larry, and Shemp try out their detective skills and attempt to rescue a damsel in distress inside a castle on a rainy night, but they have to watch out for an evil scientist, his psychopathic assistant, and a headless robot. We know that the Stooges aren't going to lose their heads, but because of how menacing the villains are, it's still nerve-wracking to see how close they come during this exciting game of hide and seek.

SOUTH PARK
PINKEYE
Airdate: October 29, 1997; Season 1

Although there are several Halloween episodes of *South Park*, none hold a candle to the first one, which includes a zombie outbreak, a school costume contest, a "Thriller" parody, and Cartman dressing as Hitler and then a Klansman.

TALES FROM THE CRYPT
TELEVISION TERROR
Airdate: July 17, 1990; Season 2

Outrageous! Seven seasons of arguably the most rewarding series of all time for horror fans and with the exception of a few measly minutes of season 6's "Only Skin Deep," our sacred holiday went completely ignored? Still, it would be equally outrageous to omit our darling Cryptkeeper from this chapter. Considering the abundance of these demented mini-movie masterpieces, it's a difficult choice, but one that works remarkably well for howling October nights is "Television Terror," which stars Morton Downey Jr. as a shock jock TV host who believes ratings gold will come once he steps inside The Ritter House, a chamber of horrors with a past that includes mass murder, dismemberment, suicide, and paranormal sightings. He wants to be the first to capture psychic phenomena on live television but he gets much more than he bargains for. Taking a tour of this cesspool of evil will fill you with the kind of crippling dread you experienced in the Overlook Hotel, Regan's cold-as-hell bedroom, and room 1408.

TALES FROM THE DARKSIDE
TRICK OR TREAT
⌨ **Airdate:** October 29, 1983; Season 1

Creepshow's success led to George A. Romero getting the chance to create his own television anthology series. It got off to a good start with its Halloween themed pilot episode, in which a Scrooge-like character goes to great lengths to protect and exploit the debts that are owed by the struggling citizens in his small town. His favorite Halloween tradition is inviting the local children to his house and promising to annul their parents' debts if they are able to find the hidden IOU's, but they always leave the house screaming and empty-handed. But one trick-or-treater that he doesn't expect is a horrifying witch who may or may not have the ability to send him straight to hell for his wicked ways. Just watching that opening theme with the positively chilling narration is enough to put you in the Halloween spirit! In the opening scene, be sure to look out for the indomitable Max Wright, who played Willie Tanner in *Alf*.

TALES FROM THE DARKSIDE
HALLOWEEN CANDY
⌨ **Airdate:** October 27, 1985; Season 2

This Tom Savini-directed episode opens with shots of trick-or-treating so classy they wouldn't be out of place in a collection of vintage Halloween postcards. There is something so fascinating about these trick-or-treaters that you wish the episode could be more about them. Each one is alone, leaves constantly crunching beneath their feet, and is adorned in a costume that might have looked cute back then (bunnies and clowns), but now would win the Scariest Costume Award at any Halloween party. Even the way they say "trick or treat, trick or treat" is absolutely precious and somehow a little sad. The episode is actually about an elderly man who hates Halloween because he doesn't like to be bothered and he despises

the sound of his own doorbell. The only candy he hands out is "goblin candy" and this is not something you want in your pillowcase! This angers the spirits of Halloween and they unleash horrors upon him that resemble the crate monster and cockroaches in *Creepshow*. There is even an athletic troll! And with a soundtrack that plays like a Sounds of Halloween cassette from the '80s, this was gearing up to be one of the best overall Halloween television episodes ever, but that all changed when I saw an ending so weak and unsatisfying I almost wanted to throw goblin candy at the TV screen.

TOM & JERRY HALLOWEEN SPECIAL
⌨ **Airdate:** October 16, 1987

Tom & Jerry's Funhouse was proving to be a successful morning addition to TBS's lineup so the wise decision was made to give the cat and mouse duo their own prime time Halloween special, and they brought lots of friends with them. Six animated shorts from 1939–1965 are shown, separated by wraparound live-action segments with child actors Josh Jarboe and Audra Lee, in which they talk about the origins and iconic images of Halloween, share corny Halloween jokes, and offer a trick-or-treating checklist and safety tips, before introducing each cartoon. The two kids are articulate and enthusiastic, and I love how they share their segments with a family of jack-o'-lanterns. And as someone who trick-or-treated in St. Louis, where it's still customary to tell jokes before getting candy, I appreciated their silly jokes because I had to tell ones like "What happens when a banana sees a ghost? The Banana splits" hundreds of times on Halloween. As for the cartoons themselves, the best one is probably "The Flying Sorceress" which has Tom unwittingly auditioning to become a wicked witch's new flying companion when all of the others fell off her broom and died. Not wanting to nap in a coffin like the witch demands, he decides to take her broom out for a late-night flying session. My other favorite was "Ghosts in the Bunk," where Bluto revamps a deserted hotel to look like a haunted funhouse, and then extends an invitation to Popeye the Sailor Man. Here we learn that the only thing scarier than an invisible man is one with spinach! The other cartoons are "Ghost Wanted" where a Casper-look-alike is tormented by evil spirits and their spine-chilling laughter, "Haunted Mouse," which has Jerry and his magician cousin playing tricks on poor ole Tom, "Hair-Raising Hare" in which Bugs Bunny meets up with a Peter Lorre-esque scientist and his Gossamer monster, and "Fraidy Cat," where Jerry takes advantage of Tom's frail state after he listens to a frightening radio station.

THE TWILIGHT ZONE

Sadly, even though there were two different Christmas-themed episodes, All Hallows' Eve never got recognition in the *Zone*. You might not consider sharing yet another holiday with this classic show because of the SyFy Network's annual Twilight Zone marathons on New Year's Day and Independence Day, but there are many classic episodes that really fit the mood on Halloween night. In "The After Hours" (Season 1), a woman named Marsha White is in a department store looking for a gift for her mother in the form of a gold thimble. The elevator operator takes her to the ninth floor, a dark and uninviting place that has only one employee and one item for sale. Things only get stranger for Marsha when she wakes up in the department store to discover she's all alone except for the mannequins. Even scarier is "Mirror Image" (Season 1) in which Vera Miles plays a woman who is experiencing one peculiar dilemma after another in a bus station on a rainy night, leading her to believe that she's either losing her mind, has a couple of lookalikes, or becoming a victim in a bodysnatching scenario. Since *Psycho* is a favorite of mine, it was a real treat seeing Vera Miles appear in such a strong episode, which is why I also have to highly recommend "The New Exhibit" (season 4), which stars Detective Arbogast himself, Martin Balsam. Here he plays a man who values his job at a wax museum more than anything else—including his marriage—due to his obsession with preserving the statues of serial killers like Jack the Ripper and Albert Hicks. When the news breaks that the museum is closing, he persuades his boss to let him keep the wax figures in his air-conditioned basement, but it doesn't take long before they start misbehaving.

YOU CAN'T DO THAT ON TELEVISION

HALLOWEEN

💻 **Airdate:** Season 5; October 9, 1984

I was probably wrong to write off this Nickelodeon sketch-comedy show so quickly as a child—I remember watching one episode and being more grossed out than amused for some reason. A couple of my friends were huge fans of this show and it took me over 25 years to understand why. I was really dreading this particular Halloween episode but to my surprise it was creative, interesting, and completely harmless. I knew this was a sketch comedy show but I had no idea it was going to unfold in awesome, fire-rapid succession à la *Robot Chicken*, not giving you a chance to feel bored during a skit since most of them last approximately 45-seconds. So what we get is about a hundred little slices of Halloween, with one established storyline involving Ross, a Halloween Grinch, who suffers from unbelievably bad luck after being "cursed" by one of the children.

THE ATTACK OF THE TOP 5 LISTS

I have made a bunch of top 5 lists for those of you with very specific tastes. These films are not ranked in order of personal overall preference, but by how effective they are as a Halloween movie. This also gives me a chance to recommend a few additional films that didn't quite make it to the final round—these titles will be listed along with their year of release.

For the youngins
1. It's the Great Pumpkin, Charlie Brown
2. Garfield's Halloween Adventure
3. Daffy Duck's Quackbusters
4. Disney's Halloween Treat
5. Scary Godmother's Halloween Spooktacular

During Halloween parties (with muted TV)
1. Terror in the Aisles
2. Haxan: Witchcraft Through the Ages
3. Boogeymen: The Killer Compilation
4. The Halloween Tree
5. House of Frankenstein

After Halloween parties
1. Fright Night
2. Evil Dead 2
3. Halloween
4. Trick 'R Treat
5. The Return of the Living Dead

If you want vampires
1. Fright Night
2. Lemora: A Child's Tale of the Supernatural
3. Near Dark
4. Black Sunday
5. Andy Warhol's Dracula/ Blood for Dracula

If you want zombies
1. Night of the Living Dead
2. The Return of the Living Dead
3. Cemetery of Terror
4. Dawn of the Dead (original or remake)
5. Spookies

If you want ghosts
1. Ghostbusters
2. Poltergeist
3. Hold That Ghost
4. Haunted
5. Mr. Boogedy (1986)

If you want a haunted house
1. Insidious
2. Poltergeist
3. Hausu
4. The Haunting
5. House

If you want witches
1. Hocus Pocus
2. Halloweentown
3. The Worst Witch
4. The Witches
5. Alucarda (1977)

If you want to be scared out of your mind
1. The Exorcist
2. Insidious
3. [Rec]
4. Dagon
5. The Haunting

If you want gore
1. Dead Alive
2. Evil Dead 2
3. Dawn of the Dead (original)
4. Wrong Turn 2: Dead End
5. Re-Animator

For a romantic evening
1. The Nightmare Before Christmas
2. Fright Night
3. A Chinese Ghost Story
4. The Midnight Hour
5. Haunted

If you want to laugh
1. Troll 2
2. Hold That Ghost
3. The Ghost and Mr. Chicken
4. Ghostbusters
5. Tucker & Dale vs. Evil (2010)

If you want Vincent Price
1. House on Haunted Hill
2. The Abominable Dr. Phibes
3. The Raven
4. Tales of Terror
5. The Monster Club (1981)

If you want Michael Myers
1. Halloween
2. Halloween 5
3. Halloween: H20
4. Halloween 4
5. Halloween 2

If you want H.P. Lovecraft
1. Re-Animator
2. Dagon
3. The Unnamable
4. In the Mouth of Madness
5. The Resurrected (1992)

If you want a quick Halloween fix (under 30 minutes long)
1. It's the Great Pumpkin, Charlie Brown
2. Garfield's Halloween Adventure
3. Spooky Bats and Scaredy Cats: A Halloween Tale
4. Pumpkin Moon
5. The Halloween That Almost Wasn't

If you want a horror anthology

1. Trick 'R Treat
2. Creepshow
3. Dead of Night
4. Black Sabbath
5. Tales from the Darkside: The Movie (1990)

If you want to show your friends something they haven't heard of

1. Hausu
2. Spookies
3. Cemetery of Terror
4. Night of the Comet
5. Clownhouse

If you want an outstanding soundtrack

1. Fright Night
2. Tourist Trap
3. Suspiria
4. The Nightmare Before Christmas
5. The Return of the Living Dead

If you want a Halloween theme

1. Trick 'R Treat
2. Halloween
3. Night of the Demons
4. The Midnight Hour
5. Hocus Pocus

If you want to heckle like characters on Mystery Science Theater 3000

1. Troll 2
2. Jack-O
3. Rock 'n' Roll Nightmare (1987)
4. Plan 9 from Outer Space (1959)
5. Hack-O-Lantern/ Halloween Night (1988)

If you want Jason Vorhees

1. Jason Lives: Friday the 13th Part VI
2. Friday the 13th Part 2
3. Friday the 13th Part VIII: Jason Takes Manhattan
4. Friday the 13th: The Final Chapter
5. Friday the 13th Part III (1982)

If you want nudity

1. The Return of the Living Dead
2. Humanoids from the Deep
3. Andy Warhol's Dracula/Blood for Dracula
4. Friday the 13th Part 2
5. Night of the Demons 2

If you want a chainsaw

1. Leatherface: The Texas Chainsaw Massacre III (1993-Unrated Version)
2. Army of Darkness
3. Dawn of the Dead (2004)
4. Texas Chainsaw 3-D (2013)
5. Motel Hell (1980)

If you want rain

1. Dagon
2. The Return of the Living Dead
3. Poltergeist
4. An American Werewolf in London
5. Hold That Ghost

If you want Stephen King

1. Creepshow
2. 1408
3. Cat's Eye
4. Silver Bullet (1985)
5. Salem's Lot (1979)

If you want a Lynchian Halloween

1. Hausu
2. Gothic
3. Lemora: A Child's Tale of the Supernatural
4. The Company of Wolves
5. In the Mouth of Madness

If you want Freddy Krueger

1. A Nightmare on Elm Street (1984)
2. A Nightmare on Elm Street 3: Dream Warriors
3. A Nightmare on Elm Street 4: The Dream Master
4. A Nightmare on Elm Street 2: Freddy's Revenge
5. A Nightmare on Elm Street 5: The Dream Child

If you want found footage

1. The Blair Witch Project
2. (REC)
3. V/H/S 2
4. Trollhunter (2010)
5. Cloverfield (2008)

If you want outer space

1. Night of the Creeps
2. Killer Klowns from Outer Space
3. Event Horizon (1997)
4. Alien (1979)
5. Aliens (1986)

If you want a beautiful-looking animated short

1. Spooky Bats & Scaredy Cats: A Halloween Tale
2. Pumpkin Moon
3. Scary Godmother's Halloween Spooktacular
4. Legend of Sleepy Hollow (1949)
5. Dear Dracula

If you want pets that turn to the dark side

1. Spooky Buddies
2. The People Under the Stairs
3. Tales from the Darkside: The Movie (1990)
4. Suspiria
5. The Boneyard (1991)

If you're not sure what kind of monster you're in the mood for

1. Spookies
2. Creepshow
3. The Cabin in the Woods
4. Trick 'R Treat
5. Suspiria

If you want Alfred Hitchcock

1. Psycho (1960)
2. Rear Window (1954)
3. Strangers on a Train (1951)
4. The Birds (1963)
5. Shadow of a Doubt (1943)

If you want killer dolls

1. Dolls
2. Child's Play (1988)
3. Curse of Chucky (2013)
4. Trilogy of Terror (1975)
5. Dead Silence (2007)

WAKING UP TO THE COLD NOVEMBER RAIN

It is nearly noon on November 1st when Johnny Myung wakes up in his bedroom where the Blu-Ray main menu for *The Nightmare Before Christmas* has been looping the same song for the past seven hours. He had been on his fourth movie of the night but by the time the trick-or-treating trio kidnapped Mr. Santy Claus, the sugar-caffeine buzz had lapsed to transform a hyper Zombie Pinocchio back into a sleepy human boy. Any chance of post-Halloween depression is immediately overpowered by the sheer joy of getting to spend the day at home while all the other kids (including the former Psycho Bunny and Vampire Tourist) are at school. Thanks to the generous "Play Hooky for one day" coupon his mom gave him as one of his birthday presents, he spends the afternoon playing video games and laughing himself silly over videos of parents participating in Jimmy Kimmel's annual "I told my kids I ate all their Halloween candy" Youtube challenge, all while a pillowcase filled with goodies remains at an arms length, looking just as precious and bulky as it did on Halloween night.

Next door, Chuck and Charlotte are returning from their annual post-Halloween shopping spree. Multiple bags filled with discounted decorations are being unloaded from the car and taken down to the basement, where they will remain until it's time to once again prepare for the House of Horrors— the newly-purchased animatronic demon baby, screaming grim reaper, and life-size Pinhead should make next year's house the scariest one yet. Then they begin the grueling process of turning their labor of love back into an ordinary house, and while it's impossible for them not to feel sad as the cobwebs are removed and the ghouls dismantled, they comfort each other and cheer up when they remember that in a few weeks, this ordinary house will once again become a Winter Wonderland.

Across the street, Jordan Petrucci awakens on his co-worker's couch to the sounds of coffee brewing and voices from the kitchen. It takes him a moment to remember where he is and why Hulk Hogan, Satan in a Snuggie™, a Gothic ventriloquist dummy, and a hippy-witch are asleep in the same room. The horror movie marathon had been such a success that Kate offered to let the soul survivors—who were wise enough to request the day off from work—sleep over. Kate sees that Jordan is awake and she brings him a cup of coffee. Ever since they bonded on Halloween night as a Candy Corn Cockroach and Jareth the Goblin Queen, they suddenly seem more like dear friends than just co-workers. The rest of the slightly-hung-over party guests wake up to the sounds of laughter, when a human cockroach attempts to drink coffee as four extra legs mirror the movements of his two arms. To his shock, the four extra extremities hadn't interfered at all while he slept. After his second cup of coffee, Jordan says goodbye to his new friends and drives home, with a Halloween mix CD still playing in his car. With the windows down, he notices that the air smells different than it had for the past few weeks. Gone was the delicious fragrance that promised otherworldly excitement, and in its place, once again, that foreboding promise of a long, cold winter. Even though he was only gone for one night, his jack-o'-lantern looks to have aged many years, and Jordan knows that later he's going to have to place his beloved gourd in the dumpster and officially close the lid on his favorite holiday. Cheering him up is the realization that pretty soon, he'll once again get to revisit Gobble Gobble Cinema like *Planes, Trains & Automobiles* and Santa Cinema like *Gremlins, A Christmas Carol* (the George C. Scott one, of course), *Home Alone*, and *Christmas Vacation*.

ABOUT THE AUTHOR

Nathaniel Tolle graduated from Webster University in St. Louis, Missouri, obtaining a Bachelor's degree in Film Studies, a program focusing on film history and aesthetics, as well as critical approaches to the study of film. He now resides in Portland, Oregon, and writes for the website Geek Legacy. His short films have been featured in various film festivals and on the official Warner Brothers *Trick 'R Treat* website.